D1715334

The Warsaw Pact

CORNELL STUDIES IN
SECURITY AFFAIRS

edited by Robert J. Art
and Robert Jervis

The Warsaw Pact

ALLIANCE IN TRANSITION?

EDITED BY

DAVID HOLLOWAY

AND

JANE M. O. SHARP

Cornell University Press

ITHACA, NEW YORK

First published 1984 by Cornell University Press.

Library of Congress Cataloging in Publication Data

Main entry under title:

The Warsaw Pact.

Includes bibliographical references and index.
1. Warsaw Treaty Organization—Addresses, essays, lectures.
I. Holloway, David, 1943–   . II. Sharp, Jane M. O.
UA646.8.W365   1984   355'.031'0947   84-7093
ISBN 0-8014-1775-9 (alk. paper)

Printed in the United States of America

Contents

[5]

Contents

Preface

Immediately after World War II, Stalin ruthlessly exploited Eastern Europe: he imposed communist governments loyal to Moscow and extracted—as reparations—resources equivalent to those which the United States poured into Western Europe through the Marshall Plan. With the signing of the Warsaw Pact in 1955, the post-Stalin leadership in Moscow sought to maintain control over Eastern Europe in an alliance framework ostensibly modeled on the 1949 North Atlantic Treaty.

In both halves of Europe in the early 1980s, the smaller powers increasingly questioned the benefits of alliance. In Eastern Europe the strains were most obvious in Poland, but economic discontent was widespread throughout the bloc and, if more muted than in the West, there was apprehension about the consequences of possible East-West military confrontation on the Continent.

This book seeks to contribute to the debate about European security and the direction of East-West relations generally by broadening understanding in the West of recent developments and future prospects of the Warsaw Pact. The chapters examine the institutional evolution of the Pact, the coordination of its foreign and defense policies, and the economic, political, and international environment in which it functions. The emphasis is less on the military capability of the Pact than on the way it works as an alliance of states.

The ten contributing authors, from a variety of disciplines, tackle a set of hitherto relatively unexplored questions as they try to measure the extent to which the Pact has developed into a genuine alliance over the past three decades. How is the Pact organized politically and militarily? How are the risks and burdens of alliance shared between the Soviet Union and the smaller East European powers and among the East Europeans themselves? Are the nationality problems that

[7]

Soviet leaders face in the fifteen constituent republics of the USSR analogous to the problems of integrating and controlling the national armies of Eastern Europe? How do the Soviets use the Pact in managing crises in the bloc?

If Eastern Europe was considered a necessary ideological and security buffer for the Soviet Union immediately after World War II, has it remained so? Or has Eastern Europe in some ways become more of a liability than an asset for Moscow? What are the costs and benefits of alliance membership for the governments and peoples of Eastern Europe? Do leaders of the smaller East European powers merely rubber-stamp Soviet policy or have they been able to use the Pact framework to press their own national interests? How, for example, has Soviet arms-control diplomacy affected the security of Eastern Europe?

The Warsaw Treaty lapses in 1985, though most analysts anticipate some form of extension. The last three chapters in this volume speculate about future developments both within the Pact and in the broader context of international relations. Despite generally bleak predictions for Eastern Europe in the near term, the authors acknowledge a perceptible trend toward looser Soviet control since Stalin's time, see the most likely impetus for innovation and long-term reform emerging from economic pressures within the bloc, and find the best hope for peaceful—albeit gradual—change in a stronger commitment to East-West detente by both the United States and the Soviet Union.

This book stems from a project of the Peace Studies Program at Cornell University. During the academic year 1981–1982 the program undertook a major study of the political, military, and economic relations between the Soviet Union and Eastern Europe. A working group met regularly through the school year, and two conferences were held at Cornell in the spring semester. The first, in April, was organized in conjunction with the Department of Economics and the Committee on Soviet Studies at Cornell and dealt primarily with East bloc economic relations; the second, in May, focused on political-military relations. This book consists of papers selected from those presented at the May conference, revised in the light of the conference discussions, and updated to take account of subsequent developments in Eastern Europe and the Soviet Union.

We express our thanks to all the conference participants, both those who presented papers and those who took part in the discussions, and to the Rockefeller, Ford, and Allen-Heath foundations, which supported the project. We are also grateful to Matthew Evangelista

[8]

and Benjamin Miller, who served as conference rapporteurs, to Jane Kellog, Karen Seferlis, and Patricia Carlson-Molan, who typed and retyped many of the chapters, and to Trudie Calvert, who polished our prose and shepherded the final version to publication for Cornell University Press.

Finally, we owe special thanks to Judith Reppy, former director of the Peace Studies Program, for her encouragement and support and for providing a congenial atmosphere in which to work.

DAVID HOLLOWAY AND JANE M. O. SHARP

Palo Alto, California
Ithaca, New York

Contributors

J. F. BROWN serves as consultant to the Rand Corporation and Stiftung Wissenschaft und Politik, Ebenhausen, West Germany. He formerly was Research Director and Director of Radio Free Europe in Munich. Brown is the author of *The New Eastern Europe: The Khrushchev Era and Beyond* (1966) and *Bulgaria under Communist Rule* (1970), as well as many articles and chapters in books.

JONATHAN DEAN, Resident Associate of the Carnegie Endowment for International Peace, has had long association with Eastern Europe and East-West issues. In the late 1950s he was a State Department desk officer concerned with the relations between West and East Germany. In the early 1960s he was First Secretary at the American Embassy in Prague. In the early 1970s he was deputy negotiator for the Four-Power Agreement on Berlin. From 1973 to 1978 he was deputy head of the American delegation and from 1978 to 1981 head of the delegation to the NATO–Warsaw Pact negotiations on Mutual and Balanced Force Reductions in Vienna. His articles on European security issues have appeared in European and American journals.

DAVID HOLLOWAY is a Senior Research Associate at the Center for International Security and Arms Control at Stanford University, on leave from the Department of Politics at Edinburgh University. He spent the academic year 1981–1982 as a Visiting Professor at the Peace Studies Program, Cornell University. He is the author of *The Soviet Union and the Arms Race* (1983) and many articles on Soviet military affairs.

CHRISOPHER D. JONES is Assistant Professor in the School of International Studies at the University of Washington in Seattle. He is the author of *Soviet Influence in Eastern Europe: Political Autonomy and the Warsaw Pact* (1981) and co-author, with Teresa Rakowska-Harmstone, of a forthcoming study of the political reliability of the Soviet and non-Soviet nationalities of the Warsaw Pact. He was formerly Visiting Research Professor at the Strategic Studies Institute of the U.S. Army War College. From 1977 to 1982 he was a Visiting Scholar at the Harvard Russian Research Center.

F. STEPHEN LARRABEE is Vice-President and Director of Studies of the Institute for East-West Security Studies in New York. He was a Visiting Professor in the Department of Government at Cornell University during 1982–1983 and served on the National Security Council staff from 1978 to 1981. He is co-editor of *Confidence-Building Measures in Europe* (1983) and has written widely on Balkan and European security issues.

MALCOLM MACKINTOSH is the Consultant on Soviet Affairs in the International Institute for Strategic Affairs, London. A researcher in Soviet affairs in the British Foreign Office since 1960, he has served as an Assistant Secretary in the Cabinet Office since 1968. From 1948 to 1960 he was Head of the Bulgarian and Albanian sections of the BBC Overseas Service. During World War II he served in the British Army in the Middle East, Italy, and the Balkans and was a member of the Allied Control Commissions in Romania and Bulgaria and liaison officer with the Soviet army. His publications include *Strategy and Tactics of Soviet Foreign Policy* (1962), *Juggernaut: A History of the Soviet Army* (1967), and *The Evolution of the Warsaw Pact* (1969).

PAUL MARER is Professor and Chairperson of International Business at the School of Business, Indiana University. He is the author of *Soviet and East European Foreign Trade* (1972), editor of *U.S. Financing of East-West Trade* (1975), co-editor (with J. M. Montias) of *East European Integration and East-West Trade* (1980) and (with E. Tabaczynski) of *Polish-U.S. Industrial Cooperation* (1982), and author of more than fifty articles and chapters on the economies of Eastern Europe, East-West trade and finance, and intra-CMEA relations. He has served as consultant to the World Bank on centrally planned economies, to the International Monetary Fund on Hungary, to the OECD and the United Nations on East-West trade and technology transfer, and to various congressional committees on Eastern Europe.

EDWINA MORETON is a member of the editorial staff of *The Econo-*

mist, specializing in Soviet and East European affairs. Her publications include *East Germany and the Warsaw Alliance: The Politics of Detente* (1978). She is co-author of *Nuclear War and Nuclear Peace* (1983) and co-editor of *Soviet Strategy in Western Europe* (1984).

CONDOLEEZZA RICE is Assistant Professor of Political Science and Assistant Director of the Center for International Security and Arms Control at Stanford University. She is a specialist on Soviet and East European foreign and defense policy and arms control and international security policy. Professor Rice was a 1980 recipient of the Ford Foundation's Fellowship for Dual Expertise in Arms Control and International Security and Soviet Studies. She is a member of the core faculty of the Stanford-Berkeley Program for the Study of Soviet International Behavior. Her publications include *Uncertain Allegiance: The Soviet Union and the Czechoslovak Army, 1948–1983* (1984) and articles on the Warsaw Pact and Soviet civil-military relations. She serves as a consultant to the Rand Corporation and to Science Applications, Inc.

JANE M. O. SHARP is a Resident Scholar in the Peace Studies Program at Cornell University, where she directed the Warsaw Pact Project in 1981–1982. She serves on the Board of Directors of the Council for a Livable World, Washington, D.C., and the Institute for Defense and Disarmament, Brookline, Massachusetts. She is the editor of *Opportunities for Disarmament* (1978) and the author of numerous articles and chapters on East-West relations, European security, and the arms-control process.

Participants in the May 1982 Warsaw Pact Conference

BENEDICT ANDERSON, Cornell University
J. F. BROWN, Oxford
LAWRENCE CALDWELL, Occidental College
RICHARD DARILEK, Rand Corporation
JONATHAN DEAN, Carnegie Endowment for International Peace
JOHN HARDT, Congressional Research Service
DAVID HOLLOWAY, Stanford University
A. ROSS JOHNSON, Rand Corporation
CHRISTOPHER D. JONES, Harvard University
CATHERINE M. KELLEHER, University of Maryland
MICHAEL KRAUS, Middlebury College
F. STEPHEN LARRABEE, Institute for East-West Security Studies, New York
FRANKLIN A. LONG, Cornell University
MALCOLM MACKINTOSH, Cabinet Office, London
PAUL MARER, Indiana University
EDWINA MORETON, *Economist*, London
DANIEL NELSON, University of Kentucky
GEORGE QUESTER, University of Maryland
TERESA RAKOWSKA-HARMSTONE, Carleton University
ROBIN REMINGTON, University of Missouri
JUDITH REPPY, Cornell University
CONDOLEEZZA RICE, Stanford University
RICHARD ROSECRANCE, Cornell University
GERALD SEGAL, University of Leicester
JANE M. O. SHARP, Cornell University
GEORGE STALLER, Cornell University
JIRI VALENTA, Center for Postgraduate Naval Studies, Monterey, California
IVAN VOLGYES, University of Nebraska

Acronyms

CBM	Confidence Building Measures
CCP	Chinese Communist Party
CDE	Conference Désarmement Européen (European Disarmament Conference)
CMEA	Council for Mutual Economic Assistance
COCOM	Coordination Committee for Export Controls
COMECON	CMEA Council for Mutual Economic Assistance
CPA	Czechoslovak People's Army
CPSU	Communist Party of the Soviet Union
CSCE	Conference on Security and Cooperation in Europe
EDC	European Defence Community
EEC	European Economic Community
ESC	European Security Conference
FLNC	Front for National Liberation of the Congo
FRG	Federal Republic of Germany
GATT	General Agreement on Trade and Tariffs
GDR	German Democratic Republic
IBEC	International Bank for Economic Development
IIB	International Investment Bank
INF	Intermediate-range Nuclear Forces
KGB	Komitet Gosudarstvennoi Bezopasnosti (Committee of State Security—USSR)
KOR	Workers Defense Committee—Poland
MBFR	Mutual and Balanced Force Reductions
MPA	Main Political Administration
MPLA	Popular Movement for the Liberation of Angola
NATO	North Atlantic Treaty Organization
NNA	Neutral and Non-aligned countries
NVA	Nationale Volksarmee (National People's Army of East Germany)
OAU	Organization of African Unity
OMNIPOL	Agency which coordinates Czechoslovak arms exports
OPEC	Organization of Petroleum Exporting Countries

PPC	Political Consultative Committee
PUWP	Polish United Workers Party
RCP	Romanian Communist Party
RKKA	Raboche-Krest'ianskaia Krasnaia Armiia (Red Army of workers and peasants—USSR)
ROPCO	Movement for the Defense of Human and Civil Rights (Polish dissident organization)
SALT	Strategic arms limitation talks
SED	Sozialistische Einheitspartei Deutschland (Socialist Unity Party of [East] Germany)
USSR	Union of Soviet Socialist Republics
WOW	Wojska Obrony Wewnetrznej (internal defense forces—Poland)
WTO	Warsaw Treaty Organization
ZOMA	Zmotoryzowane Odwody Milicji Obywatelskiej (motorized riot police—Poland)

PART I

OVERVIEW

[1]

The Warsaw Pact in Transition

David Holloway

In recent years the Warsaw Pact has received increasing attention from Western scholars.[1] Earlier neglect rested on the assumption that the Pact was uninteresting and unimportant in its own right. There were exceptions,[2] but for many of those concerned with Soviet–East European relations the Pact seemed to be little more than an instrument of Soviet domination and therefore unworthy of detailed study. To those interested in East-West relations it often appeared to be no more than an appendage to Soviet military power and thus warranted only a cursory mention in analyses of Soviet policy in Europe.

It has become increasingly clear, however, that the Warsaw Pact merits attention in both the Soviet–East European and the East-West contexts. The Pact is more than a mechanism for transmitting orders from Moscow to the East European capitals. It has a politics of its own; its members often differ on the question of sharing the economic burdens of defense. Moreover, as the crisis in Poland showed, Eastern Europe is beset by economic and political problems, and it must be asked what role the Pact plays in dealing with these and how it is in turn affected by them.

In the East-West context, too, the Warsaw Pact has attracted increasing attention. With the emergence of strategic nuclear parity between the Soviet Union and the United States, the military balance in Europe has acquired a new importance. The non-Soviet members nominally contribute fifty-five divisions to the Pact's order of battle, compared with the thirty-one Soviet divisions in Eastern Europe. But the workings of the Pact and the relations between its members need to be assessed before one can say how much the non-Soviet forces really add to Soviet military power.

In this book the name "Warsaw Pact" sometimes refers specifically

to the institutions of the Warsaw Treaty Organization (WTO); sometimes it denotes all the military ties between the Soviet Union and the
other members of the Pact, whether these are conducted through the
Pact's institutions or on a bilateral basis; sometimes it covers the
entire network of Soviet–East European military, political, and economic relationships. This triple usage is not accidental, for it is impossible to isolate these aspects from one another. The Soviet position in
Eastern Europe rests upon an ambiguous mix of bilateral and multilateral ties, and this ambiguity is an important feature of Soviet policy
in Europe. Moreover, the Pact cannot be discussed in a satisfactory
way unless it is examined in the general framework of Soviet–East
European relations. Only by placing it in that context can its significance for the military balance in Europe be properly assessed.

In this introduction I shall look briefly at some of the arguments
advanced in the chapters before going on to discuss general issues
raised by them.

THE WARSAW TREATY ORGANIZATION

Chapters 2–5 examine the structure and functions of the Warsaw
Treaty Organization. When the Pact was signed in 1955, it established
new institutions that at first had little substance beyond the articles of
the treaty. Gradually these institutions have come to acquire a real
significance in managing the military and political relations between
the Soviet Union and the states of Eastern Europe.

In Chapter 2 Malcolm Mackintosh provides a general picture of the
development of the Warsaw Pact since its foundation in 1955. He
shows how the Pact was set up to further Soviet policies and how it
has evolved as a military and political mechanism for exercising control over the Soviet buffer zone in Eastern Europe. He analyzes the
strains and tensions that have appeared among the Pact members
and the institutional reforms that have been carried out. The Polish
crisis now presents the most serious challenge to the Pact and may
lead to measures to strengthen Soviet forces in East Germany,
Czechoslovakia, the Baltic Sea, and the western military districts of
the Soviet Union.

But in spite of the problems they face in Eastern Europe, Mackintosh believes that the Soviet leaders would not willingly relinquish
control over the region because that control is central to their concept
of security. The buffer zone in Eastern Europe provides the possibility
of a defense in depth outside the territory of the Soviet Union and a

base from which an offensive could be mounted against Western Europe. Mackintosh concludes, "The Soviet Union continues to believe that the current structure and military capabilities of the Warsaw Pact are satisfactory."

In Chapter 3 Condoleezza Rice examines the mechanism for burden-sharing in the Pact, the key to which is the Soviet attempt to secure a division of labor among its members. This strategy is clearest in the development and production of weapons, for the Pact and the Council for Mutual Economic Assistance (CMEA) have special bodies for coordinating the individual countries' efforts. The same approach is evident in the policies of the East European countries toward the Third World, though here the coordination is presumably not effected by the Pact's institutions because these activities fall outside its sphere of formal responsibility.

The division of labor has considerable advantages for the Soviet Union. It helps to rationalize the Warsaw Pact's military effort, eliminating any unnecessary duplication, and thus contributes to the standardization of equipment throughout the Pact's forces. It avoids trying to impose a uniform policy on all members and recognizes that they may have different interests, which can be accommodated within the Pact's overall policy. Hence the division of labor may also be very much to the benefit of the non-Soviet members by allowing them to specialize and to pursue their own interests in the framework of the Pact's policy.

In practice, however, relations among the members are not as smooth as this picture suggests, for as Rice shows, the interests of individual states do not always coincide. Romania has pursued an independent defense policy and has played a minimal role in the military activities of the Pact. There are clear signs that the East European members have failed to respond to Soviet pressure for an increase in military expenditure. Moreover, in spite of its apparent advantages, the coordination of weapons development and production has not proved to be straightforward, for the non-Soviet members have not been anxious to place their defense industries wholly under the control of the Soviet Union.

Christopher Jones, in Chapter 4, approaches the issue of coordination and division of labor from a military angle. He suggests that the Soviet experience with national formations in the Red Army may provide a guide to Soviet policy toward the non-Soviet members of the Pact. National formations existed in the Red Army before the war with Germany but were disbanded in 1938, only to be revived for a short time during the war. Jones argues that these formations were regarded by the Soviet leaders as militarily inferior and politically unreliable. They were ultimately phased out, and the smaller nationalities were dispersed into multinational units, which were dominated by Russians.

Jones argues that the main object of Soviet policy in the Warsaw Pact has been to prevent the emergence of national armies that are prepared to defend national territory. The Soviet Union has tried to maintain the capacity for massive and rapid intervention in Eastern Europe by preventing other members of the Pact from adopting defense policies that would enable them to mount sustained national resistance to military occupation. It wants to prevent the East European countries from adopting a territorial defense strategy similar to those of Yugoslavia, Albania, and Romania because such a strategy would enable them to resist Soviet intervention and thus to assert their political independence.

The Soviet doctrine of coalition warfare calls for the forces of the other members to act, not as national armies defending the homeland, but as part of a larger force controlled by the Soviet Union. Jones argues that the non-Soviet forces would be integrated into the Soviet command structure at division level or below. The Soviet Union uses the Pact's institutions and multinational exercises to fragment the control that the other governments exercise over their armed forces. Jones concludes that "the primary role of the Warsaw Pact is to deny its East European members national sovereignty over national armed forces," and he implies that the East European forces have only marginal significance for Soviet military policy vis-à-vis the North Atlantic Treaty Organization (NATO).

In Chapter 5 Stephen Larrabee examines the major political crises that have beset Eastern Europe with cyclical regularity since Stalin's death. The military arrangements in Eastern Europe have provided the Soviet Union with the option of using armed force to deal with these crises, but the considerations that have governed the actual use of force have been complex. Larrabee notes that the likelihood of armed resistance appears to have been an important factor in Soviet decisions whether to use force. The possibility that the Polish army would resist Soviet military intervention may have affected the Soviet decision not to use its armed forces in Poland in 1956; the same consideration may have influenced Soviet actions in 1980–1981. Similarly, Alexander Dubcek's failure to prepare the Czechoslovak armed forces to resist invasion in 1968 made it easier for the Soviet Union to resort to military force.

Larrabee notes that the Polish crisis was far from resolved by the imposition of martial law in December 1981. In some ways that action worsened the situation by inhibiting fundamental economic and political reform. In that sense events in Poland are a sharp and visible sign of the problems that beset Eastern Europe as a whole. Larrabee also believes that the role of the military in governing Poland is likely to lead to a deterioration in its military effectiveness, which could present a very serious problem for the Soviet conception of coalition warfare because the Polish forces are the second largest in the Pact.

These problems, combined with the present political succession in the Soviet Union and impending leadership changes throughout Eastern Europe, are likely, in Larrabee's view, to make the 1980s a turbulent time in Eastern Europe. He concludes that the Soviet Union's old methods of control and domination will no longer suffice and that reforms will be needed in the Warsaw Pact to deal with these problems.

The main theme of these chapters is institutional development and differentiation. Little more than a paper institution at first, the Pact has evolved to acquire an important role in coordinating East European military and military-economic policies. The Soviet Union is the dominant power in the Pact, but the other members are not pliant instruments of Soviet policy. They seem to have acquired a greater say in the Pact's affairs; at any rate, more channels have been created for multilateral consultation.

There are important differences in the analyses offered by these authors. Mackintosh argues that the Soviet leaders are basically satisfied with the Warsaw Pact's structure as it stands. Jones implies that further attempts at integration will take place following the pattern of the dispersion of national units into multinational formations in the Red Army. Larrabee argues that reforms will be needed in the Pact, on the grounds that the Polish crisis may make the Soviet concept of coalition warfare impossible to realize.

If there is disagreement about the adequacy of the existing Warsaw Pact structure, there is also a major difference in the analysis of the functions that the structure is supposed to perform. Jones emphasizes the Pact's function in maintaining Soviet domination over Eastern Europe but gives little importance to its role in Soviet policy toward NATO. The other authors do not neglect its importance in underpinning Soviet control of Eastern Europe, but they also see it as a major element in Soviet policy toward Western Europe.

Soviet and East European Security Interests

Chapters 6 and 7 look at the relationship between the security interests of the Soviet Union and those of the other members of the

Warsaw Pact. Edwina Moreton emphasizes the central importance that Eastern Europe has had for the Soviet Union. This importance has grown, not diminished, as the Soviet Union has become a superpower because the region provides not only a physical guarantee of Soviet security but also the ideological basis for the Soviet claim to superpower status. It is the only region of the world where the Soviet political and economic model has taken root, however precariously.

The Soviet stake in Eastern Europe imposes a severe constraint on the ability of the governments there to pursue independent policies. But these governments are faced with serious internal economic and political challenges, which they must try to meet within the constraints imposed from outside. It is in this context of contradictory pressures, argues Moreton, that the foreign policy interests of the East European states can best be analyzed.

The most important conflicts in Eastern Europe—those in Hungary and Poland (1956), Czechoslovakia (1968), and Poland (1980–1981)—have arisen from internal developments that threatened to destroy the leading role of the Communist party. But there have been other instances when East European interests have differed from those of the Soviet Union without provoking a major crisis. Among those that Moreton examines are Romanian defiance of the Soviet Union; differences between East Germany and the Soviet Union over relations with West Germany; and disagreements about decision making in CMEA and the Warsaw Pact. These differences of interest have sprung primarily from the attempt by the East European regimes to increase their room for maneuver in maintaining economic and political stability at home.

The Soviet Union is, of course, the dominant power in the Warsaw Pact, but the other members have not always taken Soviet interests as their own. Such divergence is likely to continue and even to grow in the 1980s, as economic and political problems in Eastern Europe become more intense and East-West relations remain hostile. The foreign policy of the Pact countries will require careful coordination by the Soviet Union. The basis for this coordination, in Moreton's view, is likely to consist of three elements: the resolution of outstanding issues that have caused contention within the Pact; greater consultation between the Soviet Union and its allies; and a greater division of labor, allowing individual states to pursue their own interests within an agreed framework of policy.

Jane Sharp focuses on a closely related issue: the way the security concerns of the East European states have been reflected in the proposals that the Warsaw Pact has put forward for security and arms control in Europe. These proposals contain a large measure of propaganda, but they can throw light on the security concerns of the East European governments and on the extent to which they are taken into account in Soviet policy.

Sharp looks at three main security issues, each of which played an important role in East-West relations in the 1970s and early 1980s: the Conference on Security and Cooperation in Europe (CSCE), the Mutual and Balanced Force Reductions (MBFR) talks, and various efforts to control nuclear forces in Europe. In each of these cases, she argues, there is evidence that some of the East European states have had interests that diverged from those of the Soviet Union and have tried to pursue them within the framework of the Pact.

These three issues have different consequences for the bloc structure of European politics. At the CSCE all states are treated as formally equal, and in the early 1970s Soviet commentators foresaw the emergence of a new security system in Europe in which the two military blocs (NATO and the WTO) would either have been disbanded or play a minimal role. MBFR, on the other hand, is taking place within the existing bloc framework and thus tends to reinforce rather than threaten it. The effect of the conflict over nuclear force modernization has been contradictory. The two superpowers have tried to increase discipline and cohesion within their respective alliances. But at the popular level, a powerful current of public opinion—especially in Western Europe—now calls for an end to the division of Europe into military blocs.

As Sharp points out, the East European states have not wanted to see the existing bloc structure destroyed because their continued existence depends, to some degree at least, on the Soviet military presence in the region. At the same time, however, they have sought a relaxation of tension and an expansion of economic and political ties with the West to allow them to pursue economic and political stability at home. They do not want the blocs disbanded because that would threaten their existence; nor do they want bloc cohesion and discipline tightened because that would restrict their room for maneuver in dealing with their internal problems. There are exceptions to this generalization, however, because individual governments, depending on their situation at home, have been suspicious of the political damage that closer ties with Western Europe might do.

In spite of the sometimes divergent interests of the members of the Warsaw Pact, the basic fact remains that it is Soviet interests that predominate. As Moreton says, "When the Soviet Union considers it has vital foreign policy goals at stake and turns on the pressure, more often than not the Eastern Europeans can at best drag their feet, rather than change the foreign policy course." Similarly, it is the Soviet Union's concept of its own security that dominates the Pact's policy in Europe.

PROSPECTS FOR THE PACT

Prediction is never easy, especially about the Soviet Union and Eastern Europe. As J. F. Brown notes in Chapter 8, caution and humility are in order when discussing the future of the Warsaw Pact, for its inner workings are shrouded in secrecy. Moreover, the future of the Pact depends on the complex political, economic, and international environment in which it works. This environment is examined in the chapters in the final section of the book.

Brown looks at the three factors that will have the greatest bearing on Eastern Europe in the 1980s: Soviet policy, which is, in Brown's view, the most important, developments in Eastern Europe, and Western policy. The Soviet Union now faces very difficult economic and political problems in Eastern Europe. The "normalization" that followed the Czechoslovak crisis of 1968 had apparently succeeded by the early 1970s and led to complacency on the part of the Soviet leaders. It was shattered, however, in the late 1970s by the poor performance of the East European economies and by political turbulence in Poland. Brown argues that the Soviet Union has basically three choices: to pursue a "decolonizing" approach, which would allow the East European regimes greater leeway in their internal and external policies; to impose harsh repression; and to "muddle through."

In Brown's view, Soviet policy will most probably follow the third course, and consequently economic deterioration in Eastern Europe will continue. The most effective response would be far-reaching economic reform, but this is unlikely, Brown believes, because the party leaders fear that economic reform would weaken their political power. Two broad possibilities exist for the region. The first is a gradual shift of power from the party to the security apparatus. The second, more hopeful possibility is that political accord in Poland might point the way to political and economic renewal in Eastern Europe as a whole.

The final factor in Brown's analysis is Western policy. He argues that the West should offer the countries of Eastern Europe generous rescheduling terms for paying present debts, further credits, and economic aid on condition that "meaningful economic reforms are undertaken, their political consequences accepted, and elementary human rights guaranteed." The present circumstances are propitious for the West to pursue such a policy. Neither Western interests nor those of the people of Eastern Europe would be as well served by a complete economic embargo or by a policy of aid without strings.

In Chapter 9, Paul Marer looks at economic relations between the Soviet Union and Eastern Europe. Under Stalin, when the East European states were expected to do what the Soviet Union told them to do, Soviet policy was purely exploitive. By the 1970s CMEA had become a complex mechanism for economic integration, and the Soviet Union was providing Eastern Europe with a large implicit subsidy. Marer explains this subsidy primarily in terms of the ossification of trade patterns and the sluggishness of the price mechanism in CMEA, not as the intended result of Soviet policy. The subsidy grew rapidly in the 1970s, but the Soviet Union acted cautiously in changing its economic relations with the East European countries, evidently because it feared that any shocks inflicted upon their weak economies might lead to political instability.

Marer's prognosis for the economies of Eastern Europe in the second half of the 1980s is that they are likely to be increasingly unstable. Economic prospects, therefore, are not conducive to greater integration within CMEA or to greater cohesion in Soviet–East European relations as a whole. Marer suggests that if greater alliance cohesion is not possible, the Soviet Union may encourage the East European states to pursue economic and political viability through economic reform. Given the economic pressures in Eastern Europe, such a policy is not to be ruled out. But reform does not depend on the Soviet Union alone, for in the past the greatest obstacles to reform have been presented by the East European leaders.

In the final chapter Jonathan Dean surveys the prospects for the Warsaw Pact in the broader context of international relations. He begins with a bleak assessment of the situation in Eastern Europe. The regimes there, he argues, have not become self-sustaining (or viable, in Brown's terms) and have had to be propped up by Soviet economic aid and military-political intervention. The Soviet Union will not relinquish its hold over Eastern Europe, but its relationship with the region will evolve, and both the Warsaw Treaty Organization and CMEA will become increasingly important as mechanisms of multilateral coordination as well as of Soviet control. Dean does not foresee any far-reaching improvement in East-West relations that could affect internal developments in Eastern Europe. He concludes that it is improbable that fundamental changes in the external environment of Eastern Europe resulting in major change in the Pact system will take place.

Given that the external environment—in the shape of Soviet policy and East-West relations—is unlikely to alter, Dean sees the main impetus to change coming from economic and political conditions in Eastern Europe. Poor economic performance will create pressure for economic reform, and popular pressure for political change will be strong. By the end of the century "most Eastern European countries will have moved perceptibly closer to West European models both in decentralization of the economy and in political life." Dean concludes on an optimistic note, for he foresees that at some point it may become possible to achieve agreements to limit forces in Europe and to move toward the creation of a European security system in which the two military blocs would continue to coexist but with East-West relations in Europe insulated to some degree from Soviet-American rivalry in the rest of the world.

None of the three contributors to this section foresees any change in Soviet politics or in East-West relations that would lead to a relaxation of Soviet domination over Eastern Europe. In the absence of such relaxation, the main impetus to change in the Pact will be provided by economic and political turbulence in Eastern Europe. The Soviet Union will find the region more difficult to control and will have to employ new methods. At the very least it will probably be forced to take more account of its allies' wishes in the Pact and in CMEA. More drastically, it might try to impose a neo-Stalinist discipline on Eastern Europe or encourage economic reform.

THE WARSAW PACT AND SOVIET MILITARY POLICY

The Soviet Union dominates Eastern Europe not only because it wishes to sustain a particular social system there but also because it believes that control of the region contributes to its military security. It maintains large ground and air forces in central Europe and has integrated the air defense systems of its allies into its own air defense network. Its control of Eastern Europe gives it great defensive depth vis-à-vis NATO: if there were a conventional war in Europe, it would start at some distance from Soviet territory. Moreover, Eastern Europe provides a base from which to launch an attack on Western Europe in the event of war, and in view of the stress that Soviet military thought lays upon the offensive, this is of considerable value to the Soviet Union.

It is more difficult to assess the contribution that the Warsaw Pact's East European members make to Soviet security. Their quantitative contribution is substantial, for they maintain fifty-five divisions, compared with the thirty-one Soviet divisions in Eastern Europe.[3] Moreover, they appear to play a key role in the Soviet conception of coalition warfare in which allied forces, under Soviet command, would conduct large-scale actions across an entire theater of military operations. In a war it is probable that non-Soviet divisions would be integrated into Soviet armies (consisting of four or five divisions and support units) or non-Soviet armies into Soviet fronts (consisting of four or five armies); only the Polish army is reported to have had an independent front.[4] This theory suggests that the Soviet Union assigns a subordinate but nonetheless important role to the East European forces.

But numbers of divisions can be misleading. Not all the East European divisions are at full strength, and they are all less well-equipped than their Soviet counterparts. And doubts exist about their effectiveness and reliability. These qualifications apply particularly to the three Southern Tier countries—Bulgaria, Hungary, and Romania. Three of the Bulgarian army's eight divisions are at only 30 percent strength, and the six Hungarian divisions are at 70 percent strength. Each of the Southern Tier armies is poorly equipped by comparison with the forces of the Northern Tier. Finally, the Soviet General Staff must have doubts about the commitment of the ten Romanian divisions, which do not exercise with their allies and are trained to implement a different doctrine.[5]

The three Northern Tier countries—East Germany, Poland, and Czechoslovakia—are of much greater strategic importance because of their size and position. Their forces are better equipped and more numerous than those of the Southern Tier. There are six East German divisions, fifteen Polish divisions, of which four are at 30 percent strength, and ten Czechoslovak divisions. But the political strains and tensions in Eastern Europe have raised serious questions about the effectiveness of these forces. The events of 1968, for example, had a traumatic effect on the Czechoslovak People's Army, causing profound shock and demoralization in the officer corps. It has still not recovered completely, and the army's military effectiveness may be seriously impaired. The presence of five Soviet divisions in Czechoslovakia suggests that the Soviet General Staff has reservations about the combat capability of the Czechoslovak forces.[6]

The effects of the Polish crisis may prove to be even more profound. Senior officers have been drawn into political and admin-

istrative roles. Training programs have been curtailed and reequip-
ment slowed down. Thus the army's political role has already
reduced its combat effectiveness. Moreover, the split between state
and society that affects Poland is reflected in the armed forces themselves. The army command runs the country, but some of the junior
officers and many conscripts were affected by Solidarity's political
ideals. This split must raise doubts about the army's reliability and
presents the Soviet Union with a difficult problem in planning for a
war in Europe. The Polish army is the second largest in the Pact, and
Poland occupies a vital geographic position.[7] There is, however, little
evidence to support the claims of some Western analysts that the
Soviet Union has increased its forces in Europe—beyond a few helicopter units—since the Polish crisis began.

The Soviet Union employs various methods to try to deal with the
problems of reliability and effectiveness. It controls the institutions of
the Warsaw Pact and imposes a uniform doctrine on its members. It
educates senior East European officers in Moscow and presumably
controls the most important appointments in the allied armed forces
(with the exception of the Romanian army). The Soviet Union also
coordinates the intensive political education programs in the Pact.
These measures may ensure that the East European officer corps are
loyal to Moscow, but they will not remove all doubts, especially because the allied forces contain large numbers of conscripts, who can
hardly remain immune to the political moods and attitudes in their
societies.

Any assessment of reliability and effectiveness must be highly
speculative, of course, in view of the possible—even probable—use of
nuclear weapons in a war in Europe. It is not clear how any troops
would perform in the terrible conditions of a nuclear battlefield.
Moreover, the performance of the troops in conventional operations
would probably depend very much on circumstances. Western students of the problem have assumed that the non-Soviet forces—especially those of the Northern Tier—would fight well in defending
their own countries against a Western attack or in launching an offensive against Western Europe, as long as that offensive was successful.[8] In a protracted campaign, however, morale and combat effectiveness might well be affected by social and political strains in the
East European states. If the Soviet General Staff's evaluation of its
allies coincides with Western assessments, Soviet military planners
will be reinforced in their belief that a long war would be unpredictable and might lead to disaster and that, consequently, if there is a

war in Europe, the Soviet Union must try to achieve its goals as quickly and decisively as possible.

The reliability and effectiveness of its allies undoubtedly present the Soviet Union with problems. Just how serious these are is difficult to judge because much depends on the ability of the military organization, with its ethos of command and discipline, to overcome the strains and tensions of the wider society. It is hard to see, however, that Soviet problems would be made easier by disbanding the East European armies and creating a single multinational Pact force. The disbandment of national forces in the Red Army was accompanied by increasing centralization of economic and political power in the Soviet Union. It seems unlikely that integration on the model of the Soviet armed forces could take place at a time when a greater degree of economic and political differentiation is to be expected in Eastern Europe.

THE MILITARY IN POLITICS

The Polish crisis has provided the unusual spectacle of military rule in an East European country, where the Communist party is supposed to be the leading and directing force in society. The Marxist-Leninist tradition contains strong taboos against Bonapartism in any form, and Communist party states have created powerful mechanisms for ensuring party control over the armed forces. In Poland the army did not usurp power against the party's wishes. It was drawn into the political vacuum that had been created by the decay and disintegration of the party. Although formal martial law has been ended, there is no sign of the party's regaining vigor, and senior officers are likely to continue to occupy leading political and administrative posts for some time to come.

The imposition of martial law in December 1981 came as a surprise to most foreign observers (and to many Poles), who had assumed during the heady months of 1980 and 1981 that the army could not be used to break Solidarity because most soldiers were conscripts who might be sympathetic to the workers' movement. But this assumption ignored two important factors. It took no account of the attitudes and loyalties of the officers, who, because they have the power of command, are normally the key element in political-military relations. It also neglected the well-developed set of institutions that Poland, like other states in Eastern Europe (and most Continental European

[31]

states, for that matter), has for maintaining internal security and for repressing disorder and opposition. These forces are recruited with special regard for their political reliability. They are housed in separate barracks, and their loyalty is further reinforced by special pay and privileges. It is these forces that provide the first line of defense against internal threats to the state.[9]

These troops were used to carry out the most difficult tasks under martial law. The most important force was the motorized police, the Zmotoryzowane Odwody Milicji Obywatelskiej (ZOMO), which were used in confrontations with strikers and demonstrators. These forces are subordinate to the Ministry of the Interior, not to the Defense Ministry. The ZOMO were backed up by the Wojska Obrony Wewnetrznej (WOW), the internal defense forces, which form part of the Defense Ministry's Forces for the Defense of National Territory. These forces are responsible for defending the state against sabotage, subversion, and armed insurrection, and they are considered to be more reliable than the regular army. The main combat units of the army were assigned tasks that would bring them into only limited contact with the workers. It is clear that the criterion the authorities used in allocating roles was the political reliability of the troops. Because they had specialized forces at their disposal, they did not need to use the regular army in the tensest situations.[10]

The Polish crisis highlighted an important aspect of the power structure in Eastern Europe by showing the range of instruments the authorities have for defending the state. In his chapter, J. F. Brown argues that Poland may provide the pattern for political development throughout Eastern Europe. He suggests that the emergence of Solidarity can be seen as symptomatic of a general crisis in the political economy of East European states and that the shift of power away from the party to the agencies of repression may prove to be the common response of these states to any crisis they face. Eastern Europe, in other words, may come to be ruled by a form of military communism in which power rests with the armed forces and the security apparatus.

As Brown points out, this is only one of several possible patterns of political development in Eastern Europe, but it is one that should be taken seriously. The military is an important force in Eastern Europe and has the capacity to rule. Moreover, the Warsaw Pact provides a structure through which the Soviet Union can influence the political role of the East European high commands. It tries to ensure that these will be loyal to Moscow and can encourage them to play an active role in the event of a crisis. Consultations between Polish and Soviet military leaders preceded the imposition of martial law, thus suggesting that the Soviet leaders knew what was to happen, even if they had not pressed specifically for it. The Pact provides the Soviet Union with a political safety net in Eastern Europe by keeping open the possibility not only of intervention by Soviet forces but also of rule by the military if the party should lose control.

There are several considerations, however, that weigh against the argument that General Vojciech Jaruzelski has established a trend. The first is that although the Polish events may be symptomatic of a general crisis in Eastern Europe, the character of those events can be explained only in terms of the specific conditions of Polish society— the traditions of the working class, the role of the church, the disastrous state of the economy. The same combination of factors does not exist in the other Pact countries. Nor does the party seem to be in the same state of decay elsewhere in Eastern Europe as it was in Poland in the late 1970s. Perhaps only in Romania, with its internal unrest, weak economy, and personal rule, is a military coup possible.

Second, Soviet leaders may have encouraged the military to play the role it did in Poland, but only as a last resort. There is no likelihood that the Soviet High Command will be allowed to play a similar role. In the last years of his rule Leonid Brezhnev reasserted party dominance over the armed forces by appointing Dimitri Ustinov, a defense industries manager rather than a professional soldier and an important party figure in his own right, as minister of defense. Ustinov played a key role in Iuryi Andropov's succession, but since Ustinov is not merely a mouthpiece for the High Command, this does not indicate a shift of power to the military. The armed forces are of course a powerful force in Soviet politics, and party-military relations have been fraught with difficulty. But in recent years the central issue has been the role of professional advice and expertise in policy making, not the possibility of a usurpation of party rule. It is, therefore, unlikely that events in the Soviet Union will encourage a trend toward military rule in Eastern Europe.

Third, a crisis in party rule can create the conditions in which other political forces, including the army, come into play. In such a situation it cannot be assumed that the officer corps will be united in its political views. On the contrary, it is possible that during a crisis the military will reflect the political conflict in the society at large. That is what happened in Czechoslovakia in 1968, when both reformist and Stalinist elements could be found in the army.[11] It did not happen to the same extent in Poland because there the split was between state and society rather than within the party. Nevertheless, from the Soviet point of view the military may not always be a reliable ally in a political crisis.

Finally, military rule does not resolve the crisis that Eastern Europe faces. General Jaruzelski justified martial law for reasons of the traditional military values of order and national salvation. But he has not succeeded in working out a program for dealing with Poland's economic and political problems. This failure of military rule will discourage others from following Poland's example.

THE WARSAW PACT AND EUROPEAN SECURITY

Many people in Europe see the division of the Continent into two military blocs as dangerous and oppressive: it contains the seeds of nuclear catastrophe, obstructs political change in both parts of the Continent, and casts a blight over the whole of European culture and civilization. These themes have played an important part in the West European peace movements.[12] They have also struck an echo in Eastern Europe.

In September 1981 the East German dissident Robert Havemann addressed a letter to Brezhnev in which he argued that the division of Europe—more particularly of Germany—had brought not security but a great danger:

> In the increasing gravity of military confrontation in Europe the division of Germany plays a crucial role. Originally it seemed that a dangerous aggressor had in this way been rendered permanently powerless, thereby securing peace in Europe. But the result was the exact opposite. For if the nuclear holocaust should some day overtake us, it will result above all from the fact that the confrontation between East and West turned the two German states into bases for deployment and nuclear spearheads directed against the other. The division of Germany has not brought security: it has instead become the precondition for the most deadly threat that has ever existed in Europe.[13]

Havemann called for the withdrawal of occupation forces from both parts of Germany and for the Germans to be allowed to solve their national question.

In the early 1950s the Soviet Union did propose the creation of a reunified, but neutral and disarmed, Germany. But this has not been a goal of Soviet policy since the 1950s. It is certainly not desired by the East German leaders, who have done their best to block any East-

West deal that would undermine the position of their own state. It is, therefore, not surprising that Havemann's appeal, according to one report, "went down very badly" with the East German leaders.[14]

There is no record of what Brezhnev thought of Havemann's letter, but it is unlikely that he was favorably impressed. At a meeting in Moscow immediately after the invasion of Czechoslovakia, Brezhnev gave Dubcek a trenchant explanation of Soviet thinking about the division of Europe. According to Zdenek Mlynar, who was present at the meeting,

> Brezhnev spoke at length about the sacrifices of the Soviet Union in the Second World War: the soldiers fallen in battle, the civilians slaughtered, the enormous material losses, the hardships suffered by the Soviet people. At such a cost *the Soviet Union had gained security, and the guarantee of that security was the postwar division of Europe* and, specifically, the fact that Czechoslovakia was linked with the Soviet Union "forever."[15]

In his public utterances Brezhnev was less forthcoming, but the same view—that the division of Europe is beneficial to Soviet security—underpinned Soviet policy at the Conference on Security and Cooperation in Europe. It appears to underlie his statement to the Twenty-sixth Party Congress in February 1981 that the "military and strategic equilibrium prevailing between the USSR and the USA, between the Warsaw Pact and NATO, is objectively a safeguard of world peace."[16] It explains, too, why the Soviet Union has been so chary of that part of the peace movement that calls for the abolition of the two military blocs and the withdrawal of the superpowers from Europe.[17]

The conception that the division of Europe contributes to the Soviet Union's security rests on a number of interrelated military and political considerations. The military advantages that the Soviet Union gains from its dominant position in Eastern Europe have already been outlined. Of particular importance is the stress that Soviet military strategy lays on the offensive. In Soviet eyes the ability to station its troops in central Europe places it in a much more powerful position vis-à-vis NATO than it would be in if its forces had to remain within Soviet frontiers. The Warsaw Pact also provides, as Moreton and Dean point out, a degree of legitimation for the Soviet system because it constitutes the core of the socialist community and provides the Soviet Union with its own military bloc in a world of military alliances.[18]

The view that the division of Europe benefits Soviet security seems to be deeply rooted in Soviet military and political consciousness. But it does not appear to be consistent with the Warsaw Pact's repeated calls for the disbandment of the two military blocs. Even before the Pact was signed, the Soviet Union offered to forego the creation of the Warsaw Treaty Organization if NATO would disband itself. Since 1955 the Pact has called many times for the dissolution of the two military alliances, most recently in the Prague Declaration of the Political Consultative Committee in January 1983.[19]

The significance of such proposals is less than might appear at first sight, however, for there exists between the Soviet Union and the other members of the Pact a network of bilateral treaties and status of forces agreements that would make it possible to maintain many of the existing military arrangements in Eastern Europe even if the Pact were formally dissolved. Soviet forces could remain in Eastern Europe under the bilateral agreements, and some of the Pact's institutions could be absorbed into the Soviet General Staff. Some price would have to be paid, insofar as the Pact has acquired a multilateral character over the years. But abolition of the blocs would probably have less effect on the Pact than it would on NATO, unless the entire infrastructure of bilateral relationships in Eastern Europe were dissolved at the same time.

By pressing for disengagement by the superpowers in Europe, the peace movement has raised the question whether the Soviet Union would be willing to relax its domination over Eastern Europe if its security could be guaranteed in some other way. The proposals the Soviet Union advanced in the 1950s for a neutral Germany indicate that its conception of Europe is not immutable. But in spite of the difficulties it now faces in Eastern Europe there is no sign that it would be willing to relinquish its hold on the region. The Soviet Union evidently regards the Warsaw Pact as a more or less solid rock in the sea of its East European troubles and as an instrument through which to try to prevent the emergence in Europe of threats to Soviet security.

CONCLUSION

The Soviet Union dominates the Warsaw Pact in a variety of ways. This domination springs ultimately from the fact that the social and political systems of Eastern Europe owe their existence to the Soviet Union. It was the Red Army that liberated these countries from Nazism and then made it possible for Stalin to impose the Soviet model on them without regard to national differences. Much greater diversity now exists in the politics of Eastern Europe than there was in Stalin's last years, but the Soviet Union has used force, and the threat of force, to impose limits on change. The political order in Eastern Europe is still underpinned by the Soviet military presence there.

The Soviet Union is by far the most powerful economic and military member of the Pact. According to a Czechoslovak specialist, the Soviet Union carries about 80 percent of the Pact's economic burden (compared with the proportion of about 60 percent of NATO's costs that is borne by the United States). Similarly, the Soviet Union provides about 75 percent of the Warsaw Pact's troops, while the United States supplies around 42 percent of NATO's.[20]

The dominance that the Soviet Union derives from its political, economic, and military power is reinforced by the methods that it uses to control the institutions of the Warsaw Treaty Organization. It fills the most important positions with its own officers. It tries to impose a uniform military doctrine on the member states. It coordinates the political education programs in the Pact and controls the education of senior officers (except for those from the Romanian armed forces). In other words, it employs the standard Soviet techniques of management and control to secure its dominant position.

The Warsaw Pact was set up by the Soviet Union to serve Soviet interests, and it has to be understood primarily as an instrument of Soviet policy. In spite of Soviet dominance and control, however, the Pact is not a monolith. Romania has pursued an independent policy and has managed to evade the most important mechanisms of Soviet control. Economic difficulties in Eastern Europe have made burdensharing a contentious issue. Political crises in Czechoslovakia and Poland have had apparently profound effects on the armed forces of those countries. As Stephan Tiedtke argued in his book on the Warsaw Pact, policy differences within the Pact have sprung from the different interests of the East European leaders. These interests can be rooted in external conditions: the German Democratic Republic (GDR), for example, has a special stake in the Pact because it is only the division of Europe that guarantees its continued existence as a state. More often the different interests are rooted in internal conditions: Czechoslovak criticisms of the alliance, for example, grew out of the reformist ideas of the Prague Spring.[21] The Warsaw Treaty Organization cannot be understood in isolation from the broader economic and political conditions in Eastern Europe.

As a consequence, the Warsaw Pact has grown into a complex mechanism for coordinating the military and foreign policy activities

[37]

of its members. Its institutions have gradually acquired a substance that they lacked in 1955. The Pact is now more than an instrument for transmitting Soviet orders to the East European states. It has an alliance politics of its own, which allows the East European members to have some say in policy making, even if the Soviet Union carries most weight.

For the Soviet Union, Eastern Europe is a buffer zone, to be controlled and dominated not only because of its intrinsic importance but because it provides a defensive glacis against potential enemies. The Warsaw Pact is part of the mechanism for exercising control over Eastern Europe, but it is also intended to add to Soviet military power vis-à-vis NATO. The contribution the East European states make to Soviet security can be assessed only in the context of the Pact's organization. Soviet control makes it possible to achieve a high degree of standardization in the Pact's forces, equipment, and doctrine. At the same time, however, Soviet domination arouses political hostility and makes it difficult for the East European states to establish stable and legitimate rule. The methods the Soviet Union employs to dominate Eastern Europe also have a profound effect on its policy toward Western Europe, for they help to reinforce the cohesion of NATO and thus obstruct Soviet policy toward the West.

There is no sign that the Soviet Union is about to yield its dominant position in Eastern Europe. Control of the region has been central to its conception of its own security, and postwar history shows that it is capable of dealing, sometimes ruthlessly, with the problems that it faces there. The main challenge that the Soviet Union faces is to devise methods of domination that do not undercut the efforts of the East European leaders to secure stable rule in their own countries and do not undermine its own policies toward Western Europe.

PART II

INTRA-PACT RELATIONS

[2]

The Warsaw Treaty Organization: A History

Malcolm Mackintosh

The Origins of the Warsaw Pact

The Warsaw Pact came into being on 14 May 1955 at a ceremony in Warsaw attended by the leaders of the Soviet Union, Poland, Czechoslovakia, East Germany, Hungary, Romania, Bulgaria, and Albania and by the Chinese defense minister, who was invited to be present as an observer.[1] The official purpose for establishing the Pact was that in the previous year the Western Powers had refused to accept Soviet proposals for a European security system that would neutralize and permanently divide Germany. Instead, the West had invited the Federal German Republic to join the West European Union and was in the process of admitting her to NATO under the terms of the Paris Agreements of 23 October 1954. Four days after the ratification of these agreements on 5 May 1955, West Germany joined NATO; the Soviet and East European leaders immediately gathered in Warsaw and signed their own treaty, which came to be known as the Warsaw Pact.

There were good political and military reasons for the establishment of an organization in Eastern Europe through which the new leadership of the Soviet Union could change and improve its legacy from Stalin. The Soviet army had occupied most of Eastern Europe in 1944–1945, and the Soviet Union had imposed communist regimes totally obedient to Moscow in all East European countries except Yugoslavia. Stalin's rule in Eastern Europe, however, dominated as it was by a primitive obsession with the superiority of everything Soviet, unrestricted exploitation of all political, military, and economic resources of the area, and an anti-Yugoslav witch-hunt in the satellite countries, was not only cruel but unproductive. No attempt was made to recognize the needs or traditions of the East European peoples or to treat the countries as anything but Stalin's colonies.

Nowhere was this attitude more noticeable than in military affairs. Stalin's policy was wasteful because of his obsession with numbers of formations and men under arms and his reluctance to equip the East European armies with anything but obsolete Soviet weapons.[2] Stalin also imposed Soviet army regulations down to the most trivial details on the national armies, navies, and air forces, dispatched Soviet officers to hold key appointments (the most famous being Marshal Konstantin Rokossovskii, who became Polish defense minister in 1949), and insisted on privileges and rights for Soviet officers in each East European ally which could only be regarded as humiliating by the people of that country. Each state was bound to the Soviet Union by a bilateral defense treaty; but there is no evidence of any attempt to coordinate the training of their forces with each other or with that of the Soviet army. Stalin apparently allocated these armies little more than internal security duties; and even then he distrusted the national officer corps (especially those associated with wartime resistance movements), which he frequently purged with characteristic ruthlessness.

On the political and economic fronts, too, Eastern Europe, especially in Stalin's later years, was a wasting asset in which perhaps only the Soviet secret police developed as a flourishing industry. Stalin's successors, primarily Nikita S. Khrushchev and Nikolai Bulganin, had to get the countries of Eastern Europe moving again under appropriate Soviet direction. New and effective coordination in internal, foreign, defense, and economic policies was clearly necessary if they were to succeed.

First, the new Soviet leaders needed a political organization through which they could transmit directives to their East European allies and organize support for Soviet policies. Such an organization should at least appear to be a forum in which East European views could be taken into account by the Russians and thus help to reduce the visible signs of Soviet domination. Second, Khrushchev and Bulganin had to take into account new developments in military doctrine, not only those associated with nuclear weapons but also the buildup of NATO forces in Western Europe since 1949 and the modernization of battlefield weapons and tactics, in part based on Western experience in the Korean War.

For the European "theatre of operations," Soviet military doctrine in 1955 required Soviet and East European forces to defend the Soviet

[42]

Union's buffer zone from internal or external threats, maintaining orthodox Communist parties in power in Eastern Europe, and, in the event of war, advancing rapidly westward to destroy NATO forces and occupy NATO territory. Clearly, the East European allies had to be a part of this modernizing process. So that they could be of real value to the Soviet army, their forces had to be reorganized, reequipped, cut down to realistic strengths, provided with the necessary mobility, and, in a certain sense nationalized by replacing their Soviet commanders with reliable and efficient officers with a genuinely national background. At the same time, their activity, training, and tasks had to be coordinated under Soviet direction. The formation of a Soviet–East European High Command became a logical step in solving the problems posed by this new military doctrine.

We cannot, however, rule out the possibility that the formation of a politico-military alliance that was realized in the Warsaw Pact was a result of internal developments in the Soviet Union, including leadership struggles between Khrushchev and his allies and the more hard-line and traditionalist personalities such as Vyacheslav M. Molotov and Lazar M. Kaganovich. Khrushchev had won the power conflict over Georgii Malenkov in early 1955, but Molotov and his group were still active in the leadership and could undermine or at least delay some of Khrushchev's innovative policies. Khrushchev may well have envisioned that the creation of a new alliance structure to control Eastern Europe, embracing political, foreign policy, military, and economic issues, would give him a real and practical advantage over his rivals in this difficult and contentious area.[3]

THE ESTABLISHMENT OF THE WARSAW PACT

For all these reasons the Soviet Union set up the Warsaw Pact in May 1955. Politically, the Pact was modeled to some extent on NATO in that it had a Political Consultative Committee, which, under Article 6 of the treaty, was required to meet twice a year with each member country serving as chairman for a year. The Pact had a commander in chief drawn from the strongest power in the alliance and a Permanent Commission to recommend proposals on foreign policy "acceptable to all members of the Pact." The members of the Pact offered to disband it if NATO was abandoned by the Western Powers; until then, the Pact offered a nonaggression treaty to NATO in July 1955. Article 3 of the treaty stated that the signatories would "consult each other on all important international issues affecting their common

[43]

interests." Under Article 7, members undertook "not to join any coalition or alliance or to conclude any agreement conflicting with the objectives of the Treaty."

From the moment of its foundation, the Warsaw Pact acquired all the characteristics of a typical Soviet political and defense organization and High Command. Soviet secrecy descended on its military and political organization, its program of work, and its military planning and doctrine. As far as we know, the Political Consultative Committee met irregularly—only ten times between 1955 and 1969; its debates were rarely published, and its communiqués were usually identical with foreign policy statements issued by the Soviet Union. There is no evidence that the Permanent Commission had any role to play in the work of the Pact. The entire military organization was housed in the Soviet Ministry of Defense; the commander in chief, Marshal I. S. Konev, was a first deputy minister of defense of the Soviet Union, and the Pact's first chief of staff, Army General A. I. Antonov, was head of a chief directorate in the Soviet General Staff. Soviet military missions led by senior officers were set up in the East European capitals, but no comparable East European missions appeared in Moscow. East European officers who were attached to the Pact's staff had little say in military planning.[4]

The limited knowledge that we have of the early organization of the Warsaw Pact indicates that the Soviet Union established military headquarters which, in addition to transmitting Soviet foreign and defense policies to members of the Pact, could begin to reorganize the East European armies along more effective and up-to-date lines. The forces were reported to have been cut by 2.5 million men between 1955 and 1958.[5] After 1956 many Soviet officers serving in the East European armed forces returned to the Soviet Union or left the army; the best-known examples came from Poland and included Marshal K. K. Rokossovskii and Generals S. G. Poplavskii, and Korchits. Panchevskii, the defense minister and a former Soviet army colonel, was appointed ambassador in Peking.

These officers were replaced by younger men making their careers in their national armies; some, such as General Slavcho Trnski in Bulgaria, who had escaped Stalin's purges of members of the wartime resistance movements, assumed high positions within Warsaw Pact forces. In Poland there was even a move to recognize the services of Poles who had fought in the Home Army and in the West. This policy of renationalizing the East European armies removed some of the more obvious signs of Soviet domination and raised the prestige and attractiveness of a military career for young East Europeans. It also helped to improve the political reliability of these armies, which the Russians hoped would play an effective role in supporting the Soviet military position in Eastern and central Europe.

At the same time the Soviet Union introduced measures to formalize its right to station troops in Eastern Europe. The basis of the problem was that because the Soviet Union sought political, military, and economic cohesion in Eastern Europe with both its World War II allies and enemies, it could no longer justify the presence of Soviet troops in states such as Romania, Hungary, or East Germany under the heading of "occupation forces." Former enemy states raised understandable concern in Soviet thinking. It was therefore necessary at an early stage to devise status of forces agreements with each country which reflected and combined political realities, historical factors, and the military needs of the service chiefs in Moscow in planning military operations in Europe. Some of these agreements gave differing rights to the Soviet Union, for example, on exercises and maneuvers.

The issue of troops arose in May 1955, when the Austrian State Treaty deprived the Russians of their original authorization to keep troops in Hungary and Romania to protect their lines of communication to Austria, where the Soviet army maintained a garrison. The difficulty was overcome initially by including in the announcement of the establishment of the Warsaw Pact High Command the statement that the deployment of forces in Eastern Europe would be arranged "in accordance with the requirements of mutual defense in agreement among these states."[6] After the Hungarian rising of October 1956, new status of forces agreements were signed with Poland and East Germany, which regulated the judicial rights and limitations of Soviet troops stationed abroad, and in 1956 and 1957 with Hungary and Romania, which included at least nominally favorable conditions for the host country. Priority, however, was given in the preambles to the treaties with Poland, Hungary, and Romania to the military requirements of the Warsaw Pact.[7]

The Evolution of the Warsaw Pact 1955–1968

Within eighteen months of the foundation of the Warsaw Pact the Soviet Union faced its first major rebellion within its East European buffer zone—the Hungarian rising of October 1956. The details of this revolution are described in Chapter 5. The Soviet Union appears to have been taken by surprise by the rebellion and by the success of the Hungarians' military action, which pinned down and trapped the two Soviet divisions stationed in Hungary. This initial defeat was followed by a characteristic "pause" during which the Soviet Union issued a declaration (on 30 October 1956) suggesting that its army could be withdrawn from Hungary if all Warsaw Pact countries agreed. It is tempting to interpret this declaration as an attempt to use the Warsaw Pact as a forum for the resolution of unwanted conflicts and to stress its role in political and foreign policy relationships. Given the military evidence of the buildup of Soviet forces in southwest Russia, however, it seems more likely that the declaration was an act of deception by the Soviet leaders to gain time before launching the invasion of 4 November. When this army, commanded by General P. I. Batov, was ready, the Russians attacked with overwhelming force, destroyed the Hungarian army, and seized its leaders, who were ultimately tried in the Soviet Union and executed.

Of particular significance were the measures related to the Warsaw Pact taken by the Soviet Union as a result of the Hungarian rising. The Hungarian army was in effect disbanded: only one antitank artillery regiment in that army today bears a battle honor indicating that it supported the Soviet military action on 4 November 1956. Indeed, it was not until the mid-1960s that Hungarian divisions reappeared in the order of battle of the Warsaw Pact, and even today the Hungarian army numbers only a little over half of the eleven-division force that faced the Russians in 1956. At the same time the Soviet army doubled its garrison in Hungary from two to four divisions with air support under the command of Headquarters Southern Group of Forces.

Politically the Soviet Union also appeared to limit the role and contribution of the East European countries within the Warsaw Pact in the years after the Hungarian rising. Between the end of 1956 and February 1960 there were only two announced meetings of its Political Consultative Committee. One, in May 1958, endorsed the Soviet version of the Polish Rapacki Plan for a nuclear-free zone in central Europe and an East German proposal for a confederation of the two Germanies; the other, in April 1959, did little more than uphold Soviet policy on Germany and relations with the United States. While some of the military improvements outlined above were under way, Soviet attitudes to their East European allies seemed to be dominated by suspicion and distrust, possibly in part because of the experience of the Hungarian crisis.

Nevertheless, some progress toward military efficiency and integration was made during the early 1960s. Changes occurred in Soviet attitudes to war and military priorities associated with the growth of strategic and theater nuclear weapons in both the East and the West

[46]

and their application to Europe. In addition, Khrushchev attempted to reorganize the Soviet armed forces for the nuclear age as he understood it, a view not shared by most of his military advisers. In the course of a number of major changes made in the Soviet High Command in 1960, Marshal A. A. Grechko, at that time a protégé of Khrushchev, became the commander in chief of the Warsaw Pact forces and, with Khrushchev's backing, took effective measures to improve both the military and political efficiency of the Pact.

Marshal Grechko's appointment led in 1961, for example, to the first major multinational exercises of Warsaw Pact forces, primarily in the Northern Tier area of Poland, East Germany, and Czechoslovakia, though smaller bilateral exercises were also held with Soviet forces in the 1960s in Hungary, Romania, and Bulgaria. Romania refused to allow field exercises to be held on her territory after 1964, thus beginning the long process of "disobedience" to the Soviet Union on foreign and defense policies which has continued to the present day. Through the decade, more and more exercises in the Northern Tier were held under at least the nominal command of East European military commanders, such as those under the Polish General Marian Spychalski in 1962, Czechoslovak General Bohumir Lomsky in 1964, and the East German minister of defense, General Heinz Hoffmann in 1967.

There is evidence, too, that under Marshal Grechko the High Command of the Warsaw Pact forces finally took shape as an administrative and coordinating agency for the East European armies, but without command-and-control responsibilities. In some ways the headquarters seemed to resemble a traditional European war ministry or war office, which administers its forces but does not command them in war. The Warsaw Pact headquarters moved out of the Soviet General Staff and became an independent element within the Soviet Ministry of Defense with its own Combined Staff, although the chief of staff continued to hold the title of a first deputy chief of the Soviet General Staff. The headquarters and the Combined Staff included senior officers from all the member countries at deputy commander in chief and deputy chief of the Combined Staff level. But the commander in chief, the chief of staff, the deputy commander in chief for armaments, the head of the Combat Training Directorate, and the chief political officers were Soviet officers, as were the heads of departments or directorates dealing with control of the Soviet military missions in the East European countries and with finance and administration.

Most significant in the Pact's organization, its headquarters appeared to have no rear logistic services directorates, and the Combined Staff lacked either an operations or a transportation department. Although the Warsaw Pact included a Soviet air force general who was assigned to the Warsaw Pact countries, the actual air defense of the area was the responsibility of the Soviet Strategic Air Defense Command and was organized on a direct command-and-control link from each country to Moscow, bypassing the Warsaw Pact headquarters.

This structure was consistent with the picture described by Marshal V. D. Sokolovskii in his classic study *Military Strategy*, first published in Moscow in 1962. "In wartime," the marshal wrote, "operational units, including armed forces of different socialist countries, can be created to conduct joint operations in military theatres. The command of those units can be assigned to the Supreme High Commands of the Soviet armed forces, with representation of the Supreme High Commands of the Allied countries. . . . The chain of command would pass through the Soviet General Staff to the theatre or field headquarters established for the operation."[8]

The military growth and development in the Warsaw Pact in the 1960s coincided with a more erratic advance in the political field. Disagreements over the meaning of the Pact's political role began to appear in the early 1960s, and many of them have not yet been resolved. First was the departure of Albania from the alliance in 1961, when diplomatic relations between Moscow and Tirana were broken off and the Albanians seized the Soviet-manned submarine base at Valona on the Adriatic. Thereafter, Albania played no role in Warsaw Pact affairs and formally left the organization in September 1968.

A more important critic of the Soviet Union and the Pact, however, was Romania, whose leaders seemed intent on undermining Soviet domination of the alliance from the inside. In 1958 Khrushchev, partly as an attempt to impress the West of the sincerity of Soviet proposals for arms reductions in Europe and partly in response to Romanian wishes, withdrew the two Soviet divisions stationed in Romania. This decision may have whetted the appetite of the Romanians, for in 1963 Romania adopted the principle of noninterference in the affairs of other countries and reserved the right to take her own decisions on foreign and defense policy. In November 1964, for example, Romania reduced the length of compulsory military service from two years to sixteen months; in May 1966 Nicolae Ceausescu, the Romanian leader, called for the "abolition of military blocs, the dismantling of foreign bases and the withdrawal of foreign troops from the territory of other countries."[9] Two months later there were reports that the Romanians had turned a meeting of the Political Consultative Committee in

Bucharest into a forum for airing their grievances, which included Soviet failure to consult the Warsaw Pact allies on the use of nuclear weapons and the costs of maintaining Soviet troops on members' territory.[10] The Romanians also unilaterally established diplomatic relations with the Federal Republic of Germany in January 1967 and retained their embassy in Israel after the Six-Day War later in that year when the Soviet Union and other East European countries broke off diplomatic relations with Tel Aviv.

There is also some evidence that Czechoslovakia had doubts about the political and military nature of the Pact. In July 1966 a Czechoslovak political journal pointed out that the differing economic, social and cultural development of the Warsaw Pact states contained the seeds of disintegration and continued, "Where there are basic differences and disagreements on the interpretation of the fundamental problems of revolutionary strategy and tactics and there is no unity of view on the political part of socialist military doctrine, the cooperation of the socialist states in the military field will inevitably be endangered and even the military alliance can be seriously affected."[11]

It would be misleading to overestimate the strength of these Romanian and Czechoslovak criticisms of the Warsaw Pact in the 1960s. When, for example, the Soviet Union and the Pact faced their next major challenge from within Eastern Europe, the Czechoslovak crisis of 1968, the armed forces of the Pact seemed to be in satisfactory shape. But politically, unity of views was as diverse as ever and dissatisfaction amounting even to rank disobedience appeared to be growing within the alliance. These rumblings must have been a cause of serious anxiety to the Soviet leaders, especially in a period of crisis.

THE CZECHOSLOVAK CRISIS OF 1968

As in the case of the Hungarian rising in 1956, a detailed account of the Czechoslovak crisis is found in Chapter 5. The nature of the opposition to the established and elitist regime of President Antonin Novotny, based on intellectual and social arguments supported by both the intelligentsia and elements of the labor force, placed the Soviet Union at a disadvantage, especially in the early stages of the crisis. When by about April 1968 the Soviet leadership realized that a political and intellectual movement had become a threat to Czechoslovakia's loyalty to the Soviet Union, to Soviet communism, and to the Warsaw Pact, the Russians characteristically chose to build up a military force capable of invading the country and reimposing Soviet

[49]

control. While the concentration of forces was under way and a major exercise was held on Czechoslovak soil, the Soviet leaders negotiated with, pressured, and rallied support against Alexander Dubcek, the Czechoslovak party leader, and his colleagues in a series of attempts to persuade them to change their policies. By early August 1968 both Soviet and East European armed forces were ready for action; and with evidence in their hands that a forthcoming Czechoslovak Communist party congress would probably be dominated by members whose views were totally unacceptable to the Soviet Union, the Politburo in Moscow gave the order to invade.

There was little resistance from an unsuspecting Czechoslovak population and army, though Soviet Special Forces were available for the arrest and deportation to the Soviet Union of Dubcek and other important Czechoslovak leaders, a practice that has become part of well-established Soviet pattern in carrying out such military and political operations.[12] Our evidence about the organization of the invasion suggests that in 1968 the Warsaw Pact headquarters had no operational role. Under its new commander in chief, Marshal I. I. Iakubovskii, it assembled, exercised, and deployed the Soviet and East European forces for the invasion. But when the force was ready, its command was transferred to a forward command post of the Soviet High Command in Lignica in Poland, under army General I. G. Pavlovskii, the commander in chief of the Soviet ground forces, with the experienced General S. M. Shtemenko as his chief of staff. When the invasion was over, the Russians set up, under a treaty of 4 October 1968, a Central Group of Forces in the country of five divisions, which today provides the permanent army of occupation in Czechoslovakia.

Politically the Soviet Union justified its use of force in Czechoslovakia by what has become known as the Brezhnev Doctrine—though the Russians have never formally used this title. This doctrine maintained that a communist country has a right to self-determination only so far as the interests of other states of the "Socialist Commonwealth" are not jeopardized, that each Communist party is responsible to the other fraternal parties as well as to its own people, and that the sovereignty of each country is not "abstract" but "an expression of the class struggle."[13] In other words, the Soviet Union reserves the right to define each country's sovereignty within the Soviet bloc. By implication, at least, the doctrine gave the Russians the right to act in the defense of its allies if necessary by military force.

Successful and almost bloodless as it was, the Soviet invasion of Czechoslovakia in 1968 caused the Soviet leaders to reorganize the military structure of the Warsaw Pact to try to bring the East Europeans more directly into the working of the Pact without lessening essential Soviet control over all its activities. In the period between the invasion and March 1969 the Soviet Ministry of Defense, the Communist party leadership, and no doubt the KGB worked out what they hoped would be a minimal reorganization of the headquarters. We have no evidence on how these discussions were conducted or who took part: was there any real consultation with the Warsaw Pact Communist parties or armed forces, for example? Clearly the talks took place in conditions of characteristic Soviet secrecy in closed sessions of the organizations involved. But they must have produced a final document that was accepted by the East Europeans for it was put to a two-hour session of the Pact's Political Consultative Committee in Budapest on 26 March 1969 and received formal approval from the East European members for its recommendations.

Under the terms of the reorganization the Soviet commander in chief, then Marshal Iakubovskii, and now Marshal Viktor G. Kulikov, remained a first deputy minister of defense in the Soviet Union but was provided with two multinational committees to advise him. The senior of the two is the Committee of National Defense Ministers, composed, as its name suggests, of the ministers of defense of each member country. It meets at irregular intervals to review and approve the decisions taken by the other, more substantive body: the Military Council.

The Military Council and some of its component parts were the major innovation of the 1969 reforms. The council is modeled on the military councils that exist at high levels throughout the Soviet armed forces to control the activities of arms of service, military districts (or Groups of Forces), and fleets. The chairman of the Warsaw Pact Military Council is the commander in chief, Marshal Kulikov, and the members include the deputy commander in chief for armaments, General Fabrikov, the deputy commander in chief for air defense, General I. D. Podgornyi, the chief of staff, General A. I. Gribkov, and holders of a number of new posts created since 1969: the deputy commanders in chief for the air force, General A. N. Katrich, and the navy, Admiral V. V. Mikhailin, and the assistant to the commander in chief for rear (logistic) services, all of whom are Soviet officers, as well as the senior Soviet political officer. The council also includes senior officers of lieutenant general or vice-admiral rank from each of the East European countries. As before the 1969 reforms, East European officers of major-general or rear admiral rank are deputy chiefs of the Combined Staff.

[51]

This reconstruction of the Warsaw Pact High Command suggests that the Soviet Union has given the East European member states a greater presence in the headquarters with perhaps more say in the preparation of official statements, policies, military training, and the participation of their own countries in the activities of the Pact. That many senior Soviet officers are drawn from the main branches of the Soviet forces suggests that the Soviet Union may have delegated more authority to these areas to the Pact as an organization. This development may, in fact, provide a greater role for the Military Council, which could explain its apparent importance and the significance given to its decisions and communiqués. At the same time, it is clear that in operational areas Soviet military control over the Pact has probably been tightened. Such a move would be logical in Soviet thinking not only to ensure political loyalty and reliability but also to increase the efficiency of the alliance in the light of increasingly modern weaponry and the need for speed in operations and in command-and-control techniques.

The conclusion which this evidence suggests is, therefore, that the Warsaw Pact's military headquarters, as constituted at present on the basis of the 1969 reforms, is still primarily an administrative, training, and coordination authority for the joint multinational forces deployed under Soviet command in Eastern Europe. This organizational form does not rule out the possibility that the existing force structure and command-and-control machinery available to the Soviet Union in western Russia and Eastern Europe for use in the event of a major conflict in Europe does not overlap or make use of Warsaw Pact facilities and possible headquarters. Our evidence is inadequate to make a judgment on that point, though such coordination seems likely.

Certainly in wartime the Soviet High Command, supported by the Soviet General Staff, would take command of whatever East European forces are available, properly trained, and considered politically reliable for the task in hand. The Soviet Union continues to believe that the current structure and military capabilities of the Warsaw Pact are satisfactory. The troops appear to be well-armed and exercised, and the most senior officers have been trained in the Soviet Union. Military service is an accepted part of life for the overwhelming majority of the young people in Eastern Europe. Morale and the sense of motivation obviously vary from country to country and are at present clearly low and inadequate in Poland, where a government made up of professional soldiers imposed martial law in December 1981 in order to retain a communist regime in that country. Although martial law has formally been suspended, it continues to be the effective means of governing Poland today. But it seems likely that if a solution to the Polish crisis acceptable to the Soviet Union is ultimately achieved, the Soviet leaders probably consider that the existing Warsaw Pact alliance is at least consistent with their buffer zone concept of defense and offense. The problems that are likely to arise will, however, almost certainly be connected with the growing importance of national characteristics of the East European countries in the years ahead.

THE FUTURE OF THE WARSAW PACT

This discussion is very speculative, but it can begin with a list of at least some of the main factors that are bound to be central in any analysis of the future of the Warsaw Pact and the role of the East European countries in the alliance. Surely the first of these must be the unchanging need for Soviet political control over all the countries of Eastern Europe, ensuring the predominance of Soviet ideology and the preservation of the Soviet system of party and government control in all members of the Warsaw Pact. This factor might include the hope that in due course both Yugoslavia and Albania might return to the fold, either voluntarily or as a result of Soviet or Warsaw Pact action, directly or indirectly. Eastern Europe must also remain a political and military buffer zone, protecting the Soviet frontiers and allowing Soviet forces continuing freedom to deploy for defensive or offensive purposes. In other words, Soviet military control over the area must be retained—and it must be effective.

Following these assumptions, any analysis of the future of the Warsaw Pact has to include some international issues, primarily the future Soviet-American political, military, and commercial relationship, the likely state of arms control negotiations, the strength or weaknesses of the Western alliance in Europe, and the future East-West balance of power on the Continent. Economic factors relevant to the Warsaw Pact in the 1980s, the financial and commercial status of Warsaw Pact countries, and the energy situation in Western and Eastern Europe, especially the oil and gas requirements of East European countries, are all important factors in this analysis. Indeed, the role of energy in underpinning East European dependence on the Soviet Union may be of great importance in the evolution of the Warsaw Pact. But the most important factor will be the attitudes, needs, and policies of the individual East European countries and their likely future relationship with the Soviet Union on political and military issues.

Let us therefore look first at the largest of the Soviet Union's allies in Eastern Europe: Poland. Poland's central geographical position in Eastern Europe and along the Soviet frontier would give it this priority, even if the revolutionary events of 1980–1982 had not taken place. The Soviet Union has always had to base any analysis of Poland on the history of Russian–Polish relations and the centuries of conflict between the two nations in Europe. After the creation of a working relationship on a reasonably acceptable ideological basis between Russia and Poland since 1955, which survived dangerous moments of crisis in 1956, 1970, and 1976, it was most unfortunate, in Soviet eyes, that a trade union movement known as Solidarity developed in Poland and assumed the role of a new political party. Solidarity rivaled the official Polish Communist party, which, according to Marxism-Leninism, should be the sole element of authority and exercise the leading role in a communist country allied with and subordinate to the Soviet Union. Characteristically, as soon as the crisis reached serious proportions, the Soviet Union prepared an army to invade the country and, as in Hungary and Czechoslovakia, reimpose orthodox pro-Soviet party rule. Early in 1981, the Russians decided not to invade, probably because the Soviet government realized that the Poles would resist and because the Russians were reluctant to assume the responsibility of administering an occupied Poland, particularly given that country's traditions, history, and economic difficulties.

The Soviet Union maintained (and still maintains) strong forces around and in Poland in case invasion had become or becomes inevitable; such an operation would certainly use the facilities, communications, and resources of the Warsaw Pact. It seems likely that the Russians also prepared a fallback plan in which only Soviet forces would be used without employing the Pact's forces or structure. But the Russians exerted as much pressure as they could on the Polish military authorities who took over all government and party posts in 1981 to solve the crisis themselves. The Polish soldiers took control, at least in immediate and practical terms, by declaring martial law on 13 December 1981 and suppressing Solidarity as a real political force.

The Polish crisis, whatever its outcome, presents any Soviet leadership with its major problem in the Warsaw Pact. The Soviet Union will surely insist that Poland's territory must at all costs remain effectively within the Warsaw Pact and militarily under Soviet control. If the Polish armed forces were to be suspected of disloyalty, even if the Polish Workers' party resumes its leading role, they could be reduced in strength—as happened in Hungary in 1956—and limited to internal guard duties. Such a decision would create even greater difficulties for the Soviet Union in ensuring that Poland was administered effectively and played some military role in maintaining the buffer zone. A permanent Soviet military occupation is clearly unthinkable; so, on a very speculative basis, it is possible that the Soviet leaders might reluctantly have to fall back on the maintenance of a long-term regime of martial law in Warsaw. Military rulers might at least enjoy the traditional Polish respect for the armed forces and could probably ensure that Soviet land, sea, and air communications were safe and effectively in the hands of the Warsaw Pact.

At the same time the Soviet military position in East Germany, Czechoslovakia, and the Baltic Sea could be strengthened, and Soviet forces in western Russia might be built up and reorganized into stronger and more mobile formations, which, in the event of war, could be moved very rapidly, with or without Polish agreement, across Poland to link up with Soviet troops in East Germany and Czechoslovakia. Although, of course, there would be many other aspects of a future Soviet-Polish relationship involving the Warsaw Pact, this may be one option of a purely military nature which could form part of the evolution of the Warsaw Pact in the years ahead.

Czechoslovakia, now firmly in the hands of obedient pro-Soviet hard-liners such as Gustav Husak and Vasil Bilak, has never shared Poland's form of opposition to Soviet rule. Its opposition to Soviet domination has been intellectual and political. Czechoslovakia may have to assume a more important role in Warsaw Pact military-operational planning, and much Soviet attention will be paid to improving Czechoslovak efficiency and reliability, which may be doubted in Moscow because of the armed forces' lack of combat experience. But Czechoslovakia will almost certainly maintain its loyalty to a Warsaw Pact modeled on the present alliance, and Soviet trust in Czechoslovakia as an ally is not likely to be weakened in the foreseeable future.

Hungary has proved more difficult to keep within the Soviet orbit. The suddenness of the Hungarian rising in 1956 took the Russians by surprise; when the rising was over, the Soviet Union's initially harsh discipline and methods eventually gave way to a more flexible attitude to Hungarian nationalism, particularly in the economic and commercial fields. Today, Hungary's economic and trade policies, under the direction of Janos Kadar, seem to be the most liberal in Eastern Europe. Hungarians and Russians are deeply suspicious of each other for national reasons, however: the language barrier is almost insurmountable, and Hungarians have strong affinity for Western Europe through their historical and national traditions. But, especially if current economic progress continues, Hungary will likely remain a politically and militarily stable member of the Soviet bloc and will not press for change in the present Warsaw Pact arrangements, if Soviet control of the alliance remains effective and unimpaired.

In the Balkans, Romania creates serious difficulties for the Russians. The Russians know that the Romanians are of mixed race: part Latin (like their language), part Slav, and part Turkish, with elements of long-forgotten Asiatic tribes that settled in the Danube valley in early medieval times. Romanians have tended to regard themselves as West European, close to France and Italy; their political character has been shaped by centuries of Balkan history. Romania's present leader, Nicolae Ceausescu, is ruthless and authoritarian, and his communist regime is marked by unwavering rigidity. Romania, under Ceausescu's leadership, is in many senses a rebel against Soviet rule, but Ceausescu is a skillful rebel and has avoided giving the Soviet Union an excuse to expel or overthrow him even on issues of defense expenditure, in spite of the attraction this option may have had for Soviet leaders in the past.

The Romanian leaders, however, were dismayed by some aspects of the Polish situation and may have preferred a return to single-party control under Soviet authority to prevent a spread of Solidarity tendencies into their country. The Romanians may hope for a continuation of the present, somewhat predictable Soviet military domination of the Warsaw Pact organization. They have, after all, learned to outwit the Soviet Union on political and military matters in the last decade, using traditional Balkan tactics. Though the Romanians like to demonstrate in public a degree of independence from the Soviet Union, the present leaders would probably rather continue to follow these policies in circumstances they understand than have to face up to new and unknown forces that might appear if the Warsaw Pact changed its character significantly in the wake of the Polish crisis or if serious economic problems shook the foundations of the Soviet bloc in the next decade.

Little needs to be said about Bulgaria's future position or role in the Warsaw Pact, for Bulgaria has never given the Soviet Union any real trouble. Since 1944 the Bulgarians have been docile and subservient to the Russians, to whom the ordinary Bulgarian feels a sense of respect and even friendship—unlike the Poles or the Romanians. The Bulgarians are hard workers and traditionally disciplined and responsive to authority. They can be expected to continue their allegiance to the Russians indefinitely, under their present rulers, and would accept any form of Warsaw Treaty Organization sponsored by the Soviet Union. At a time of considerable uncertainty within Eastern Europe in 1982, Bulgaria successfully hosted a major multinational Warsaw Pact exercise (Shield 82) in which all but the Romanians took an active part, including a small contingent of elite Polish troops.

The East German role in the Pact would reflect some of the traditional ambivalence shown by the Russians for their hardworking, disciplined, authoritarian, and exceptionally efficient former opponents, whose separate state they set up after World War II. The Russians know well that East Germany has moved into a phase of economic and industrial development, which is not only efficient but of considerable value to the Soviet economy; their very efficiency must be a matter of envy to the Russians. Some aspects of East German militarism which have manifested themselves in recent years may cause disquiet among Russians and other East Europeans: the East Germans, for example, instituted the new rank of marshal of the DDR in 1982. East German leaders show no visible tendencies to question Soviet domination; if anything, especially on local, German matters, they seem to support a hard line, sometimes more extreme than that of the Soviet Union itself. East German loyalty should not obscure, however, their potential to cause problems for the Russians, who are very careful to keep the East German party and government under close observation and control.

The Soviet Union regards the presence of a large number of Soviet forces on East German soil as absolutely essential to the control of its buffer zone and its ability to exert military pressure on Europe. The East Germans also need those forces to maintain their existence as an independent state, as one of two Germanies. East Germany would certainly oppose any change in the status or organization of the Warsaw Pact and would play an active part in preventing any such alterations resulting from the crisis in Poland.

From this brief analysis of likely future developments, it seems probable that the Warsaw Pact countries, under their present or similar succession leaderships, would prefer the Pact's existing structures and Soviet control to remain broadly unchanged in the next decade. The uncertain factor, at the moment, is the situation in Poland, and any Soviet leadership, conscious of the concept of worst case scenarios, would certainly conclude that a worsening situation in Poland, one of the bastions of the Warsaw Pact in Eastern Europe, could threaten the existence of the alliance. This danger may indeed have brought some members of the Pact, who previously emphasized differing priorities, to an awareness of the risks of change.

Any interpretation of Soviet planning remains uncertain, if only because of the secretive character of Soviet policy making and the uncertain future of the Polish situation. Whatever happens in Poland, the pressures to retain the discipline and control of the existing Warsaw Pact structure will continue to be very strong in Moscow. It is possible to speculate that the Soviet Union may decide to refashion some part of its military doctrine and its force deployments to enable it to pursue its policies in Europe with reduced dependence on Polish facilities and cooperation in spite of the inevitable defects in military capabilities caused by such adjustments. It is certain, however, that whatever option is pursued (and there are many possible variations to those described above), the Soviet Union will never give up its political and military control over Eastern Europe: the buffer zone is here to stay.

Clearly, however, in the longer term, there will continue to be stresses and strains within the Warsaw Pact on political, economic, and military issues. So far the Russians have been able to keep dissatisfaction under control. It would certainly be unwise for any existing or future East European leadership to underestimate the Soviet Union's power to control, dominate, and, in the last resort, overcome any serious resistance from the East European countries. But each of the East European countries is a nation in its own right. Each has a history, a tradition of relations with Russia and of dealing with a large and dominating power; each has a national language, a culture, an economy, and economic resources as well as a political attitude that have been, and can be again, of great importance to the future of Eastern Europe. The Soviet Union cannot ignore these distinctions and differences, and in the medium and longer term East European nationalism will be one of the Russians' fundamental problems in maintaining their military posture within their own zone and in pursuing their general aims in Europe as a whole.

[3]

Defense Burden-Sharing

CONDOLEEZZA RICE

The issue of burden-sharing is at the core of alliance planning for collective defense. In NATO, burden-sharing is often contentious, marked by frequent complaints from the United States that the West Europeans are not pulling their weight. Among the signatories to the Warsaw Pact, public signs of disagreement are rare. With the notable exception of Romania, East European states frequently and dutifully proclaim their willingness to share the burden to "defend the gains of socialism." In practice, however, East European contributions to the Pact vary considerably, reflecting, as in NATO, the different resources of each country and differing assessments of the threat and of the appropriate level of defense spending. The economic burden, the protection of defense industries under the weight of Warsaw Pact standardization, and demands to support extra-European security interests of the Soviet Union are all potentially divisive issues within the Pact. In spite of protestations to the contrary, the interests of the Soviets and their East European allies are not necessarily the same.

Although the decision processes of the Warsaw Pact on burden-sharing are hidden from view, this chapter tries to shed some light on the process by assessing the extent to which East European interests may or may not be served by various burden-sharing arrangements. The ways the smaller Pact members balance their own concerns against the demands of the Soviet Union will be analyzed. Four aspects of burden-sharing are examined: defense spending; weapons standardization and its impact upon domestic production; division of labor in mission responsibility; and collective security or the use of East European forces outside the European theater.

Defense Spending

The military budget is a visible raw measure of a state's commitment to defense, and alliances usually set targets for military spending, which have great symbolic value. Failure to meet a target is tantamount to failure to live up to the obligation of alliance membership.

Unfortunately, budget data for Eastern Europe are unreliable at best, and it is difficult to assess the defense commitments of Warsaw Pact states on the basis of military spending. Official military budgets often exclude some expenditures. Differences in valuation of costs for civilian and military goods further complicate the task of establishing the real level of expenditure. Western analysts such as Thad Alton have adjusted East European defense spending data by computing dollar estimates of the costs, and those data are used here.[1] Currency conversion and many of the problems of valuation are addressed, but no attempt is made to reconcile the problem of hidden expenditures. Consequently, the data must be used with care and are not, for example, employed here to discuss the impact of defense spending on East European economies. On the other hand, broad trends and differences in the level of expenditure within the alliance can be established. In sum, the *economics* of defense spending (actual costs) are difficult to assess using these data, but they are adequate to address the *politics* of burden-sharing.

The Political Consultative Commission (PCC) of the Warsaw Pact first attempted to coordinate the allocation of resources to defense in January 1965.[2] In accordance with Soviet plans for more efficient use of the alliance, the allies were asked to support collective defense on the basis of ability to pay and to participate actively in building a new, more integrated defense system. According to Soviet sources, the socialist states, reacting to "aggressive moves by NATO, adopted a concrete, collective strategy for their protection, based on the devotion of the resources of the individual states to a collective defense."[3]

Poland, Hungary, and Bulgaria reportedly endorsed the integrated defense plan.[4] Soviet sources even claim that an enthusiastic East Germany or German Democratic Republic (GDR) actually convened the meeting.[5] On the other hand, Romania, which had already signaled her divergence in 1964 by unilaterally cutting the term of national service, was unhappy.

Czechoslovakia's position was more complex and is the only verifiable case of intraparty dissension. Antonin Novotny, the party general secretary, embraced the idea, but some within his party did not.

[60]

He encountered considerable difficulty in selling the plan in Prague, and the announcement of his Five-Year Plan for defense generated an intense public debate about defense spending. At times, the Czechoslovak press was openly critical of the high defense burden and argued that the recommended share was out of line for a small state.[6] In answer to the critics, Novotny demanded a full evaluation of Czechoslovakia's "willingness to defend socialism."[7] In response to tremendous public pressure, the minister of defense announced in 1968 that Czechoslovakia would unilaterally declare a moratorium on increases in defense spending.[8] Czechoslovak defense spending, it appears, has never again reached the pre-1968 level.

Only a few references to actual targets for defense spending have appeared since the coordinated effort began. In 1978 the Warsaw Pact members apparently were asked to increase defense spending by 5 percent.[9] The data show that most of the East European states have failed to make substantial increases, and in both Czechoslovakia and Poland defense spending has declined since 1965 (see Table 3.1). Czechoslovak spending, which was 4 percent in 1965, declined and has stabilized at just over 3 percent of the GNP, while Poland's contribution has dropped from a high of 3.8 percent in 1970 to 2.6 percent. Hungary's contribution, never above 3 percent, has also declined and reached a new low in 1976. Hungary has been reluctant to increase defense spending, opting for steady devotion of resources to consumer goods and light industry. This trend, when using data converted to dollar values, shows a marginal real increase and an actual decline in percent of budget allocated to defense. On the other hand, Bulgaria's commitment to defense has been growing. In both percentage of GNP and dollar value, Bulgaria has substantially increased its spending, though the percentage to GNP has not yet topped 3.5 percent. Romania, the most outspoken critic of Warsaw Pact targets, has held defense spending at just over 2 percent since 1965. There was a modest rise between 1968 and 1970, which might be explained by Romania's increased preparation for self-defense following the Soviet invasion of Czechoslovakia. These trends have not changed significantly in the 1980s.[10] Ceausescu of Romania has made no secret of his opposition to spending increases. In 1978 he openly criticized the 5 percent target increase and, according to Western sources, he walked out of the 1978 meeting of the PCC (see the discussion in Chapter 6). Other states have been less vocal, simply ignoring the targets, but occasional criticism of Soviet pressure for increased spending has occurred. A Czech commentator, after thanking the Soviets for their tremendous contribution to socialist defense, warned that further de-

Table 3.1. Share of GNP devoted to defense expenditure in East Europe

	Percent of GNP		
	In domestic currency	In dollars	Index in current dollars
Bulgaria			
1965	2.6	12.0	100.0
1966	2.5	11.2	103.3
1967	2.4	10.6	106.6
1968	2.3	10.4	110.7
1969	2.4	10.1	118.8
1970	2.4	10.2	133.5
1971	2.6	10.4	148.4
1972	2.7	10.6	165.0
1973	2.7	11.1	188.9
1974	2.8	11.7	224.8
1975	3.0	10.5	240.7
1976	3.0	10.4	261.2
1977	3.2	10.7	278.9
1978	3.2	9.8	283.0
Czechoslovakia			
1965	4.0	8.9	100.0
1966	3.9	7.6	101.1
1967	3.8	7.5	107.4
1968	3.7	7.2	112.5
1969	3.4	7.0	117.1
1970	3.4	6.3	113.6
1971	3.4	6.7	130.5
1972	3.3	6.6	140.5
1973	3.2	6.7	155.5
1974	3.0	6.5	172.2
1975	3.2	6.3	187.5
1976	3.1	6.1	191.8
1977	3.1	5.8	203.8
1978	3.1	5.8	222.0
German Democratic Republic			
1965	3.0	5.4	100.0
1966	2.9	5.3	104.9
1967	3.1	5.5	114.3
1968	3.9	6.4	146.4
1969	4.0	6.5	159.4
1970	4.2	6.7	176.8
1971	4.2	6.7	190.1
1972	4.1	6.7	205.2
1973	4.1	6.9	231.3
1974	4.0	6.7	257.2
1975	4.0	6.8	296.6
1976	4.1	6.7	317.6
1977	4.0	6.6	339.0
1978	4.1	6.6	372.8
Hungary			
1965	2.6	7.6	100.0
1966	2.2	6.8	97.2
1967	2.1	6.2	96.5
1968	2.3	6.4	105.1

Table 3.1. (Continued)

| | Percent of GNP | | |
	In domestic currency	In dollars	Index in current dollars
1969	2.3	6.4	115.2
1970	2.9	7.2	137.9
1971	2.6	7.0	143.5
1972	2.3	6.9	151.4
1973	2.1	6.7	163.3
1974	2.2	6.8	185.5
1975	2.3	6.5	199.3
1976	2.1	6.0	194.8
1977	2.1	5.5	198.5
1978	2.3	5.5	221.6
Poland			
1965	3.4	8.0	100.0
1966	3.5	7.4	102.1
1967	3.4	7.4	108.0
1968	3.6	7.4	119.4
1969	3.8	7.7	130.0
1970	3.8	7.4	139.2
1971	3.5	7.7	162.1
1972	3.3	7.3	171.4
1973	3.0	7.4	199.0
1974	2.9	7.1	220.7
1975	2.8	6.9	245.6
1976	2.6	7.1	279.2
1977	2.7	6.6	280.9
1978	2.6	6.3	297.7
Romania			
1965	2.1	8.5	100.0
1966	2.0	7.4	100.0
1967	1.9	6.5	94.3
1968	2.1	6.6	102.2
1969	2.2	6.9	118.5
1970	2.4	7.1	131.2
1971	2.3	6.1	134.1
1972	2.2	6.4	157.1
1973	2.1	6.2	165.4
1974	2.1	6.2	188.2
1975	2.2	5.9	210.1
1976	2.2	5.5	230.5
1977	2.1	5.3	241.0
1978	2.1	5.0	260.4

SOURCE: Thad P. Alton et al., "East European Defense Expenditures, 1965–1978," *East European Economic Assessment* (Part II), submitted to the Joint Economic Committee of the Congress of the United States (Washington: U.S. Government Printing Office, 1981). Alton's group used official statistics for the percentage of GNP in local currency devoted to defense. The dollar estimates of defense spending involve applying U.S. pay scales to the manpower component of total spending.

mands on the smaller states might be inappropriate and should not be made.[11]

While other WTO members ignore the targets, the GDR has enthusiastically increased its commitment to defense. In 1965 3 percent of its GNP went to defense, but the level jumped to 4 percent within three years. The index in dollars, with 1965 as the base year (100), was 378 in 1978. Figures for 1980–1982 show a continued steady rise in East German spending. These data support the thesis that East Germany is now the Soviet Union's most valuable ally.

The ability of some of the states to resist Soviet pressure on defense spending casts doubt upon the commonly held assumption that the WTO is run by Soviet fiat. The Soviet Union should enjoy considerable leverage because of the dependence of the East Europeans on Soviet trade, subsidies, and other goods. The employment of these levers, however, has been difficult (see the analysis in Chapter 9). William Reisinger has also shown that it is difficult to predict East European defense expenditure on the basis of a dependency index.[12] (The dependency index equals the standard score on two variables—the percentage of the state's total trade with the USSR plus the state's international debt service as a percentage of exports.) Poland's decreasing percentage of the GNP allocated to defense despite increased subsidies cannot be explained. One conclusion is that the East Europeans have been able to press their cases on the basis of economic incapacity. Poland, for example, was reportedly officially excused from the 5 percent in 1980 on that basis.[13] Nonetheless, there are signs that the Soviets are not completely satisfied with the contributions of their allies. A 1975 Soviet discussion of the development of the Warsaw Pact acknowledges the difficulties inherent in preparing for defense and admits that progress in the devotion of resources to defense "has not been as rapid as expected."[14]

The Soviets shoulder an overwhelming share of the burden for the maintenance of the Warsaw Pact, and it is difficult to imagine that the readiness of the Pact is endangered by meager East European defense spending. The Czech source cited above sets the Soviet contribution at over 80 percent, and Western sources would put this estimate higher. Therefore, the argument can be made that it is less the meager economic contribution that troubles the Soviets than the political issue of East European commitment to the alliance. With East Germany shouldering a disproportionate share of the burden among the East Europeans, Hungary, Poland, Romania, and, to a lesser extent, Czechoslovakia could be accused of passive "free-riding." Obviously, the East Europeans, who are devoting resources to defense in spite of enormous economic difficulty, may not share this view. But for the Soviets, the trend for few increases must be disturbing. Moreover, facing shrinking resources at home, the Soviets may have hoped for a greater contribution from the East Europeans and may well press for those increases in the future.

WEAPONS ACQUISITION AND STANDARDIZATION

Military budgets provide only a partial picture of the contribution of the allies to the common defense. A related issue is the activity of the East Europeans as arms producers and suppliers.

Tight integration and standardization of weapons is considered one of the Warsaw Pact's advantages over NATO. All of the states of the Warsaw Pact have some capacity for the production of weapons. The manner in which standardization and coordination of production are achieved is more complicated than the commonly held notion that the Soviet Union simply transfers weapons and/or blueprints to its East European allies. There are visible tensions between indigenous production and the demands of alliance integration. In recent years the Soviets have pressed not only for the standardization of weapons produced in the bloc but for a division of labor among the arms producers in Eastern Europe. Since 1970, strong pressure has been exerted upon the East Europeans to abandon comprehensive arms production and most forms of indigenous weapons production. After a brief exploration of arms production before 1970, we will examine the Soviet policy of specialization and the reaction of the East Europeans to it.

The modern era of defense production for the central European industrial powers began shortly after communist rule was consolidated. Czechoslovak and Polish weapons production capacity recovered slowly after the war, in part because of the uncertain political environment of 1946–1948 in both countries and efforts in Czechoslovakia by both the communists and the social democrats to control this important economic sector. The Czechoslovak communists actually suggested disbanding the industries and transferring the assets to the Soviet Union.[15] This was not done, of course, but until the coup d'etat of 1948 the plants were used primarily to repair old German and Russian war material.

The situation changed drastically in 1949. In conjunction with the militarization of Eastern Europe and the defense buildup in the Soviet Union, Czechoslovakia's arms industries were rejuvenated. The catalyst for rejuvenation of Polish industries was the Korean War. The Czechoslovak and Polish industries were given new socialist names such as the Lenin Works at Plzen and equipped with new machinery and Soviet technicians. The influx of Soviet technicians into Czechoslovakia was so massive that housing complexes had to be built in Brno and Plzen, two centers of arms production. The situation was similar in Poland, but the Polish industries continued to lag behind those of Czechoslovakia.

Cooperation with the Soviet Union began in earnest in 1951, when the first coproduction license outside of the USSR was granted to Czechoslovakia for the manufacture of jet engines for the MiG-15 fighter. Within a few years, the Czechoslovaks were allowed to build entire MiG fighters. The year 1955 was another turning point in the development of East European industries with the formation of the Warsaw Pact and the extension of socialist power in the Third World through the Egyptian arms deal. That transaction had an immediate impact as Czechoslovakia and soon Poland began supplying domestically produced arms to the Third World.

Since the formation of the Warsaw Pact in 1955, standardization of weapons and cooperation in defense research and development have been pursued through a number of multilateral and bilateral arrangements. There were two distinct phases in this development: the first in which much of the standardization and coordination was fostered by CMEA's technical committee, functioning as a defense-industrial arm of the Warsaw Pact's planning commission, and the second, more advanced stage, when the Joint Technical Committee of the Warsaw Pact was formed in 1970 to facilitate planning, coordination, and development. These multilateral efforts are supported by bilateral arrangements between industries in the USSR and in Eastern Europe.

In the first stage, military cooperation consisted primarily of granting increasing numbers of coproduction licenses to East European industries, but technology-sharing and indigenous design modification lagged. This pattern can be seen in the production of aircraft, armored vehicles, and artillery.

Aircraft

A number of coproduction licenses were granted to Czechoslovakia and Poland. Almost as quickly as it had begun, however, one of the most visible programs in Poland, the production of parts for jet fighters under license, was cut back and finally eliminated in 1959. In 1964

Mikhail Suslov, who helped to engineer Khrushchev's removal from office, criticized Khrushchev's decision to close down this Polish industry.[16] He noted the dislocation of fifteen thousand personnel and the danger which the reduction in orders apparently posed to Poland's Mielec Aircraft Corporation. The reduction led to a redirection of production to the development and sale of basic jet trainers. Mielec began production of 240 TS-8 Bies and research and development work on the TS-11 Iskra.[17] Orders were also given for the production of a utility helicopter and eventually, after Khrushchev's ouster, for another light utility plane. This redirection of production caused one major problem, however; Czechoslovakia had had a virtual monopoly on jet trainers in the Eastern bloc, but by the mid-1960s the Polish trainers were competitive and presumably threatening to take a share of the market. The same fate befell East German aerospace industries, in which the cutback in the development of jet engines and production of the IL 14M put twenty thousand people out of work.[18] Additionally, the faculty for aviation construction at the Technical University of Dresden was closed and the students asked to choose other courses of study.

The licensing of jet fighter production continued in Czechoslovakia, which became the only state outside the Soviet Union to produce and retrofit complete fighters, apparently benefiting from Poland's loss of licenses in 1959. The MiG-21 (Fishbed-AC), the first major production version of the MiG-21, was begun in Czechoslovakia almost simultaneously with its production in the USSR. Additionally, Czechoslovakia engaged in research and development on engines for the fighters, culminating in the development of Fishbed-F (1968).[19] Czechoslovak engine design was integral to the new version of this fighter.

Poland's loss of licenses to produce fighters resulted in a second redirection of production in 1961 and 1964. Poland and the USSR signed an agreement in January 1964, which made Poland a major producer of civilian and military helicopters. The Mil Mi-2, first flown in 1961 in the USSR, was turned over to Poland for "further development and production."[20] Production began in 1965 with orders for three hundred helicopters from Czechoslovakia, Romania, the USSR, and several West European and developing countries. The production rate has been held at about three hundred per year, and there are enough contracts to ensure production to 1985.

Armored Vehicles and Artillery

Cooperation in the production of tanks, artillery, and other armored vehicles was also primarily through coproduction and licensing among the Warsaw Pact nations in the early period. Attention was given to standardizing features of the artillery—especially ammunition requirements—but little cooperation was evident in design and development. Soviet designs were generally transferred after prototypes had been built.

Czechoslovakia was the most active producer in this area, building several kinds of artillery (field guns and howitzers), amphibious landing craft, tank recovery vehicles, trucks, and armored personnel carriers. Battle tanks were also produced under license throughout the Warsaw Pact and even in Bulgaria, where the T-54 was produced under license.[21]

At least one coproduction venture excluded the USSR. An agreement between Czechoslovakia and Poland for research and development of an armored personnel carrier resulted in production of the OT-64 in 1964.[22] The OT-64 carrier did not, however, become a standard weapon of the Warsaw Pact, though it was deployed with the Czechoslovak and Polish forces. East Germany and Hungary also purchased a number of these personnel carriers.

THE JOINT TECHNICAL COMMITTEE, 1970 TO THE PRESENT

The Joint Technical Committee was created as a part of the institutional reform of the Warsaw Pact in 1969–1970. It was apparently a Czechoslovak suggestion and was intended to give the East European states greater participation in weapons research, development, and production.[23] Other states, particularly Poland, trumpeted this and other changes in the Warsaw Pact machinery as a means for greater consultation and cooperation.[24] The committee has been used for two primary purposes: coordination of research and development and implementation of a coordinated division of labor for weapons production and acquisition which leaves only the Soviet industries with comprehensive arms production programs.

On the whole, the purpose of coordinating research and development was to address the concerns of the smaller states. Methods of cooperation to enable the East Europeans to enter the process of research and development at earlier stages have proliferated, though the East Europeans are reportedly still unhappy with Soviet unwillingness fully to share technology. A former Polish officer has stated that the Soviets transfer technical documentation for weapons only after serial production has begun in the USSR.[25] Charges have also been made that East European innovations in weapons design have been rejected in early stages simply because they are not Soviet. In addition to ill will and wounded pride, this chauvinism presents two problems for the East Europeans. First, basic research and development are almost isolated from weapons development, so there is no spin-off to benefit the technological base of the society as a whole. Second, CMEA statutes reserve to the primary developer the right of export veto,[26] and assuming that this policy is enforced in the WTO as well, Soviet dominance of the process provides yet another legal restriction on East European arms export. Moreover, though the methods of cooperation exist, the East Europeans continue to encounter difficulty in using them. In addition to direct sale of Soviet weapons and production licenses from the USSR, the East Europeans may now receive licenses to produce by Soviet plan but to modify and develop, with exchange of documentation; engage in joint production with joint research and development, including reciprocal transfer of documentation; or continue to design weapons indigenously but with standard features and interoperability.

The third and fourth strategies, which include exchange of documentation, have been employed sparingly. Only one agreement under the joint production arrangement can be documented. In 1978 an agreement between the USSR and Poland for production of the transport plane An-28 (NATO code name CASH) was signed. Although the An-28 is produced in civilian and military versions, the agreement does not openly differentiate.[27] The first prototype was seen in 1972, but the An-28 never entered into serial production in the USSR. The first exports of An-28 to the USSR were scheduled to begin in 1983. The Soviet Union has agreed to buy at least twelve hundred such planes by 1990.

Production agreements involving joint research and development are difficult to document. The only one that has been publicized was between Poland and Czechoslovakia for the development of the OT-64 armored personnel carrier, and this was concluded before the formation of the Joint Technical Committee. Nonetheless, though the specifics are not known, there are unconfirmed reports of collaboration with the Soviet Union on engine development by Czechoslovakia, radar development by Poland, and radio equipment by Hungary. Coordination apparently exists between certain advanced civilian industries, such as the East German optics industry and Czechoslovak chemical industries. The value of cooperative agreements between the smaller states is probably limited because of Soviet dominance of research and development. In determining why there are so few joint development projects between the smaller states, one example from the civilian sector is instructive. Czechoslovakia indefinitely postponed a joint production agreement with the GDR for a new front-wheel-drive automobile because of slow research and development on the part of the GDR. Defending the decision to rely completely on Czechoslovakia's own development base or perhaps on technology purchase from the West, the commentator noted that differences in the level of the research base made cooperation impossible.[28] He also remarked that export to nonsocialist countries would be easier in the long run if there were no CMEA technology-sharing arrangement.

The fifth strategy calls for indigenous production, tight integration, and standardization, but these are not always complementary. The Soviets have reduced the number of totally indigenously produced weapons in Eastern Europe. Apparently, the Soviets have reason to be concerned because there is evidence of cases—especially with small arms—in which standardization has not been upheld. For example, it is said that there are so many national versions of the Kalashnikov assault rifles and machine guns that it is impossible for personnel of various armies to use all versions easily. The Czechoslovak and Soviet versions do not have interchangeable magazines. Czechoslovakia also produces its own self-propelled, 152mm gun, for which Soviet ammunition may need modification.[29]

The second function of the Joint Technical Committee has been to enforce a specialization scheme whether weapons are produced indigenously or by license. Actually, some division of labor has always existed. Only Czechoslovakia and Poland produce significant numbers of tanks and armored fighting vehicles (see Table 3.2). Both states received licenses for the production of the T-72 tank in 1980 and will produce about twelve hundred before 1990. Naval equipment is produced exclusively by Poland and East Germany and helicopters and aircraft by Poland and Czechoslovakia. But over time the Soviets, convinced that too much redundancy and too many national designs of weapons still exist, have pressed for even more restrictive specialization. Under such a division of labor, Czechoslovakia would produce the widest array of equipment but would concentrate on armored vehicles, artillery pieces, transport equipment, and jet trainers. Poland would produce only a few armored vehicles under license, helicopters, and ships. The GDR would produce munitions and a few small ships, and Hungary would concentrate on bridge-laying equipment and a few transport vehicles. This plan would require the GDR to phase out a substantial heavy transport production capacity and Po-

Table 3.2. Production of ground forces materiel, USSR/Non-Soviet Warsaw Pact

	1978		1979		1980		1981		1982	
	USSR	NSWP	USSR	NSWP	USSR	NSWP	USSR	NSWP	USSR	NSWP
Tanks	3,000	800	3,500	800	3,100	700	2,000	520	2,500	600
T-55	500	800	500	800	–	700	–	500	–	500
T-72	1,500	–	2,000	–	2,300	–	1,400	20(CZ)	400	100 of which 50(CZ) 50(PL)
Other armored vehicles	5,500	1,800	5,700	1,625	6,300	1,450	5,200	1,250	4,500	1,450
Towed field artillery	1,300	110	1,500	160	1,400	160	1,600	210	1,700	260
Multiple rocket launchers	550	150	600	150	700	150	700	150	700	100
Towed artillery	100	200	–	200	–	150	–	250	–	200

SOURCE: United States Department of Defense, *Soviet Military Power* (Washington, D.C.: U.S. Government Printing Office, 1983), and Stockholm Peace Research Institute, *World Armaments and Disarmament Yearbook* (Stockholm: SIPRI, 1983).

land to drop production of jet trainers and utility aircraft. All of the arms manufacturers would continue to produce small arms.

The Soviets defend this strategy on the grounds of efficiency. It is not possible, one Soviet commentator noted, for the national industries to build everything: "Only the USSR can achieve this. It is better for the socialist countries to specialize."[30] Whatever the rationale for a division of labor, the policy has not been a total success. An element of national pride is undoubtedly a contributing factor. Czechoslovakia and Poland were arms producers well before their membership in the Soviet bloc. East European industries are already far less sophisticated and comprehensive than they were before the establishment of the Joint Technical Committee. Only Czechoslovakia continues to produce sophisticated, indigenously designed heavy weapons. And even heavy weapons production under license has suffered. For example, the high point for tank production in Czechoslovakia was 1968, and that level has not been reached since the establishment of the joint committee. Moreover, as the phase-outs in the 1950s showed, the phase-out of industries can produce considerable dislocation and temporary unemployment, requiring retraining of a sizable work force. Consequently, redundancy continues, and there are few signs that the East Europeans are convinced of the wisdom of this policy.

Czechoslovakia and Poland, the largest producers, have been the most reluctant to carry through with the policy. One Czech commentator, discussing the debate on the virtues of tracked versus wheeled armored vehicles, explained that specialization and joint decisions on the appropriate direction of new developments take time and ought not to be made hastily.[31] Poland, for instance, continues to produce jet trainers (TS-11 ISKRA), and Czechoslovakia continues to develop helicopters. Poland also produces light utility aircraft, the PZ1-104 (Wilga-32), which competes with the Czechoslovak Z-43. The PZL-194 is used in the USSR, Bulgaria, and the GDR, whereas the Z-43 is used in Hungary, Romania, and the USSR. Moreover, though Hungary is supposed to dominate the market in bridge-laying equipment, national versions of this equipment abound. Poland and the GDR use the East German–made BLG-60, Hungary uses its own version, Bulgaria apparently uses the Soviet type, and Czechoslovakia persists in building the MT-55, the largest tank-launched scissors bridge in the Warsaw Pact.

One area in which the Soviet Union has pressed for a tight plan of coordination and specialization is in the production of wheeled vehicles, but nevertheless many designs persist.[32] East Germany has been asked to stop production of buses and heavy transport, and Poland has acquired the task of producing flat-bed trucks and semitrailers. Hungary will produce primarily parts. Czechoslovakia will produce the heavy vehicles for the use of armed forces. Numerous agreements have been signed between East Germany's vehicle firm, IFA, and the Soviet ZIL Works and between the Schumen works in Bulgaria and Skoda in Czechoslovakia to support this effort.[33] Still, Czechoslovakia continues to produce almost all types of vehicles (TATRA line), and Hungary has contracts for production with MAN of West Germany and other West European and Canadian firms.

In spite of the only partial success of specialization, it may ultimately serve the East Europeans well by securing intra-Pact markets. Indigenously developed weapons are clearly at a disadvantage in the Warsaw Pact because of Soviet preference for Soviet-designed weapons. But specialization could conceivably increase the incentive for smaller Warsaw Pact states to conclude agreements among themselves. A carefully controlled strategy that assured East Europeans that their weapons would be purchased by Pact members could be useful. One wonders, for instance, what market there is for the Polish TS-11 Iskra since Czechoslovakia's L39 AERO is the standard weapon of the Warsaw Pact. Moreover, the Soviets have shown a sensitivity to East European concerns for markets in their willingness to buy East European small arms, amphibious landing vehicles, and trucks. The Soviets even admitted implicitly that an East European weapon was superior when the monopoly on standard weapons was finally broken in 1976 with the adoption of the Czechoslovak L-29 AERO trainer as the standard trainer of the Warsaw Pact. Perhaps miffed that the TS-11 Iskra was not so designated, the Poles did not buy the L-29 AERO or the upgraded "queen of the Paris air show," the L-39 AERO. This victory was apparently not without its costs because Soviet requirements for the L-39 were so restrictive that production was slowed by several months. Nonetheless, the L-39 continues to be the greatest victory for Czechoslovak production and a successor is already planned.[34]

Hungary and Romania seem to be pursuing different strategies than Poland and Czechoslovakia in coping with specialization and standardization. While continuing to produce a few small arms and significant amounts of engineering equipment, the Hungarians have begun to divert resources and to emphasize production of nonmilitary goods in the search for markets in the West. Scaling down its production of buses and trucks, especially for military uses, Hungary successfully pursued a strategy in automotive production of sub-

[73]

contracting for Western firms and recently announced similar plans in aerospace. The Hungarians intend to begin primarily with agricultural aircraft but hope to branch out into other aerospace areas. Technika, the coordinating agency, claims that it will seek contracts that "encourage quality work rather than providing high employment" and look for "good partners." Western cooperation is clearly the target. Hungary is attempting to entice Western producers with the high skill level of its work force, favorable industrial conditions, and government support for such endeavors.[35]

Romania, on the other hand, has sought extra-Pact cooperation for some time, producing a number of goods for military use under license from the West. The main truck of the Romanian air force, for example, has been built under license from Renault for over a decade.[36] Romania has also received licenses to produce helicopters and utility planes from France. But Romanian efforts to break dependence on Warsaw Pact production for weapons have been partly frustrated by hard currency problems and western restriction imposed by the Coordinating Committee for Multilateral Security Export Controls (COCOM).

The Romanians are also seeking extra-Pact markets for indigenously produced utility planes. At present, a number of agricultural aircraft dominate Romanian plans. The aircraft are tested with two different engines, one built in the West (PTA34AG/Canada) and the other in the East (PZL3-S/Poland). But in a bolder move, the Romanians are testing a jet trainer with both the Canadian engine and the Czech Walter M601B. The trainer, the IAR825, is presently targeted for the Romanian air force. It is less advanced than the Czech L-39 AERO, but the Romanians hope to market it abroad. Its main competitors for Third World markets will be the Swiss PC-7 and Brazilian Embracer PO27. Finally, the Romanians produce two French helicopters, the Alouette 3 and the Puma. Romania has limited sales rights but can reportedly negotiate with the French if potential customers appear.[37]

All of this activity is a part of an extensive growth effort in the Romanian aerospace industries. Other projects include production of the Pilatus Britter–Norman BN2 and the Rombac 111 transport plane under license from Britain. The plans for exclusive military production include manufacture, under license, of the Soviet Yakovlev YA-S2 aerobatic trainer and of the Yugoslav IAR-93 subsonic strike fighter. If this strategy is successfully pursued, Romania's aerospace industries will probably be the most diversified and advanced in Eastern Europe.

Romania's ability to operate outside of the Warsaw Pact's specialization scheme may ultimately make it a more competitive arms dealer than the traditional leaders in that area, Czechoslovakia and Poland. Romania's arms-exporting activity has increased over time but still represented only 0.9 percent of all Romanian exports in 1978.[38] Romanian activity is apparently increasing, however, and it may turn increasingly to export of arms and equipment as a hard currency source in the future.[39] A dramatic rise in Romanian exports would probably require increased production capacity, however.

For the other East European arms suppliers, specialization could be a mixed blessing in the search for extra-Pact markets. One problem the Czechs and Poles face as arms suppliers is high per unit cost, which makes their larger weapons uncompetitive. The only completely indigenously designed and produced large weapon of the Warsaw Pact that seems to do well in Third World markets is the Czech L-39 AERO. The Polish OT-64 APC and its variations have not fared well against the Soviet BTR-60.[40] Specialization could conceivably allow Czechoslovakia and Poland to produce more weapons within fewer lines of equipment, decreasing per unit costs. A second problem that specialization might address is redundancy and resultant intra-Pact competition for the same Third World markets. Indicative of this problem was an incident in 1978, when India broke off negotiations with Czechoslovakia for the purchase of the L-39 AERO and turned to the Poles for the TS-11 Iskra. With standardized features there is little to distinguish one supplier from another.

On the other hand, specialization will give arms producers fewer lines of weapons to offer customers. It is instructive that Czechoslovakia, the state most active in the arms trade, has failed to eliminate any equipment lines since 1970. And Poland and Czechoslovakia have turned, since 1972, to the production of a few models of their weapons exclusively for export as another way of reconciling Pact policies with the demands of the market. A few Czechoslovak small arms and one infantry gun are examples. The Czechs even reportedly developed an export version of one weapon that fires NATO ammunition. A number of copies of NATO small arms and artillery pieces are produced by the Czechs and the Poles, and the Czechs reportedly produce some of these copies for export.[41]

Whatever the impact of Pact policies on exports, the East Europeans continue actively to pursue customers. Czechoslovak arms transfers to the Third World have increased so rapidly that 8 percent of all Czechoslovak exports are arms, and since 1980 more than 40 percent of Czechoslovak arms exports have gone into non-Warsaw Pact markets.[42] Omnipol, Czechoslovakia's arms export coordinator, employs its own publicity agent and has a wide array of glossy advertisements for Czech weapons.[43] Poland, too, has increased exports to the extent that it is now a leading arms merchant, but in 1978 only 1 percent of Polish exports were arms. The East Europeans' favorite customers are the oil-rich states of the Middle East, and these purchasers are encouraged to pay in hard currency. An oil-for-arms deal with Iran was pending in 1978, shortly before the shah's demise. Czechoslovak arms exports to the Third World totaled $112 million from 1979 to 1981, a substantial increase over the previous three years. The total for all other East European countries between 1978 and 1981 was $101 million. Most of these are Polish and East German transfers.[44]

These numbers probably underestimate the value of East European arms exports. In addition to licensed exports through its arms merchant, Omnipol, Czechoslovakia is notorious for black market transfers. Czechoslovakia produces excellent small arms, which are of great interest to terrorist groups, and Czech arms have been identified with the Palestine Liberation Organization, (PLO), Black September, and the Irish Republican Army. The embarrassment of having Czechoslovak arms turn up on both sides of innumerable conflicts led to an effort in 1976 to harness Omnipol.[45] Licensing was put under the Ministry of Interior with instructions to be vigilant in checking customers. But the black market is not the only problem. Disagreements with the USSR over the political nature of arms sales surfaced in 1973, when the Czechoslovaks reportedly concluded an arms pact with General Augusto Pinochet in Chile, only to have Moscow veto the deal. East European arms are, of course, sold to political customers who cannot pay in hard currency. Presumably, gifts are still made to Vietnam, Ethiopia, and perhaps Central America. A distinction should be drawn between these gratis deliveries and those that appear to be more economically motivated. The lure of the arms market is self-evident; the Czechs in particular have been candid about the search for hard currency. A deputy minister of defense explained that Czech weapons are very popular abroad and could be sold even though other Czechoslovak goods could not be.[46]

The East Europeans have thus pursued different strategies to cope with the problems of standardization and indigenous production. Though some argue that they do so at a loss, their eagerness to export arms suggests that there is money to be made in arms sales and, in some cases, hard currency, which cannot be obtained through other trade. Presumably, the Soviets want to see the East European defense industries survive, providing excess capacity for the alliance. Therefore, weapons standardization and coordination is a complicated process in the Warsaw Pact. The Eastern bloc has had to reconcile the demands of domestic weapons production and sale in peacetime with the needs of military efficiency.

DIVISION OF MISSION RESPONSIBILITY

Although in theory the forces of the Warsaw Pact function as one, missions and tasks for the national units are differentiated. The nature of those tasks seems to be a function of the size and technical merit, geographic position, and, perhaps, reliability of the individual forces. Thus the image of the non-Soviet Warsaw Pact forces as a large infantry leg in support of Soviet forces is erroneous. Over time, East European forces have acquired important military missions, particularly in the Pact's Northern Tier: Poland, Czechoslovakia, and East Germany.

The largest and most uniformly advanced forces of Eastern Europe are those of Poland. All components of the more than three-hundred-thousand man force are well developed, possessing modern equipment and high standards of training. Poland's most advanced arm is the air force, which is equipped for offensive and defensive missions. Poland is the only East European state to base with its own forces the fighter-bomber Su-20 (a nuclear-capable delivery vehicle), but it is not known whether the Polish air force would fly nuclear missions. Poland's forces, however, were the first to simulate training in a nuclear environment, and they still devote considerable time to such training. Further, Poland's air force is well-equipped to carry out important air defense missions, and indigenously designed radar is employed for these purposes.

Poland's forces are expected to fight on an external front, that is, outside of Poland and are devoted to service of the joint armed forces of the Warsaw Pact.[47] A. Ross Johnson and his colleagues have noted, however, that the Poles have also been trained to fight on an independent Polish front. Two of the three armies on this front would advance across the North German Plains to the Low Countries, while the third army occupies Denmark. Reportedly, in preparation for this front, there are Danish-speaking units in the Polish army. The authors caution, however, that the Soviets seem to have doubts about the value of an independent front and, though using it as a dominant scenario in Soviet-Polish staff exercises, may intend to ignore it in reality.

[77]

The military forces of Czechoslovakia were once considered to be the best of Eastern Europe. Though they are still second only to Poland's in size, their modernization and growth was halted for a time by the tremendous dislocation of the Prague Spring. More than eleven thousand officers were purged, and the educational level of the Czech forces declined markedly, especially in the air force. For a while fears about the reliability of these forces prompted the leadership to build up the militia rather than the regular military, and the modernization of the armed forces was halted.[48] After 1975, the military-political leadership claimed that the forces had been normalized. Since 1975, a great deal of effort has gone into recruitment, and it may finally be paying off. Czechoslovak forces have been modernized substantially during the last five years, with long-delayed deliveries of the T-72 and MiG 23 finally made.[49] (These planes entered service in Poland and the GDR much earlier.) The Czech forces are deployed along the southwest border of the Warsaw Pact. The ground and air forces are equipped for various advanced defensive and offensive missions, but there seems to be little specialization in the Czechoslovaks' role.

The East German army, on the other hand, seems to be on the rise. Though the forces of the GDR are the smallest, numbering just under 160,000, they are well-equipped and armed, and they have improved steadily in the 1980s. Efficient and modern, they are deemed by Western analysts to be the most reliable and valuable of the East European forces. Their value is increased by their association with the elite Group of Soviet Forces in Germany (twenty Soviet divisions in a high state of readiness) and by their subordination directly to the joint command of the Warsaw Pact. These regular forces, which would see early action in a conflict with NATO, are a valuable asset on the front line. In addition to their sizable regular forces, the East Germans have a number of well-trained paramilitary forces, border forces, and border guards that could prove important. These forces, in addition to the officer corps, have been very important in East German activities in the Third World.

Finally, it is important to note that the forces of the Northern Tier are trained to fight in both nuclear and chemical environments, in accordance with Soviet insistence on preparation for combined arms operations in any conceivable military environment.

The Hungarian, Bulgarian, and Romanian forces are small and not very well-equipped, though there has been an effort to modernize them in recent years. From 1975 to 1978, there was a significant increase in the rate of growth of nonpersonnel costs in Bulgaria and

Hungary and a rapid introduction of replacements for aging artillery and armored fighting vehicles.[50] Romania's forces should be discounted as a militarily valuable arm of the Warsaw Pact. They are neither well-trained, integrated, nor reliable from the Soviet point of view. The Bulgarians are geographically isolated because of Romania's refusal to participate in the Warsaw Pact's military training and are therefore of only marginal use. It is expected that they would perform primarily defense or garrison operations in the Balkans in case of war, although they might be valuable in intervention against Romania or Yugoslavia. Hungary contributes excellent engineering and construction corps and is especially well-known for bridge-building in support of amphibious operations.[51] Hungarian industries build bridging equipment under license from the Soviet Union, Czechoslovakia, and the GDR, which is an important and complete, if limited, mission for Hungary, whose contribution to the Pact is often ignored.

Finally, there are trends to suggest tighter coordination, specialization, and division of labor in mission responsibility in the future. Under the integrated joint command of the Warsaw Pact, the East European forces (with the exception of the GDR) retain their national integrity. In recent years, however, individual units of national armed forces have exercised with units of the Soviet armed forces without distinction. The Druzhba exercises of 1982 are an example; functional units such as artillery units of the Soviet, Czech, and Hungarian forces exercised together. Similar cooperation occurred with bridge-laying units of the same three forces, which did not exercise with their national armies. Finally, there was extensive training of chemical troops of the Soviet Union and Czechoslovakia during the 1979 Druzhba exercises in isolation from the maneuvers of the national armed forces.[52] Some have suggested that these exercises mean that the Soviets will siphon off reliable units of East European forces and use them as supplementary personnel with Soviet forces. Though the evidence is far from conclusive, trends that are contrary to maintenance of the national integrity of the forces should not be dismissed.[53]

Finally, mention should be made of naval forces, especially those of Poland and the GDR, which are the largest and best equipped in Eastern Europe. They are expected to support the Soviet navy in coastal defense and perform intelligence-gathering functions. The navies are equipped with a wide array of mine-laying and detection equipment, as well as amphibious support capability. According to one specialist, "Poland's Navy is charged with surveillance of its own coastline in peacetime, but in wartime it would operate jointly with the Soviet Baltic fleet and East German Navy, to augment amphibious lift capability . . . and to defend the country's coast."[54] It could conceivably carry out support functions for antisubmarine warfare as well.

One final and recent development in the division of responsibility is noteworthy. Under the direction of Marshal Nikolai V. Ogarkov, the Soviet General Staff has become interested in and is exploring intensively the prospects for automated troop control. The Czechoslovaks, East Germans, Poles, and perhaps Hungarians have been involved in the development of computer models for various levels of troop control. Though information is scarce on these activities, the proliferation of scholarly papers on the military uses of computers, particularly for troop control suggests that this is an area in which the East Europeans may continue to play an important role.[55]

These differentiated missions suggest that the non-Soviet Warsaw Pact forces are of considerable military value. Clearly, there is a question as to how reliably they would perform their missions given the host of social, political, and economic difficulties in the states they serve. After the recent upheavals in Poland, for example, the reliability of Polish forces upon whom so much rests is a big question mark.

COLLECTIVE SECURITY

One of the most difficult issues facing an alliance is the coordination of foreign policy outside of the primary theater of conflict. European members of the NATO alliance have responded coolly to suggestions that support for the foreign initiatives of the United States outside of the European theater is a matter of alliance solidarity. The independent and sometimes contradictory interests of the Western allies in dealing with their former colonial possessions of the Third World has been a source of tension.

Foreign policy coordination for the Warsaw Pact is, on the surface, a less contentious point. Members of the Pact rarely criticize Soviet policy outside the European theater (see Chapter 6). But willingness to pay lip service to Moscow's initiatives is one thing and active support for those initiatives through commitment of resources is another. Along the spectrum of cooperation, devotion of military resources to efforts outside of Europe is a sign of significant commitment to the foreign policy goals of the Soviet Union. Such a commitment involves political risks, including soured relations with Western states over the expansion of socialist power in the Third World, and is a significant drain on military resources.

It should perhaps not be surprising, then, that the widest variation in commitment of resources is observable in this area. Moreover, given the costs of Third World involvement, great care has been taken to separate the activity of the individual states from the Warsaw Pact because use of the Pact machinery outside Europe would carry with it risk of involvement in far-flung global conflict. Nevertheless, the Soviets continue to press the East Europeans to aid their extra-European activities, and unconfirmed reports suggest that Vietnam and Cuba have on occasion been proposed for membership in the Warsaw Pact, which would change the European character of the alliance.[56] More recently, the Soviets called a meeting to discuss coordination of socialist policy on Afghanistan, but to date this activity has been carefully separated from the framework of the Warsaw Pact. For example, the meeting was called, not by Marshal Kulikov of the Warsaw Pact Command, but by Marshal Alexei Epishev of the Main Political Administration.[57]

The separation of the alliance machinery from the socialist extension of power should not overshadow the military contributions of individual members of the alliance to Soviet policy in the Third World. Hungary and Poland have contributed primarily economic assistance, though Poland has transferred significant numbers of arms to Third World states and for a time maintained a military mission in Syria to train forces using Polish and Czech equipment. In general, however, Poland has been reluctant to become involved in the Third World, and Polish foreign policy focuses primarily on East-West arms control issues.

Bulgaria provided economic assistance to the Third World through the decade of the 1970s. The rapid industrialization and growth of the Bulgarian economy after the establishment of communist rule could be held up as a model of the value of socialism for developing countries. Recently, Bulgaria's activities have reportedly expanded into the military sphere. A growing number of Bulgarian military technicians and advisers have been particularly active in black Africa.[58] Bulgarian military activities are still modest, however, reflecting perhaps the meager military resources of Todor Zhivkov's regime.

The most active military programs in the Third World are maintained by Czechoslovakia and East Germany. Czechoslovakia established early military links with the Third World as an outgrowth of the 1955 Czechoslovak-Egyptian arms deal. Initially foils for Soviet involvement, the Czechoslovaks became deeply involved in military assistance, particularly in Egypt, resulting in a relationship that was so close that Egyptian officers often trained in Prague rather than in Moscow. Also indicative of the great depth of Czech involvement is the fact that during the 1956 Suez crisis, Czechoslovak pilots flew MiG fighters out of trouble for the Egyptian air force.[59]

Throughout the 1960s, Czechoslovakia actively supported Soviet military assistance programs throughout the Third World. Czechoslovak arms industries produced ideal weapons for Third World states, including small arms and, under license, fighters and tanks. Arms sales and military assistance continued into the 1970s, but then the emphasis shifted toward sales, and the number of Czechoslovak officers sent to the Third World began to shrink. There are several possible explanations, but a compelling one is that the Czechoslovak People's Army was considered unfit for extranational duty following the upheaval of 1968. The tremendous problems of morale and efficiency, which plagued the armed forces until at least 1975, undoubtedly kept the Czech government and military leadership preoccupied with problems at home. Another explanation is that the Czechoslovaks, having become deeply involved in Egypt, were burned badly by the break in Egyptian-Soviet relations after 1973. They had invested a great deal of money, expertise, and political capital in Egypt and were just beginning to reap the benefits when the break occurred; for example, Czechoslovakia was Egypt's principal trading partner in a number of commodities at special prices.[60] The web of economic and military ties, built over fifteen years, suddenly collapsed when Moscow and Cairo parted. The Czechoslovak government is clearly still bitter about the losses and continually assailed Egypt under Anwar Sadat with greater vigor than did the USSR. Having been burned once in devoting resources to the socialist extension of power, Czechoslovakia undoubtedly is now more circumspect.

Czechoslovakia's military contribution to developing nations is still substantial but is heavily focused on arms sales, though a few technicians accompany the more advanced weaponry. The Communist party daily newspaper has defended Czechoslovak involvement, stating that "many developing countries do not have their own military industry or the possibility of training their own military personnel; therefore, if they ask . . . for this kind of help in the anti-imperialist struggle, aid cannot be refused."[61] Czechoslovak arms are found in numerous Third World states, usually in support of Soviet initiatives. The new socialist states—Ethiopia, Vietnam, and Angola—apparently receive arms at low prices for political reasons. Czechoslovakia also reportedly supplies several fringe groups. The PLO has been a steady customer. But the propensity of the Czechoslovaks to mix business and politics—searching for hard currency sales—has led to a concentration of arms sales in the Middle East, particularly Syria and Iraq. Syria has been a very active customer, buying a wide array of weapons, including many of the T-72s which the Czechoslovaks produce under Soviet license.

Czechoslovakia's role as a junior ally has been eclipsed, however, by the more intensive and pervasive activity of the GDR. The East Germans have been willing and able to undertake activities in support of Soviet policy far beyond those of any other East European state. Apparently, the East Germans feel that the gains of Third World involvement outweigh the costs. Activity in the Third World has given East Germany a foreign policy identity, not to mention an enhanced hold on the attention of the Soviet Union, grateful for the assistance in the costly extension of power. Moreover, from the Soviet point of view, the East German armed forces, small, efficient, and thoroughly controlled by the Soviet Union, are a more reliable partner than the Czechs ever were. It is hard to imagine deviation by the East German armed forces with twenty Soviet divisions on the territory of the GDR. The involvement of the East Germans in Soviet activities in the Third World seems certain to continue and perhaps intensify.

The East Germans have primarily, but not exclusively, focused on the emerging socialist states of Africa: Ethiopia, Angola, and Mozambique. East Germany furnishes less equipment to these states than does Czechoslovakia but maintains active military training and advising missions. East Germany is known to have military missions in Algeria, Angola, Ethiopia, Guinea, Iraq, Libya, Mozambique, South Yemen, and Syria and is believed to have military assistance treaties in addition to friendship treaties with Angola, Ethiopia, Mozambique, and perhaps South Yemen.[62] These treaties are more entangling than arms transfer agreements and demonstrate the depth of East German involvement.

There are no indications that the East Germans have been involved in combat, but some Western analysts believe that on at least two occasions they have planned military actions. East German advisers (numbering about one hundred) were called into Angola to train the FLNC forces following their defeat in Shaba I. In Angola, the East Germans were reportedly involved in planning Shaba II.[63] They may also have helped evacuate fleeing FLNC forces, providing tank cover from inside Angola.

The East Germans have also been active in Ethiopia. In 1979, fifteen hundred East German military experts were dispatched to Ethiopia to provide aid against the Eritrean Liberation Front.[64] The height of the East Germans' advisory involvement was reportedly in the dramatic airlift operation in 1979, which turned the tide toward Ethiopia. Extensive training of security forces by East Germans in these areas has also been reported.

This East German involvement suggests coordinated efforts of Soviet allies in military conflicts unparalleled before the 1970s. East German advisers presumably work closely with their Soviet counterparts. The coordination and the use of the collective resources of several bloc countries are what make the East European contribution significant. There has even been one report of Bulgarian, East German, Czechoslovak, Cuban, and Vietnamese forces fighting alongside Soviet forces in Afghanistan.[65]

In sum, the contribution of the allies to the socialist extension of power in the Third World is substantial. The East Europeans (primarily Czechoslovakia, Poland, and the GDR) have trained more than sixty-four hundred Third World officers in the period from 1955 to 1979 and contributed large numbers of arms.[66] Given their meager resources, this is a significant gesture of support for Soviet efforts. The difference in the range of activities, however, is a reminder that the collective effort may mask different agendas. The broad East German effort is in support of goals quite different from Czechoslovakia's sale of arms, which has strong economic motivation. Confluence of interest should not be confused with identity of interest. And in cases such as arms sales, there is the potential for conflict and tension between Soviet goals and East European tactics.

More than in any other area, then, it appears that East European military involvement in the Third World is voluntary. Whether East Europeans will be able to draw the line clearly in the future depends on the Soviets' perception of the balance between costs and gains in pressing their allies. Twice in recent months, the Soviet bloc met to discuss coordination of matters of international policy. The Soviets, pressed for resources, may decide to turn to their allies for help. How hard they push depends upon Soviet perceptions of the relative costs involved in demanding greater coordination of policy outside the European theater. Until now, the strategy apparently has been to accept the East European contributions in whatever quality and form they come. After all, the Achilles heel of the Eastern bloc's Third World effort is its embarrassingly sparse economic aid and, as a consequence, many unhappy clients. It may be more beneficial to encourage the Hungarians, Poles, Bulgarians, and even Romanians, to increase their economic aid.[67]

For the most part, the arrangements adopted for burden-sharing within the Warsaw Pact are characterized by formal policies to maximize the contributions of the non-Soviet states and increase the use of their resources in support of Soviet goals. These policies attempt to create a division of labor and enforce specialization and integration. Only the Soviet armed forces retain the ability to act as independent, integrated national forces.

In practice, the arrangement is more complicated. In the areas of defense spending and weapons procurement, burden-sharing falls considerably short of the formal decrees. Defense spending is well below the target in all East European cases except the GDR and has shown little growth in recent years. The weapons procurement process is complicated, and specialization and standardization requirements have often lagged. In this area, which has the potential for conflict between the need to protect East European industries and the demands of specialization, compromise is most apparent.

Conflicting Soviet and East European interests are less apparent in the case of mission responsibility. One could argue that the increasingly specialized roles for East European forces, even to the point of integration of certain units with their Soviet counterparts, severely constrains the ability of the forces to act in their own national interest should it conflict with that of the alliance. An integrated socialist army is indeed an effective way of limiting the independence of united East European parties and militaries. But for the East Europeans, already strapped for resources, limited missions may be more supportable, and there are excellent military arguments for integration and division of labor.

Compromise in collective security efforts is more obvious. The activity of the East Europeans in the Third World varies widely and is seemingly a matter of Soviet acceptance of East European contributions, ranging from East Germany's pervasive activity to Hungary's rhetorical support and economic assistance. East European and Soviet interests are not necessarily identical in these areas, but the GDR and, to a lesser extent, Czechoslovakia have pursued interests that are generally consonant with Soviet goals.

Consequently, burden-sharing is not a simple matter for the Eastern alliance in spite of the minimal leverage the East Europeans can employ within the alliance. As leverage they can use their domestic economic and political problems, and the Soviets must listen for it would not be prudent to press the East Europeans too far beyond their ability to comply. Weakness can be a source of power under some circumstances, as demonstrated by the East Europeans' ability to maneuver on the issue of burden-sharing.

[4]

National Armies and National Sovereignty

CHRISTOPHER D. JONES

This chapter will challenge the widely held assumption that the primary mission of the Warsaw Treaty Organization is to mobilize East European military personnel for participation in a Soviet offensive against Western Europe. This orthodox view arises from the preoccupation of NATO countries with *Soviet* nuclear forces capable of annihilating Western Europe and with offensively oriented *Soviet* conventional forces. Although NATO analysts have frequently expressed skepticism about the political reliability of the East European forces of the WTO, they have generally not considered the possibility that the Warsaw Pact has a mission other than to mobilize East European armies for an assault on Western Europe.

Two other important missions for the WTO will be identified: maintaining a Soviet capability for rapid military intervention in Eastern Europe and preempting the capabilities of East European armed forces to lead sustained national resistance to a Soviet military occupation. The military and political elites of the loyal members of the WTO rely on the Soviet capability for military intervention to intimidate their domestic opponents. They also rely on Soviet military power to deter West Germany and the United States from offering military support to these internal opponents.[1]

In arguing that the WTO has developed in response to internal threats to the political security of the Soviet Union and the pro-Soviet elites of Eastern Europe, this chapter will focus on three topics: (1) the threat posed to the Soviet control system in Eastern Europe by independent national armed forces; (2) the fragmentation of national control over national armed forces within the loyal members of the WTO;

and (3) the historical function of national formations, both within the Union of Soviet Socialist Republics and in Eastern Europe.

THE THREAT POSED BY EAST EUROPEAN
DOCTRINES OF TERRITORIAL DEFENSE

Three East European communist states, Yugoslavia, Albania, and Romania, have withdrawn from participation in the Soviet military alliance system by adopting national strategies of territorial defense. These Balkan strategies are directed mainly against the Soviet army. Yugoslavia never was a member of the Pact but both Albania and Romania were signatories of the Warsaw Treaty of 1955. Albania formally left the alliance in 1968. Romania remains a member but does not participate fully in the integrated military command structure. The examples of Yugoslavia, Albania, and Romania have demonstrated that national control over national armed forces is the prerequisite for the exercise of sovereignty by an East European communist state in domestic and foreign policy.

The deployment of territorial defense systems by each of these states has followed the seizure of the local Communist party by a domestic faction that has freed the party of its political dependence on Moscow by cultivating local support for an assertion of sovereignty against the USSR and for the development of a distinctly national form of communism. Moscow has feared that the success of a domestic faction of an East European party in seizing control will infect the remaining pro-Soviet parties in the region and perhaps even the national Communist parties of the adjoining union republics of the USSR.

Since the early 1960s the principal military threat to Soviet political security in Eastern Europe has been the possible contagion of the doctrines of territorial defense adopted by Yugoslavia, Albania, and Romania in the late 1950s and early 1960s. These territorial defense strategies are designed to deter Soviet interventions against the domestic factions of the three national parties by preparing for the mobilization of the entire adult populations of their countries for prolonged resistance to a military occupation.[2] These strategies do not seek military victory over a Soviet expeditionary force but political stalemate between the native resistance movement and a native occupation regime championed by the Soviet army. For each of these three rebellious communist regimes, political survival depends on the credibility of their national defense systems, the maintenance of a mutually deterrent East-West military balance in Europe, and the cultivation of sufficient domestic legitimacy to stand without Soviet support.

The Yugoslavs call their strategy "General People's Defense." The Romanians call theirs "War of the Entire People." To the Soviets, these military doctrines defend neither the territory nor the people of an East European state but the rebel leader of its national Communist party. In the event of the internal collapse of an East European communist regime, a national capability for waging a war of territorial defense could be used to defend whatever regime the local officer corps chose to recognize as the legitimate bearer of national sovereignty.

The possibility that East Germany might adopt such a doctrine is particularly unnerving to the Soviets because of the likelihood that the successor regime would be the Federal Republic. Had Poland had the capability for waging a prolonged war of national resistance to military occupation, the internal and external dynamics of the crisis that began in August 1980 probably would have been different. Pro-Soviet regimes in the Warsaw Pact have been no less anxious than Moscow to reject East European doctrines of territorial defense because they fear that national defense systems based on such doctrines will shield their domestic opponents, both inside and outside the local parties, from the threat of Soviet military intervention in support of the local Muscovites.

Alternative Security Policies for East European States

Even if the territorial defense systems of Yugoslavia, Romania, and Albania were not used to deter Soviet interventions, they at least made the national armed forces of these states unavailable to the Soviets for exerting military pressure against NATO countries in southeastern Europe. The existence of these defense systems also demonstrates the practical possibility for an East European communist state to disengage its armed forces from the Soviet military alliance system and to pursue independent military missions, security policies, and foreign policies. The Soviets have faced challenges on security policies not only from these three nations but also from three other East European states: Hungary, Poland, and Czechoslovakia.

Imre Nagy, the prime minister of the new Hungarian government, proclaimed the restoration of a multiparty democracy on 30 October 1956. The following day he proclaimed Hungary's withdrawal from the Warsaw Pact and declared Hungary a neutral state. A historian of the Hungarian revolution, Ferenc Vali, rejects the conventional argument that Nagy's withdrawal from the Warsaw Pact prompted the Soviet invasion of 4 November. Vali suggests just the opposite: the imminent threat of Soviet intervention against Nagy's multiparty noncommunist government prompted Nagy to withdraw from the WTO in order to generate international pressure against a Soviet military invasion.[3]

In Poland in October 1956, when Wladyslaw Gomulka prepared to call soldiers and civilians to defend him against a threatened Soviet intervention, there is evidence that certain officers of the Polish armed forces began to take preliminary steps toward disengagement from Soviet control mechanisms. In the late 1950s General Zygmunt Dusynski headed a group of high-ranking officers who attempted to draw up plans for establishing within the Warsaw Pact a separate, compact, well-defined "Polish Front" intended as an exclusive theater of operations for the Polish armed forces. Dusynski's plans also called for the formulation of a specifically Polish military doctrine, an independent national defense system, and a separate armament industry.[4]

During 1957 and 1958, Gomulka's foreign minister, Adam Rapacki, advanced a series of proposals which may have been aimed at the creation of a military-political basis for a Polish Front manned exclusively by Polish soldiers. The Rapacki Plan of 1957 called for the creation of a nuclear-free zone in central Europe. Rapacki's principal concern appears to have been to prevent the deployment of U.S. nuclear weapons in West Germany and comparable Soviet nuclear weapons in Eastern Europe. In 1958 Rapacki proposed limited withdrawals of foreign troops from the two Germanies and Poland. Gomulka again raised the issues of the Rapacki proposals in the early 1960s.[5]

In the spring of 1968 the commandant and several department heads at the Gottwald Military-Political Academy in Prague drafted a document that became known as the Gottwald Memorandum. This memorandum, which appeared in the Czechoslovak army newspaper on 2 July 1968, offered three possible security policies for Czechoslovakia:

> The coalition principle (the alliance with the Soviet Union and the other states of the Warsaw Pact on which our defense system is currently based) is subject to development and it is necessary to reconsider its validity in the coming 10 to 15 years.

It is possible to think about coordinated defense in Central Europe without the military potential of the USSR (some kind of military analog to the political Little Entente "in a socialist form" or some kind of collective security organization without a class determination).

The possibility of neutralizing one's territory and of pursuing a policy of neutrality by relying on one's own means of defense.[6]

The third option identified by the Gottwald Memorandum, that of proclaiming Czechoslovakia's neutrality and of "relying on one's own means of defense," is the military-political basis of the defense system of Yugoslavia. The second option suggested a collective security organization made up of two possible sets of members: a group of communist and noncommunist states in central Europe or a group of states constituting a "military analog to the Little Entente 'in a socialist form.'" The members of the Little Entente, a military alliance of the 1930s, were Czechoslovakia, Romania, and Yugoslavia. The Little Entente was directed against Hungary, which had territorial claims against Czechoslovakia, Romania, and Yugoslavia. Its revival "in a socialist form" may well have contemplated Hungary not as an enemy but as a potential member. Adjoining both Hungary and Czechoslovakia is a nonaligned noncommunist central European state which relies on a territorial defense system: Austria. Austria in turn borders on a similar nonaligned central European state, Switzerland.

Within three weeks of the drafting of the Gottwald Memorandum Marshal A. A. Grechko, the Soviet minister of defense, came to Prague specifically to discuss Soviet-Czechoslovak military cooperation "in the framework of the Warsaw Pact."[7] Within six weeks, Marshal I. I. Iakubovskii, the WTO commander in chief, led Soviet troops into Czechoslovakia for hastily scheduled Warsaw Pact exercises.

Marshal Iakubovskii's troops were able to enter Czechoslovakia easily in June 1968 and again in August because during the early 1960s Marshal Grechko, then WTO commander in chief, had closed off the military exits from the Warsaw Pact. In 1961 Grechko introduced a system of regular joint military exercises, which belatedly attempted to reverse Romania's decision to deploy a territorial defense system and to preempt the possibility that any Warsaw Pact state could take advantage of a Rapacki Plan or Gottwald Memorandum to copy the Romanian and Albanian examples of disengaging national military forces from Soviet control mechanisms.

FRAGMENTATION OF NATIONAL CONTROL OVER NATIONAL
ARMED FORCES: WTO EXERCISES AND WTO AGENCIES

The joint exercises which Marshal Grechko began in 1961 were for
the purpose of drilling the armies of the Warsaw Pact for nuclear
offense against NATO and also to render them incapable of conventional defense against the Soviet Union. He also began to prepare
Soviet forces for interventions in Eastern Europe. Several aspects of
the joint exercises support these conclusions. Albania refused to participate in the exercises although it maintained formal membership in
the WTO until 1968. After 1964, Romania refused to permit WTO
exercises on its soil or to send troop contingents to exercise outside
Romania. Several map exercises of Soviet, Bulgarian, and Romanian
staff officers in a map room of the Romanian defense ministry have
been allowed, but since 1964, Romania has sent to WTO exercises
only staff officers, whom the Romanians have described as observers
and the Soviets have described as participants.[8]

The exercises facilitated Soviet intervention in the participating
states by fragmenting national armed forces into components assigned
to bilateral and multilateral coalition groupings. These multinational
groupings make the components of any one national military dependent on the components of other militaries to execute a given mission.
In the WTO there are four basic types of military groups for ground
forces: the subunit (in Russian, the *podrazdelenie*); which is a battalion,
company, or smaller entity; the unit (*chast'*), which is usually a regiment or similar self-contained entity; the formation (*soedinenie*), which
is a brigade, division, or corps; and the superformation (*ob"edinenie*),
which is either an army (about five divisions) or a front (several
armies). The terms subunit, unit, formation, and superformation are
used in other WTO service branches for equivalent entities.

Although WTO sources occasionally speak in vague terms about
the interaction of allied formations and superformations,[9] the available evidence from Soviet and East European accounts of WTO exercises suggests that the publicly visible levels of integration are the
division, the unit, and the subunit. This conclusion may reflect a
deliberate WTO policy of not publishing information about the interaction of national formations and superformations. The un-
classified materials available from Soviet and East European military
publications nevertheless document the existence of a highly developed system for combining Soviet and East European divisions,
units, and even subunits into bilateral and multilateral formations.

In its discussion of the participation of the Hungarian armed forces in WTO exercises, the text on the WTO edited by the current Warsaw Pact Commander, V. G. Kulikov, declares, "There is not a single major exercise which fails to provide for the joint actions of Soviet and Hungarian units and subunits."[10] The available evidence suggests a similar pattern in the cases of the other national armies of Eastern Europe. A Czechoslovak major reported in a 1970 article on cooperation between the Central Group of Soviet Forces in Czechoslovakia and the Czechoslovak army, "Frequently the subunits of the two friendly armies participate in joint combat actions, constituting a monolithic striking force."[11]

Even in the two largest WTO exercises ever held, the Oder-Neisse maneuvers of 1969 and the Brotherhood in Arms exercise of 1970, Soviet sources reported interaction at the level of the subunit and unit but at no higher levels. In its discussion of the Oder Neisse exercises the Iakubovskii text on the WTO declared, "In all stages of the exercise there was extensive interaction and mutual assistance among the subunits and units of the allied armed forces in carrying out common missions."[12] Another Soviet text described a similar level of integration in the Brotherhood in Arms maneuvers. This volume, edited by a former commander of the Group of Soviet Forces in Germany, E. F. Ivanovskii, declared that in these 1970 maneuvers, "the interaction of the friendly armies was carried out not only on the level of troop staffs, but also among units, subunits and even among aircraft and other technical crews."[13] This study noted a joint action executed by German and Soviet tank companies and a joint battle waged by subunits of German paratroopers with subunits of Bulgarian and Czechoslovak tank forces. It also mentioned a joint naval landing conducted by subunits of Soviet, Polish, and German naval infantry supported by subunits of paratroopers from each country. This account in addition chronicled the concluding phase of the exercises in which WTO soldiers surround and then destroy enemy forces. This action was the work of units and subunits of tank forces drawn from the armies of the Soviet Union, Poland, Hungary, and East Germany, supported by Bulgarian paratroopers and Czechoslovak troops landed by helicopter.[14]

In a discussion of the Shield 72 exercises in Czechoslovakia, a joint Soviet-Czechoslovak study reported an action in which Hungarian artillery began shelling an enemy position after which unspecified Polish and Czechoslovak forces fought "shoulder-to-shoulder" while supported by Soviet mechanized infantry. When the "enemy" brought up reinforcements, Soviet tank, artillery, and air forces rushed to the battle and annihilated the opposing forces.[15]

Accounts of more recent WTO exercises, such as the 1982 Friendship maneuvers in Czechoslovakia, also testify to the interaction of subunits of the participating armed forces. A *Krasnaia Zvezda* account of Friendship 82 discussed the interaction of the officers and personnel of two tank battalions, one Soviet and one Hungarian. These two subunits participated in an action which also required the services of a Czech tank battalion, an unidentified air force grouping commanded by a Soviet major, and Czechoslovak aircraft sufficiently numerous to require the command services of two lieutenant colonels. In addition to these forces, whose officers were identified by name, *Krasnaia Zvezda* noted the participation of unidentified subunits of artillery and motorized infantry.[16]

Several other characteristics of joint exercises serve to fragment national control over national armed forces. One of them is the practice of assigning the planning and evidently the conduct of joint exercises to the WTO staff, rather than to purely national staffs. The Kulikov text on the WTO declares that the WTO staff is responsible for "the working out and conduct of joint maneuvers, exercises, and military games of diverse scale—from the operational-strategic level to the level of troops and special forces."[17] The occasional mention of the directing staff in WTO accounts of joint exercises invariably points out the multinational composition of the staff.

The joint exercises also deny national defense ministries the opportunity to drill large formations of national troops for actions on national soil. For any given East European army, no more than one-third of its WTO exercises have been conducted exclusively on national territory, and at least one-third have taken place entirely on foreign and national territory. Of the one-third of the exercises conducted at home, many have been large multilateral affairs in which several WTO armies have practiced entering the national territory and seizing military objectives.[18]

The armed forces of a given country have been under the supreme command of one of their own officers in no more than one-third of the exercises. In at least two-thirds of the exercises in which they have participated, national troops have found themselves under the ultimate command of a foreign officer, sometimes Soviet and sometimes East European.[19] In the joint exercises, joint political activities, which take place during pauses in simulated combat, have been directed mainly at justifying the presence of foreign soldiers on national soil. These political activities, conducted with both military and civilian personnel, have proclaimed the common obligation of the WTO soldiers to defend the "gains of socialism" in each fraternal country against both external and internal enemies.[20]

The system of joint exercises introduced by Marshal Grechko in 1961 activated the central WTO agencies established in 1955. After the Soviet intervention in Czechoslovakia, the WTO created in 1969 a series of formal agencies which appear to have functioned on an ad hoc basis during the mid-1960s. These central organs parallel corresponding agencies of the East European states and are in a position to fragment East European control over national defense ministries, with the exception of the Romanian defense ministry, which maintains only formal links to the central Warsaw Pact administrative bodies. The Committee of Defense Ministers, nominally the supreme administrative agency of the WTO, meets once a year for a two-day session. Its membership consists not only of the seven WTO defense ministers but also the WTO commander in chief and his first deputy, the chief of the WTO staff. The Military Council meets twice a year to plan and review joint programs of training and military exercises. Its members, drawn from the Soviet and East European personnel assigned to other central agencies of the WTO, often meet in a joint session with officers from all the WTO armed forces.

The Joint Command, directly subordinate to the WTO commander in chief, consists of East European officers who hold the formal titles of deputy commanders of the WTO and Soviet officers responsible for coordinating the interaction of national service branches and special services. In addition, the WTO commander has at his disposal a separate group of liaison representatives to each of the loyal East European defense ministries. These representatives are high-ranking Soviet generals.

The Joint Technical Committee and Technical Council of the WTO are concerned with the research, development, production, and deployment of advanced weaponry by the WTO armed forces. The Sports Committee of the Fraternal Armed Forces organizes an extensive program of bilateral and multilateral sports events.[21]

The real locus of military authority in the Warsaw Pact is the WTO staff, the administrative organ of the WTO commander and his first deputy, the chief of staff. Both of these officers come from the Soviet army. Two sets of officers work on the WTO staff: East Europeans, headed by East European officers with the title of deputy chiefs, and Soviet officers appointed by the Soviet government.[22] As the working organ of both the Committee of Defense Ministers and the Military Council, the WTO staff has within its purview all the joint activities of the WTO. By far the most important of these is the planning, directing, and evaluating of the joint programs of troop training and military exercises.[23] The WTO staff is also responsible for organizing regular meetings of corresponding national service agencies.[24] The number, frequency, and scope of these meetings is such that they virtually constitute part of the WTO administrative structure. Both the Iakubovskii and the Kulikov texts on the WTO report regular meetings of national general staffs, staffs of service branches, and corresponding agencies throughout the Warsaw Pact.[25] A Soviet-Bulgarian study published in 1969 said that by 1968 the WTO had conducted more than twenty-five hundred meetings of military specialists devoted to military-technical, military-political, and military-historical questions.[26]

WTO sources frequently refer to unidentified "other organs of administration" subordinate to the WTO commander.[27] The available evidence suggests that three of these organs are an agency to coordinate military doctrine, an agency to coordinate WTO political administrations, and an agency to coordinate officer education within the Warsaw Pact. Like the publicly identified organs, these agencies penetrate into key bureaucracies of East European defense ministries and fragment national command over national armed forces.

The WTO Directorate for Military Doctrine

The WTO conducts frequent conferences to coordinate the formulation of alliance doctrine for its loyal members. These conferences draw their participants from national administrative agencies, research institutes, and military academies.[28] Such consultations are not mere academic exercises. A Soviet officer observes that "as a result of cooperation in the area of military theory" the fraternal armies have been able to adopt common norms for "regulations, military administration, and training manuals."[29] Despite the joint conferences, WTO doctrine turns out to be synonymous with Soviet doctrine. In a discussion of allied cooperation in the working out of WTO doctrine, Marshal Grechko observed, "The availability of the extremely rich military experience of the Soviet armed forces, of its first-class material-technical base, and of its well-trained military cadres—all this guarantees Soviet military experts a vanguard role in the resolution of the problematic tasks of military science."[30]

Soviet doctrine has two components: the military-political and the military-technical. The military-technical component consists of highly detailed discussions of four theories: military art (strategy, operations, and tactics), military economics and rear services, and the organization and development of a national defense system.

The authors of Soviet military doctrine claim that the military-political component is the more decisive in the formulation of a state's military doctrine. In the case of the Warsaw Pact, this claim is entirely justified. For the five loyal East European members, accepting a common set of military-political axioms is the prerequisite for accepting the Soviet conceptions of military art, troop training, military economics and rear services, and the organization of a national defense system. For Romania and Yugoslavia, the basis for the rejection of the military-technical component of Soviet doctrine is rejection of the military-political component. The military-political axioms of Bucharest and Belgrade declare that each socialist state must rely on its own forces to defend national sovereignty on national soil against a very large army. In comparison with the loyal East European members of the WTO, Romania and Yugoslavia have very different conceptions of military art, troop training, military economics, and the organization of a national defense system. The practical application of these conceptions results in national control over national armed forces.

The framers of the military-political component of Soviet doctrine reject any socialist military doctrine that does not require the interaction and mutual support of allied socialist armies. According to a volume on the ideological struggle in military questions by the chief of the Soviet Main Political Administration, "The military doctrines of the countries of the socialist confederation proceed from the fact that it is possible to prevent the outbreak of a new world war only by joint efforts of the fraternal socialist countries." This study by General A. A. Epishev vociferously condemned an exception to this rule, the Maoist heresy that a socialist state can defend itself by "reliance on one's own forces."[31] The Kulikov text on the WTO specifically declares that the "Maoist preaching of 'reliance on one's own forces' is intended exclusively for export and is also intended to disrupt . . . the unity and solidarity of the socialist countries."[32]

The military-political axioms shared by the armed forces of the loyal members of the WTO require a military-technical doctrine that eschews reliance on one's own forces and facilitates the fragmentation of national armed forces into units available for assignment to bilateral and multilateral formations. The common doctrinal propositions of the WTO states also serve as the basis for the conduct of joint exercises. In turn, the joint exercises provide the Soviets with the means of enforcing the conformity of the participants to the military-political and military-technical components of Soviet doctrine.

[97]

WTO sources report frequent meetings of the chiefs of the WTO political administrations, their deputies in central agencies of national main political administrations (MPAs), and corresponding MPA agencies for national service branches. There are programs for the exchange of MPA lecturers, journalists, and historians.[33] During both bilateral and multilateral troop exercises the fraternal armies form joint staffs of political officers to organize meetings of fraternal units and subunits, meetings of allied soldiers with the local population, and programs of "agitation-propaganda" and "cultural enlightenment." During the larger exercises, the joint group of WTO political officers also supervises a joint press center, a joint multilingual newspaper, joint multilingual radio broadcasts, and a joint cinematography group.[34]

Colonel V. Semin of the Soviet army writes that "as a rule" political activities take place during pauses in military action. "When the situation permits," the joint operational group of political officers organizes joint discussions by units and subunits on military and political themes, speeches by propagandists, and the exchange of films and stage performances. The joint meetings of soldiers and civilians sometimes include performances by choral groups, dance troupes, and orchestras.[35] Judging by accounts in Soviet sources, Warsaw Pact exercises evidently anticipate a conflict in which a series of rapid troop movements and nuclear strikes will alternate with a series of political rallies, musical performances, and visits to sites of historical and cultural interest. During the largest WTO exercise ever held, the Brotherhood in Arms maneuvers of 1970, there were more than forty meetings of allied military units, more than two hundred political rallies involving soldiers and civilians, and about three hundred cultural programs.[36]

The available evidence suggests that most of the joint political activities of the Warsaw Pact consist of bilateral Soviet–East European programs. According to the Kulikov text on the WTO, the number of joint political activities involving personnel from the Group of Soviet Forces in Germany, the East German army, and GDR civilians "every year amounts to between 30,000 and 35,000 joint measures."[37] According to an officer of the Czechoslovak People's Army, the Soviet garrison in Czechoslovakia and the Czechoslovak MPA synchronize their programs of political indoctrination: "Our army has the possibility of drawing directly upon the rich experience of the Soviet armed forces through direct cooperation with the commanders, political organs, party and Komsomol organizations of the Central Group of Soviet Forces. We make good use of such possibilities on the basis of a joint plan of the Main Political Administration of the Central Force Group and the Main Political Administration of the Czechoslovak People's Army."[38]

Romania does not participate in the synchronized programs of political indoctrination in the WTO. One reason is that the structure of the Romanian political agencies does not correspond to the structure of such agencies in the other WTO states. The organizational structure of the Romanian political agencies is virtually identical with that of the Yugoslav armed forces. The principal mission of the political administrations of the loyal members of the WTO is to prevent the party and military hierarchies of any WTO member other than Romania from uniting on a program that would resist fragmentation of national military forces by WTO agencies. The MPA systems of the Warsaw Pact carry out this mission by monitoring the practical applications of the shared military-political axioms of the WTO.

The WTO Directorate for Officer Education

In the extensive WTO program of educational exchanges, East Europeans send officers to study in the USSR and the Soviets send lecturers and textbooks to Eastern Europe. Romania, Yugoslavia, and Albania have each declined the hospitality to East European officers by Soviet military academies and educate all their officers at home, where they study the problems of waging a war of territorial defense. The Iakubovskii and Kulikov texts call attention to the special role of the East European graduates of Soviet institutions in the military affairs of the WTO: "Thousands of officers and generals of the fraternal armed forces have studied in Soviet military academies and higher military educational institutions. These generals and officers constitute the backbone of national military cadres and have played an important role in the establishment and development of their national armed forces."[39]

East European undergraduate military colleges train the great majority of East European junior officers. A limited number of East European officer candidates attend some of the 133 Soviet undergraduate military colleges, but the principal points of entry into the Soviet military education system for WTO officers are the 16 mid-career academies of the USSR, which accept captains and majors bound for senior command responsibilities. Many of these elite institutions offer highly specialized three-to-five-year curricula in fields such as chemical defense, communications, rear services, antiaircraft systems, and artillery forces. With the possible exception of several Polish academies and institutes, comparable specialized academies do not exist in Eastern Europe. The East European states do, however, have mid-career academies for combined arms commanders and for political officers.

The Frunze Academy for combined arms commanders and the Lenin Military-Political Academy appear to compete with their East European counterparts for East European applicants. Each of these academies has special programs designed to prepare East European officers for joint activities.[40] The WTO may reserve certain commands and certain MPA positions for the graduates of the Frunze and Lenin acadmies. In a speech commemorating the fiftieth anniversary of the Frunze Academy, the commandant of the Polish counterpart of Frunze declared, "Just as in the Soviet army, the graduates of the M. V. Frunze Academy hold responsible leading posts in the armed forces of the socialist states."[41] In 1971 the president of Czechoslovakia decorated the Lenin Academy for "aid in the establishment and training of the party-political apparatus of the Czechoslovak People's Army."[42]

The WTO officer education system limits formal training in strategic doctrine to the Voroshilov General Staff Academy in Moscow, an institution which accepts colonels, generals, and admirals from all WTO service branches for a two-year course. The strategy taught by the Voroshilov faculty is that of waging a coalition war by allied armed forces.[43] The only WTO institution that offers instruction in an alternative strategic doctrine is the General Military Academy in Bucharest.

The available evidence suggests that the alumni of the Voroshilov Academy enjoy a virtual monopoly on the highest-ranking posts in Eastern Europe and on command and staff positions in the multinational exercises of the WTO. The Soviet history of the Voroshilov Academy, published in 1976, reports that at the time of publication four of the five loyal WTO states had Voroshilov alumni as defense ministers; all five had Voroshilov graduates as chiefs of national general staffs; and four had Voroshilov officers as chiefs of main political administrations. Each of the five loyal East European members of the WTO has decorated the Voroshilov Academy for its services in training command personnel. Romania has not conferred any such decoration. When he presented Bulgaria's decoration to the Voroshilov Academy, the Bulgarian ambassador to the USSR declared, "In this most authoritative educational institution there has taken place the training of almost the entire leading staff of the Bulgarian People's Armed Forces.''[44]

It does not appear that the Soviets rely on the educational process to implant pro-Soviet loyalties in the East European alumni of Soviet military academies. It is more likely that the admissions process is used to identify officers who have decided to advance their careers by accepting openly Soviet hegemony over the alliance. Attending a Soviet academy means spending two to five years in the USSR, acquiring proficiency in the Russian language, and developing a capacity for practical daily cooperation with Soviet officers. If education in a Soviet military academy fails to generate genuine loyalty to the Soviet defense ministry, it probably succeeds in arousing expectations of Soviet patronage after graduation. The Soviet officers who administer the central agencies of the WTO have ample opportunity to dispense such patronage in the course of joint alliance activities. In turn, the beneficiaries of this patronage assume the obligation to maintain the devices that permit the Soviets to fragment national command over the national armed forces of Eastern Europe.

Such a set of reciprocal obligations may explain the prominence of graduates of Soviet military academies on the Military Council of National Salvation, which proclaimed martial law in Poland on 13 December 1981.

The chairman of the council, General Vojciech Jaruzelski, is an alumnus of the Voroshilov Academy, as is the deputy chairman, Florian Siwicki, who also serves as chief of the Polish General Staff. At least four other members are also Voroshilov graduates, each of whom was graduated from the USSR with a gold medal for outstanding academic work: Tadeusz Tuczapski, the head of the Polish civil defense system; Tadeusz Hupalowski, who serves both as the General Staff deputy for mobilization and as the minister of (civilian) administration; Joszef Wlodzimierz-Oliwa, the commander of the Warsaw Military District; and Czeslaw Piotrowski, the chief of military research and technology. According to a *Who's Who* published in the West, at least three other members of the council have degrees from Soviet academies: Michael Janiszewski, an alumnus of the Budennyi Academy of Military Communications; Ludwik Janczyszn, a graduate of the Lenin Military-Political Academy; and Eugeniusz Molczyk, the recepient of a degree from an unidentified Soviet military academy.[45] The Polish cosmonaut on the council, Miroslav Hermaszewski, apparently does not hold a Soviet degree but must have close ties to military and scientific colleagues in the Soviet space program.

The Soviet officers who command the central agencies of the WTO can influence the promotion of the East European alumni of Soviet military academies because they evaluate the performance of WTO officers in joint exercises, joint agencies, and bilateral activities. At a minimum, the military-educational network of the WTO denies East European officers training in the theory and practice of territorial defense. This network also enables the Soviets to compete with the political leaders of Bulgaria, Hungary, East Germany, Poland, and Czechoslovakia for the obedience of the upper echelons of the officer corps of these five countries. At most, the military-educational network of the WTO inducts high-ranking East European officers into a greater socialist officer corps commanded by Soviet marshals and assigned the joint mission of the defense of the gains of socialism against internal and external enemies.

NATIONAL MILITARY FORMATIONS IN SOVIET MILITARY POLICY

The joint programs and agencies of the WTO which fragment national control over national armed forces ostensibly focus on the conduct of joint actions against NATO. If these programs are in fact preparations for war with NATO as well as devices to immobilize East European armies in the event of Soviet military interventions in Eastern Europe, then the WTO evidently plans to integrate East European regiments and smaller subunits into multinational divisions or, at best, to integrate East European divisions into multinational armies. Such a program of integration for combat forces presupposes identical organizational structures, training programs, weaponry, support services, and, above all, a series of bilingual officer corps capable of functioning in both Russian and East European languages.

The alternative pattern of mobilization would of course be to entrust national armies with distinct national missions, as in NATO. The available evidence indicates that the only East European forces that have been organized for the execution of distinct national missions are those of Yugoslavia, Albania, and Romania.

There are clear precedents in the history of the Soviet army for two processes corresponding with the current policies of the WTO: the formal recognition of national military units whose political function is to legitimize the presence of Soviet military forces in "independent" political entities and the integration of ethnic units into multinational divisions and/or army groups. There are also precedents in Soviet military history for the development of the organizational structures to integrate ethnic units into a multinational force and for the development of a bilingual officer corps to command multinational formations.[46]

In 1923 the Twelfth Party Congress, which met after the establishment of the Union of Soviet Socialist Republics in 1922, decreed the organization of four distinct components of the Workers' and Peasants' Red Army (RKKA): a relatively small cadre army consisting mainly of Great Russians and russified Slavs; a large reserve force of territorial-militia divisions, which were much less expensive to maintain than regular cadre divisions; a relatively small number of regular cadre "national" military divisions recruited from the larger union republics and "autonomous" national districts; and inside cadre divisions, ethnic companies, battalions, and regiments recruited from the smaller nationalities,[47] in particular the Tatars and Bashkirs, two nationalities that had traditions of military service under the tsarist regime.

On the basis of the decisions of the Twelfth Party Congress, in 1924 the RKKA raised four Ukrainian rifle divisions, one Belorussian rifle division, two Georgian rifle divisions, one Armenian rifle division, and one Azerbaidjani rifle division.[48] According to a Soviet military scholar, in the fall of 1924 there were ten national-territorial divisions and seven separate national-territorial "units" (probably regiments). At this time, these ethnic detachments constituted about 10 percent of all Soviet military personnel, including the militia formations.[49] A five-year plan designed largely by M. V. Frunze was adopted in 1924 to establish national divisions made up of Kazakhs, Uzbeks, Turkomans, and Tadzhiks. The RKKA also planned to raise additional ethnic "units" for service within multinational cadre divisions.[50] According to research by Ellen Jones, the non-Russian ethnic units integrated into cadre combat divisions constituted close to 19 percent of Soviet manpower in 1924, in addition to the 10 percent serving in the national divisions.[51] According to a Soviet officer, the concentration of non-Russians in ethnic units within RKKA divisions made it possible to conduct political work in the native languages of Red Army soldiers, a policy that he claims greatly enhanced the effectiveness of such work. He added that one goal of political work was to overcome "manifestations of national prejudice" among the multinational personnel of the RKKA.[52] A resolution of the Twelfth Party Congress had specifically directed the political officers of the RKKA to improve ideological work in national units on the themes of the friendship and brotherhood of the nations that made up the Union of Soviet Socialist Republic.[53]

These policies bear a clear resemblance to the current WTO programs of political indoctrination aimed at cultivating friendship and brotherhood among the national components of the Warsaw Pact. Another parallel to the current policies of the Warsaw Pact was the Soviet decision to establish native-language officer schools to train a cadre of non-Russian officers, some of whom would eventually graduate to the Russian-language mid-career academies of the Soviet army. A Central Committee resolution of 1924 decreed: "It is now necessary to begin establishing military schools in the republics and national districts for the quick recruitment of command staff from local personnel who are able to serve as the nucleus of national troop units. In this matter, it is understood that the party and social composition of the national units, especially of the command staff, must be assured."[54]

The Soviet official who assumed the primary responsibility for organizing the two types of ethnic formations within the Soviet Army was M. V. Frunze, who held a series of high-level military and party posts from 1922 until his death in 1925. In the period following the Twelfth Party Congress, Frunze made a number of public declarations on the political necessity of maintaining such units as devices which legitimized the RKKA as a federal army. He also frankly acknowledged the questionable military utility of such national formations. In a speech to the Military Academy of the Red Army in late 1924, Frunze, in his capacities as commandant of the academy and chief of the RKKA General Staff, observed: "It is unknown as to which is better: to have ten divisions made up of Russian soldiers, well trained and well disciplined; or to have only five good divisions and five national divisions which are poorly trained and of low quality. From the point of view of the overall long-term perspective, it is very possible that the second alternative will prove more advantageous."[55]

The principal justification that Frunze advanced for the maintenance of national military formations of questionable military value was the political utility of giving formal recognition to the autonomy of the federal components of the USSR. "We cannot organize our army in any other way," Frunze declared to a meeting of army political workers on 17 November 1924. "A Union republic justifiably requires the creation of such units." Frunze added, in a declaration frequently cited in Soviet texts, "We never considered our Red Army as a "Russian" army, an army of one nationality. The great Russian nationality has constituted and will constitute the nucleus of the army and the basis of all its strength. But this has not and will not deprive all other nationalities of the Soviet Union of the right and responsibility to defend the Soviet land with weapons in hand."[56]

Frunze's military career suggests an unspoken corollary to this declaration: the right and responsibility of the non-Russian nationalities to bear arms does not deprive the Great Russian nucleus of the Red Army from the right and responsibility of defending Soviet rule in the non-Russian republics of the USSR. During the Red Army campaigns of 1919–1920 in Central Asia, Frunze worked out the dynamics of legitimizing the military presence of Soviet troop formations made up largely of Russian personnel by introducing these forces as the fraternal allies of the native communist military and political organizations. Frunze's success in eliminating native anti-Soviet military forces stands in clear contrast with the failure of the Red Army to prevail over the anticommunist native military forces of the Baltic states. Frunze further refined the techniques of preempting anti-Soviet nationalism during his tours of duty in various official capacities in the Ukrainian Soviet Republic, including an assignment as chief of the delegation that negotiated a treaty between Turkey and the Ukrainian Republic, at the time (1921) a nominally independent state.

In his arguments in favor of maintaining national troop formations, Frunze frankly acknowledged, "Among some comrades in some localities there are tendencies to transform national formations into the nuclei of national armies." Frunze dismissed these concerns by declaring that the RKKA had adequate command and control devices to preempt any such development toward autonomous national military foces: "We do not permit the existence of national armies in any separate *oblast'* or republic." He explained that the RKKA preserved its integrity as a federal army by imposing standard administrative structures, regulations, and doctrinal conceptions which converted national formations into components of "a single national entity."[57]

Frunze called attention to the possibility that the creation of large territorial militia forces might lead to the creation of an independent national military force in the western regions of the Ukraine. He noted that some unnamed comrades saw "political danger" in the possibility that the introduction of the territorial-militia system "will lead to the transformation of the majority of the Red Army in the Ukraine into a national Ukrainian army." Frunze argued that it would be a greater political risk not to give formal expression to Ukrainian sovereignty in the form of both territorial-militia units and national Ukrainian cadre divisions. He argued that the threat posed by incipient Ukranian nationalism could best be contained by the imposition of standardized administrative structures, energetic political indoctrination, and, above all, the recruitment of a Soviet command cadre capable of using both the Russian and Ukrainian languages.[58]

In 1935 the Soviet army began dismantling both its national-territorial divisions and its territorial-militia forces. A Soviet political officer writes that these changes were made to prepare for the possibility of war with Germany and Japan.[59] This explanation implies that the Soviets had little or no confidence in the reliability of their national formations in combat with a formidable external opponent. It also implies that the Soviets never intended to use these formations for external objectives. In March 1938, in conjunction with changes in the new USSR Constitution, a joint decree of the Party Central Committee and the Soviet of People's Commissars abolished all national divisions and units and reassigned their personnel to multinational cadre divisions.[60] According to a study of the Soviet armed forces edited by Marshal Grechko, the Soviet government abolished national detachments because of linguistic difficulties that arose in preparing regulations and manuals and because the national detachments "were unavoidably tied to their own territory, which prevented their training for action under different climatic, terrain and tactical conditions."[61] Grechko's explanation also implies that the RKKA never seriously contemplated the use of national formations in combat against an external enemy.

National Formations during the Great Fatherland War

By the end of 1941 Nazi armies had occupied almost all of the western regions of the USSR and much of central Russia. The Soviet command, deprived of the manpower of Belorussia, the Ukraine, and much of Russia, was forced, in a reversal of its policy of 1938, to mobilize national divisions recruited from the nationalities of the Caucasus, Kazakhstan, Central Asia, and Siberia. Although it deferred to the necessity during 1941–1942 of training non-Russian soldiers in national units, the Soviet command demonstrated distrust of the reliability of such formations in combat. As the war progressed, the Soviets followed a policy of dispersing ethnic personnel in ever smaller units within multinational cadre divisions made up predominantly of Russians and Slavs. The available evidence suggests that in 1941–1942 the Soviets organized non-Russian personnel into ethnic divisions, regiments, battalions, companies, and even smaller subunits. After 1943, when the Soviets launched a counteroffensive against the Nazis, the Soviets virtually dismantled all the national divisions and regiments.

According to one Soviet historian, by 1943 the Soviets had mobilized about 1,250,000 native personnel from the Caucasus, Central Asia, Kazakhstan, and Siberia.[62]

K. Tskitishvili, a Soviet Georgian historian, writes that a total of thirty-three rifle divisions were recruited in the Caucasus during the war. In this account, in the first year of the war the Soviets raised sixteen divisions, each recruited mainly from one national group: eight Georgian divisions, five from Armenia, and three from Azerbaidjan. Later, the Soviets raised seventeen divisions which bore the names of Caucasus republics, but each of these was organized as a multinational rather than mononational division. Tskitishvili writes that Georgians, Armenians, and Azerbaidjani collectively made up 60–70 percent of nine of these seventeen divisions.[63]

A Soviet Kazakh historian, M. K. Kozybaev, writes that during the first year of the war the Central Asian republics sent to the front thirty-seven rifle and cavalry divisions and twenty-seven separate brigades.[64]

The evidence available from Soviet sources suggests that the Soviet command assigned personnel from the Caucasus, Central Asia, Kazakhstan, and Siberia to distinct ethnic regiments, battalions, and companies.[65] As in the earlier national formations of the RKKA, this practice helped to solve the linguistic and cultural problems of both military training and political indoctrination. There is abundant evidence from Soviet sources that the existence of distinct ethnic units and subunits was critical to the wartime programs of conducting political indoctrination in the native languages of the non-Russian personnel.[66] There is also some evidence that the Soviets pursued a policy of assigning non-Russian command and political officers according to the relative proportion of a given non-Russian nationality in a given military unit or subunit, down to the levels of platoons and squadrons. In a discussion of an elite Kazakh Division, the Eighth Guards Rifle Division, a Soviet historian noted the following assignment of personnel during October 1943:

> The assignment of command and political cadres in the division was carried out in such a manner that in each subunit there were representatives of several nationalities.
>
> For example, the commander of the Seventh Company of the Nineteenth Regiment was a Tatar who knew Russian well. The political officer was a Russian. The head of the party organization was a Kirghiz. The deputy of the political officer was a Kazakh.
>
> When the commanders of platoons or squadrons were Russians or representatives of other nationalities who did not know the languages of the peoples of Central Asia, the most well-prepared Red Army men of

[107]

Kazakh, Kirghiz, Uzbek, or other nationalities were assigned as their deputies.

Such assignment of leading military cadres provided the opportunity to conduct work in the combat training and ideological-political upbringing of multinational personnel more correctly and in a more differentiated manner.[67]

The Dissolution of the National-Territorial Divisions of the Caucasus, Kazakhstan, and Central Asia

There is not enough evidence from Soviet sources to answer the question of whether the Soviet high command was satisfied with the combat reliability of the national divisions, regiments, and smaller subunits recruited from the Caucasus, Kazakhstan, Central Asia, and Siberia. When the victories at Stalingrad and in the North Caucasus enabled the Soviets to launch a counteroffensive in late 1943, the proportion of native peoples in the divisions named for the non-Russian republics dropped so precipitously that these divisions became indistinguishable from regular cadre divisions in the national composition of their personnel.[68] The Soviet historian A. P. Artem'ev notes,

> In the rifle divisions which were established in the Central Asian republics and in Kazakhstan, the proportion of the representatives of the Kazakh, Uzbek, Turkoman, Kirghiz, and Tadzhik peoples was comparatively great.
>
> In many formations, they made up from 40 to 50 percent of all personnel.
>
> But in the course of military actions the personnel of these divisions departed and dispersed into other military units.
>
> These divisions received new reinforcements and in this manner were transformed into ordinary formations of the Red Army which had in their composition only an insignificant portion of soldiers from the national republics for which the divisions were named.[69]

In a discussion of five "national" divisions of the Caucasus, Artem'ev, citing archives of the Soviet defense ministry, claims that in early 1943 native soldiers made up from 30 to 90 percent of the personnel of their respective divisions. But, by mid-1944, the proportion of any one Caucasus nationality in a division carrying the name of its republic ranged from a low of 2 percent to a high of only 15 percent. Artem'ev offers the following explanation:

[108]

To the degree that these divisions went further and further from their republics, it became more complex to reinforce their personnel in the required time with representatives of the corresponding nationalities.

And furthermore, there was not the same kind of necessity, as in the initial period of war, since the soldiers of non-Russian nationality had by 1943 received good military tempering and experience, and many of them had mastered the Russian language and received a good internationalist training.

This in no small degree facilitated their blending with the soldiers of all other nationalities.[70]

The evidence available on the national divisions of the Soviet army during World War II suggests that the Soviets preferred to disperse distinct national military units inside larger multinational divisions in which each non-Russian nationality was a small minority. The evidence available from WTO exercises, discussed in a preceding section, suggests that the Soviets have developed within the WTO organizational devices for dispersing East European military personnel into multinational WTO formations made up largely of Soviet personnel. It is likely that such a policy within the Warsaw Pact is based on the previous Soviet experience of integrating non-Russian personnel into multinational combat formations.

CONCLUSION

Romania, Yugoslavia, and Albania have demonstrated that national sovereignty in Eastern Europe is based on national control over national armed forces. The primary mission of the agencies and programs of the WTO is to deny national control over national armed forces to the political and military elites of the loyal East European states. These pro-Soviet elites support the WTO policy of denying independent military capabilities to their armies because this policy preserves the assured capability of the Soviet army for rapid military interventions in the internal affairs of the loyal East European states. The pro-Soviet elites of Eastern Europe rely upon the Soviet army as a shield against challenges from their domestic opponents, both inside and outside the local parties.

The Soviet experience with the techniques of depriving national military forces of national missions goes back to the origins of the Red Army. The principal peacetime function of the former national military forces of the union republics of the USSR and of the national armies of the socialist republics of Eastern Europe has been to serve as hosts who legitimize the presence of Soviet troops and the right of Soviet troops to defend the "gains of socialism" on non-Russian soil.

The Soviet experience with the techniques of mobilizing national military formations for combat with an external opponent suggests that the Soviets have been willing to send such forces into battle only after dispersing them inside predominantly Russian multinational formations. The organizational pattern of WTO agencies and programs suggests that the preferred Soviet plan for mobilizing East European national forces against NATO is to disperse elite East European forces, at the level of divisions and perhaps even smaller units, into larger military formations made up predominantly of Soviet personnel. The marginal role allotted to the East Europeans under such a pattern of mobilization suggests that the primary role of the Warsaw Pact is to deny its East European members national sovereignty over national armed forces.

[5]

Soviet Crisis Management in Eastern Europe

F. Stephen Larrabee

Since the end of World War II the Soviet Union has faced a series of challenges to its hegemony in Eastern Europe. The most serious occurred in East Germany in 1953, in Hungary in 1956, in Czechoslovakia in 1968, and in Poland in 1980–1981. Though the dynamics differed, military force was used each time to resolve the crisis.

The Polish crisis in 1980–1981 differed from the others in that the Soviet Union did not intervene directly but sought to use Polish forces to suppress the challenge posed by Solidarity. The recent Polish example thus raises questions about the nature of Soviet power and crisis management in Eastern Europe. Did the Soviet decision not to intervene directly in Poland in 1980–1981 indicate a change in Moscow's basic approach to crisis management in Eastern Europe or is it the exception that proves the rule? What are the implications of this most recent reaction for the Soviet Union's approach to Eastern Europe in the future?

In attempting to answer these questions it may be useful first to look at previous crises in Eastern Europe and Soviet efforts to manage them in comparative perspective. Particular attention will be focused on the process of crisis management. What political and military means did the Soviet Union use to resolve each crisis? To what extent did Moscow act unilaterally and to what extent did it coordinate its actions with and consult its East European allies in each crisis? What role did the Warsaw Pact play in the process of crisis management? Finally, has there been an evolution in the Soviet approach to managing crises in Eastern Europe? The final section of this chapter will draw some tentative conclusions about Soviet crisis management over time and the prospects for the future.

[111]

F. Stephen Larrabee

EAST GERMANY 1953

The uprising in East Berlin in June 1953 was the first violent challenge that the Soviet Union faced in Eastern Europe.[1] It was a direct product of de-Stalinization. Stalin's death in March 1953 unleashed widespread uncertainty in Eastern Europe about the future directions of Soviet policy. At home Stalin's successors initiated a program of limited de-Stalinization, highlighted by a reduction in terror and the introduction of the New Course. Abroad an interest was expressed in a relaxation of tensions with the West that was most obvious in the Soviet willingness to explore a possible settlement of the German question.

This willingness was reinforced by the deteriorating situation within the GDR, which by the spring of 1953 had become critical. The policy of forced industrialization adopted by the Ulbricht regime at the Second Conference of the Socialist Unity party (SED) in July 1952 had led to a serious deterioration of the economy and growing popular dissatisfaction. Discontent was particularly strong among the industrial workers as a result of the SED's decision in May 1953 to increase the work norm by 10 percent.

Faced with rising social and economic tensions in the GDR, and unable to provide economic assistance because of their own economic difficulties, the Soviet leaders in early June ordered Walter Ulbricht to introduce the New Course. The implementation of reforms provoked widespread confusion and demoralization within the SED, which had not been politically or psychologically prepared for the dramatic shift in policy. It also aroused expectations among the workers that the hated work norms would be abolished. When the party did not repeal the norms, protests broke out among the construction workers in East Berlin on 16 June.

As in Hungary in 1956, the protests in the GDR were spontaneous and were an expression of accumulated frustrations and dissatisfaction that had been building up for some time. Initially, the demonstrations were orderly and the objectives were primarily economic—a lowering of the work norms and a reduction of prices. Later, as the demonstrations grew larger, they became more violent and took on greater political content. They quickly spread to the rest of East Germany.[2]

Strike committees were set up in many factories, but they were badly organized and had no clear-cut objectives beyond a repeal of the work norms. In contrast to Hungary and Poland in 1956, however, the intellectuals did not come forward with a coherent political platform and act as articulators of popular grievances. Nor was any effort made to set up revolutionary councils to take over local civil administration or control traffic and telephone communications—essential prerequisites for any serious bid for political power.

Soviet Intervention and Crisis Management

The Soviet reaction to the outbreak of the strikes was prompt but cautious. Early on 17 June the Soviets took over the important transport and communication positions, but they did not use troops and tanks to disperse the crowds until late in the day, when the uprising had taken on a popular character. In the coal and uranium areas in Saxony, where they had troops stationed, the Soviets appear to have intervened fairly quickly and succeeded in nipping the insurgency in the bud; in areas where no troops were stationed, several hours elapsed before they intervened because troops had to be transported from field maneuvers to various trouble spots.

In general, the Soviet troops acted with restraint, and there were few casualties. Commanders appear to have been instructed to avoid bloodshed if possible; for instance, Soviet soldiers generally shot over the heads of the demonstrators. Soviet intervention did not represent a crucial turning point, however, for by the time troops were employed the uprising had already begun to subside.[3]

In short, because it was essentially a spontaneous protest against economic conditions and lacked well-defined political goals, the uprising quickly fizzled and never posed a major threat to Soviet interests in the GDR. The brevity of the crisis allowed no time for consultations with Moscow's East European allies. Even if there had been time, however, it is unlikely that Moscow would have consulted with other countries in the bloc. The Warsaw Pact had not yet been formed, and no institutional mechanism for policy coordination existed. Moreover, as a victorious power in the war against fascist Germany, Moscow felt it had a legitimate right to intervene unilaterally in Germany to protect its interests.

The West was caught off guard by the uprising, which was not at first reported by Western news agencies because they doubted its authenticity. When it became apparent that the demonstrations were part of a genuine popular revolt, Western action was remarkably restrained. Both the Western powers and the Adenauer government took pains to avoid actions that might be interpreted as interference in the affairs of the Soviet Union or the GDR.[4]

As in later crises, divisions within the Soviet leadership affected the

Soviet response. Some leaders, notably Georgi Malenkov and Lavrent Beria, appear to have favored dumping Ulbricht and exploring the possibilities of a negotiated settlement of the German problem so as to head off Bonn's entry into the European Defense Community (EDC), which had been ratified by the Bundestag in March 1953.[5] They seem to have encouraged opposition to Ulbricht within the SED leadership, headed by Wilhelm Zaisser, SED Politburo member and minister of state security, and Rudolf Herrenstadt, editor in chief of the party paper *Neues Deutschland* and a candidate member of the Politburo.

HUNGARY 1956

The crisis in Hungary in 1956 differed considerably from that in the GDR in 1953 and posed very different problems for the Soviet Union. The uprising in the GDR was essentially a spontaneous outburst of pent-up anger against the failure of the government to revoke the work norms. Its goals were relatively limited and primarily economic in nature, though they quickly expanded to include political demands. It had no coherent political platform or organization. As a result, it ended when the Soviet troops were introduced.

The revolt in Hungary, on the other hand, was a genuine national uprising. It had a concrete program, which aimed not only at introducing wide-ranging political and economic reforms but also at recovering a degree of national sovereignty and restructuring relationships with the Soviet Union. It was also more vehement and radical. Popular resentment was directed not only against the party but against the political police, some of whom were rounded up and hanged.

The uprising in Hungary also had a stronger basis of support among the population. Intellectuals, centered in particular in such institutions as the Petöfi Circle, a discussion club associated with the party youth organization, and *Iradalmi Ujsag*, the organ of the Writers' Association, played a prominent role in spearheading the reform movement and voicing criticism of party policy. After the second Soviet intervention on 4 November the workers took over leadership of the revolution, putting up stiff resistance and calling nationwide strikes. Workers' councils were set up throughout the country and exercised formal governing powers for a brief period in some areas.[6] Students also were prominent in the opposition.

Another important difference was the length of the crisis. In the

GDR it lasted only a day and a half. The revolt in Hungary, on the other hand, was the culmination of protracted conflicts within the Hungarian party, originating in the de-Stalinization process. In contrast to the GDR, however, the introduction of the New Course in Hungary by Imre Nagy, who replaced Matyas Rakosi as prime minister in June 1953, did not provoke an immediate outbreak of disturbances. Rather, it accentuated deep-seated differences within the leadership between the reformers, centered in the government bureaucracy, and the Stalinists, located mainly in the party, and led to a prolonged crisis which significantly weakened the party and undermined its authority.

A third important difference was related to the nature of the Communist parties. The Hungarian party was wracked by deep divisions between "home" communists, who had spent the war years in the underground in Hungary, and "Muscovites," who had been in exile in the Soviet Union during the war. Although factions existed in the SED, they were no means as deep. Moreover, the purges that occurred after the expulsion of Tito from the Cominform were far more severe in Hungary than in the GDR. Whereas in the GDR they led to dismissal of a few second-level functionaries, in Hungary they resulted in the execution or imprisonment of many of the most prominent home communists.

The introduction of the New Course, therefore, had a more profound psychological impact in Hungary than in the GDR and led to a great sense of indignation and moral outrage against past abuses. The party's authority and cohesion were further weakened by Khrushchev's famous "secret speech" at the Twentieth Congress of the Communist Party of the Soviet Union (CPSU) in February 1956, which accentuated ferment within the ranks of the party and among the intellectuals. By October 1956 the party was so weakened and discredited that in the early days of the uprising it virtually disintegrated. A power vacuum was created that made the task of crisis management significantly more difficult for the Soviet leadership than in the GDR, where the party remained essentially intact.

A final important difference was that the Hungarian revolt broke out after the formation of the Warsaw Pact in May 1955. It was also part of the larger effort undertaken by Khrushchev to dismantle the most odious elements of direct Stalinist rule and replace them with more indirect mechanisms for exercising Soviet hegemony in Eastern Europe. Initially, however, little effort was made to foster meaningful political or military integration within the Pact, and up until the 1960s it remained largely an empty shell. Its most important purpose was to legitimize the stationing of Soviet troops on Hungarian and Romanian soil after the ratification of the Austrian State Treaty in 1955.

Crisis Management

The Soviet leadership did not decide immediately upon a full-scale invasion of Hungary. Rather, the decision to intervene evolved over a period of days in response to changing events within Hungary and the international system. The Soviet handling of the crisis can be divided into two phases. The first began on 24 October, when in response to a request by Hungarian First Secretary Erno Gerö (who had replaced Rakosi in July 1956) a limited contingent of Soviet troops that had been stationed outside Budapest entered the city. The troops numbered only a few thousand and were designed as a psychological show of force to back up the efforts of the Gerö government to quell the unrest. The troops moved to protect party headquarters, the Parliament, bridges, and the Soviet embassy. Although these troops sustained some casualties, in general they tried to avoid engaging the Hungarians in combat.

In retrospect, the introduction of Soviet troops at this point was a tactical blunder which severely complicated Moscow's task of crisis management. It associated the Soviets directly with the hated Gerö government and transformed an essentially domestic protest into a genuine popular uprising with distinct anti-Soviet undertones. Moreover, the number of troops was too small actually to suppress the uprising. Once having introduced troops, however, the Soviets could not easily withdraw them without losing face and giving the insurgents the false impression that they had won, thus further fueling their revolutionary élan.

The Soviet handling of the crisis during the first phase was marked by indecision, vacillation, and hesitation, some of which can be attributed to the fluidity of the situation in Hungary and the dynamism of the crisis. As in the case of the GDR, however, divisions within the Soviet leadership also played a role. Some members appear to have pressed for extending "fraternal assistance" (sending more troops) while others appear to have hoped the crisis could be settled by political means.[7] In fact, the Soviets appear to have vacillated regarding intervention right up until the last second, changing their minds more than once.[8]

Initially, they adopted a conciliatory approach, apparently hoping that the situation could be brought under control without armed intervention. On 24 October—the day the first limited contingent of

Soviet troops entered Budapest—two members of the Politburo, Anastas Mikoyan and Mikhail Suslov, were dispatched to Budapest to consult with the Hungarian leadership. While in Budapest they agreed to the appointment of Nagy as prime minister—one of the key demands of the students—and the replacement of Gerö as first party secretary by Janos Kadar, who had spent several years in prison as a victim of Rakosi's purges in the early 1950s.

Mikoyan and Suslov returned to Budapest on 29 October with a copy of a Politburo declaration which offered to withdraw Soviet troops from Budapest and open negotiations with the Hungarian leadership for a withdrawal of Soviet forces from Hungary. The declaration also admitted past "mistakes," promised to base its relations on "strict Leninist principles of equal rights," and offered to reconsider "together with other socialist states" the question of Soviet advisers stationed in East European countries and "to review" (again with "other socialist states signing the Warsaw Pact") the question of Soviet troops in Eastern Europe, including Hungary.[9]

The conciliatory tone of the declaration suggests that at this point the Soviets still had not decided upon invasion. It is unlikely, however, that they ever seriously entertained the idea of withdrawing their forces from Hungary. They probably saw the offer as a tactical maneuver designed to dampen tensions and buy time until the situation had stabilized. Negotiations could be prolonged until the crisis had subsided, at which point Moscow would be in a better bargaining position and under less pressure to make meaningful concessions.

Initially, Nagy did not embark upon a radical course or take actions that precluded a political solution. On the one hand, he tried to restore calm and get the insurgents to lay down their arms, promising a return to the basic elements of the New Course and a restructuring of Soviet-Hungarian relations. On the other, he tried to convince the Soviets that changes were necessary and that these measures offered the best prospect for reestablishing order. The uprising quickly took on a dynamic of its own, however, making much of his program obsolete and forcing him to adopt more radical measures in an effort to try to stem the tide of revolution.[10]

The critical turning point in the crisis was not 1 November, the day Nagy declared Hungary's neutrality and withdrawal from the Warsaw Pact, as is often assumed, but 30 October. On that day Nagy, reacting to popular pressures, proclaimed the establishment of a multiparty system based on the coalition of parties that had emerged at the end of World War II. At the same time, he announced the formation of a new cabinet in which the Communists held only three out of seven seats.

Nagy's announcement of a return to the multiparty system initiated the second phase in the Soviet approach to the crisis. Up until 30 October the Soviets had tentatively backed Nagy and appear to have been willing to give him a chance to bring the unrest under control. His announcement of a return to a multiparty system, however, dramatically changed the nature and dimensions of the challenge, posing a direct threat to Soviet interests in Hungary and in Eastern Europe as a whole. It would have severely reduced the importance of the Communist party in Hungarian politics and deprived Moscow of the main instrument for maintaining control in Hungary. Moreover, it might have had an echo throughout the region, leading to similar pressures in other East European countries.

The announcement of the introduction of a multiparty system seems to have tipped the balance in favor of invasion. The first turnaround of Soviet troops, which had begun withdrawing on 28 October, was reported by Defense Minister Pal Maleter on 30 October.[11] Thereafter the Soviets began steadily reinforcing their troops. Key installations including the airport were surrounded, and Budapest was encircled.[12]

Nagy's announcement of Hungarian neutrality and withdrawal from the Warsaw Pact on 1 November must be seen against the background of the change in Soviet policy on 30–31 October. As Ferenc Vali has pointed out, Nagy's declaration did not provoke the invasion; it was a reaction to Soviet actions which constituted a breach of agreement by the Soviets to withdraw their troops. During the course of the day (1 November), Nagy tried in vain to reach Khruschchev and Mikoyan in Moscow to obtain clarification of the meaning of the troop reinforcements and other actions. He also sought clarification from the Soviet ambassador in Budapest, Iuryi Andropov, but received evasive and unconvincing answers. It was only after he failed to obtain a satisfactory explanation from Soviets that Nagy declared Hungary's neutrality.

It is unlikely that Nagy—a lifelong Communist who had lived in the Soviet Union and was familiar with its ways—was so naive as to believe that the Soviets would accept Hungarian neutrality. His declaration was most likely a last desperate gamble aimed at mobilizing international public opinion to try to forestall what he rightly saw as preparations for an invasion. It also provided the legal basis for Western aid or intervention, which previously would have been incompatible with Hungary's status as a member of the Warsaw Pact. At this point, Nagy had little to lose; for all intents and purposes the invasion had already begun.

The Soviets continued for several days to engage in deception while putting the final touches on the preparations for the invasion. Negotiations with the Hungarian military delegation about the withdrawal of Soviet troops from Hungarian soil were initiated. During the negotiations, the Soviets took a relatively accommodating stand, which lulled the Hungarians into a false hope that perhaps the crisis could be settled peaceably. These hopes were dashed on the night of 3 November, when the Hungarian military delegation, which was meeting with the Soviet delegation at Soviet military headquarters, was arrested by Soviet security forces. Shortly thereafter the invasion began in full force. Resistance was wiped out in less than three days, though some units of the Hungarian army continued to fight for another week before retreating into Austria.

As in the GDR, the Soviet military intervention was carried out almost exclusively by Soviet troops. In contrast to the East German situation in 1953, however, the Soviets consulted with their East European allies as well as with the Chinese and the Yugoslavs. Except for those with the Chinese, these consultations appear to have taken place after the decision to invade had been made.[13] Nonetheless, the fact that the Soviets felt the necessity to consult with their allies at all is significant and underscores the importance the Soviet Union attaches to the process of consultation and consensus-building.

International factors also probably influenced the Soviet decision to carry out the second invasion. Of particular importance was the extremely cautious U.S. reaction. President Dwight D. Eisenhower, concerned that the Soviets might be prompted to take extreme measures to maintain their grip on Hungary and provoke a conflict, sought to reassure Khrushchev that the United States would not attempt to make Hungary a military ally.[14] These assurances were undoubtedly welcomed by the Soviet leadership and probably influenced the decision to go ahead with the invasion.

A second important factor was the outbreak of the Suez crisis on 31 October, which divided the West and deflected its attention away from Hungary and Soviet actions there. With the West absorbed in its own problems, the chances that it would take a strong stand against Soviet actions were greatly reduced. Moreover, the moral force of the West's criticism of Soviet actions was undercut by French and British intervention in Egypt to protect key national interests.

The Soviet decision to invade was probably also influenced by the situation in Eastern Europe as a whole. At the time, Poland was in the midst of a crisis, although it was showing signs of stabilizing, and the situation in the rest of Eastern Europe remained unstable. Reports had been arriving about disturbances in Romania and Czechoslovakia, and there was even news of demonstrations in favor of Hungary in Soviet universities. There was thus a real danger that if the uprising was not contained it might accentuate instability elsewhere in Eastern Europe and further undermine Soviet hegemony in the region. As Khrushchev noted in his memoirs, "If the counterrevolution did succeed and NATO took root in our midst, it would pose a serious threat to Czechoslovakia, Yugoslavia, Romania, not to mention the Soviet Union itself."[15]

Finally, Khrushchev was on weak ground politically and appears to have feared that his enemies within the Soviet leadership would hold him responsible for the "loss" of Hungary.[16] And, in fact, some of his opponents—principally Molotov but probably others as well—apparently did try to blame the problems in Hungary on his policies.[17] He therefore could not afford to appear weak and indecisive when he was under attack from enemies who were looking for an excuse to undermine or remove him.

CZECHOSLOVAKIA, 1968

The Soviets faced a very different challenge in Czechoslovakia in 1968 than they did in Hungary in 1956. The Hungarian revolt was a spontaneous uprising, which took on a dynamic and momentum of its own. The party virtually disintegrated, and power passed quickly into the hands of the workers' councils and the insurgents. Nagy was never in control of events; rather, he was driven by them.

The challenge in Czechoslovakia, by contrast, was more gradual, less violent, and more ambiguous, making it difficult for the Soviet leadership to define the exact point at which the situation became unacceptable. Moreover, in Czechoslovakia, the reform movement was led by the party rather than directed against it, as was the case in Hungary in 1956.

Another important difference was that the Soviet Union had no troops in Czechoslovakia as it had in Hungary in 1956. Moscow therefore lacked an important instrument of pressure. Troops had to be moved in from the outside, which created diplomatic and military complications, or they had to be exercised along the borders, which was less effective.

A final important difference was related to developments within the Warsaw Pact. The revolt in Hungary broke out less than a year and a half after the formation of the Pact, and little effort had been made to integrate the East European forces into it. Thus little effort was made to use the Pact as a forum for crisis management. By 1968, however, the East European forces were more fully integrated into the Pact militarily, and Moscow had undertaken efforts to upgrade their military capabilities. Political integration had also been enhanced. As a result, Moscow was able to use the Pact mechanism for policy coordination and crisis management.

Soviet Interests and Perceptions

The Soviet response to the crisis in Czechoslovakia was influenced by a number of factors. Perhaps the most important were the growing polycentrism in Eastern Europe that began to manifest itself in the wake of Khrushchev's fall and the new *Ostpolitik* of the Federal Republic of Germany (FRG). Indeed, there was a direct relationship between the shift in Bonn's policy and the Soviet invasion of Czechoslovakia. *Ostpolitik* tended to reduce the potency of the German threat, which had traditionally been one of the most important means of maintaining cohesion in Eastern Europe. As long as West Germany remained wedded to the policies of the Adenauer era, the Soviet Union had little to fear. Once Bonn joined the great Western march toward detente, however, it posed a major threat to Soviet interests. This threat became particularly acute after Romania broke ranks and established diplomatic relations with the FRG in January 1967, a move Moscow feared might spark a "mad rush to Bonn."

Moscow's concern about the impact of developments in Prague was reinforced by pressure from Ulbricht, who was adamantly opposed both to Bonn's *Ostpolitik* and to liberalization in Czechoslovakia. To Ulbricht, Dubcek's course in Czechoslovakia was doubly objectionable, for it might prove contagious and infect the GDR and it threatened to lead to a breach in the wall of hostility that had been erected to isolate the Federal Republic.[18] Thus backed by Gomulka, Ulbricht sought to press Moscow to take a firmer line against both Prague and Bonn.

The new Soviet leadership was faced with growing restlessness among its own intelligentsia, many of whom followed the course of liberalization in Prague with great interest. The unrest in Czechoslovakia also was having an impact in some areas of the Soviet Union, particularly the Ukraine,[19] and to a lesser extent in some of the Baltic republics. Thus there was a danger not only that developments in

[121]

Czechoslovakia would spill over into Eastern Europe but that they might infect the Soviet Union as well.

The crisis in Czechoslovakia emerged against this background of gradual erosion of control both at home and abroad. Pressure for change had been gradually growing in Czechoslovakia more or less unnoticed by the Soviet leadership for several years before 1968.[20] This pressure culminated in the ouster of First Secretary Antonin Novotny, one of the last of the Stalinist leaders in Eastern Europe, in January 1968. Novotny's replacement by Alexander Dubcek paved the way for the introduction of a comprehensive program for economic and social reform, which was embodied in the Action Program, approved by the party in April 1968. These reforms went further than those introduced by Nagy in Hungary in many areas. Among the most important provisions were those for greater intraparty democracy, greater guarantees for human and civil rights, greater autonomy for the Slovaks, and a decentralization of economic decision making. In addition, Dubcek abolished censorship, a move which particularly alarmed the Soviet leadership.

Unlike Hungary, however, Czechoslovakia made no attempt to withdraw from the Warsaw Pact or to declare neutrality. On the contrary, Dubcek continually stressed Czechoslovakia's loyalty to the Pact. Nor was there an attempt to establish a multiparty system, as Nagy had been willing to do. The Action Program, in fact, specifically underscored the importance of maintaining the leading role of the party.

Crisis Management

The gradual and ambiguous nature of the challenge in Czechoslovakia, together with the strong support Dubcek enjoyed within the party, complicated the Soviet task of crisis management. Initially, the Soviets adopted a policy of "watchful waiting." As the process of reform gathered momentum, particularly after the publication of the Action Program in April, Soviet concern mounted and the Kremlin leaders engaged in a conscious campaign of political, psychological, and military pressure designed to induce the Czechoslovak leadership to arrest the process of reform.

But whereas in Hungary the Soviets had acted essentially alone, consulting with their allies only at the last second or after having made the decision to invade, in Czechoslovakia they acted from the beginning in concert with their allies. The Warsaw Pact served as an instrument of policy coordination and implementation. The Warsaw

Pact summits in Dresden (March), Warsaw (July), and Bratislava (August) were used by the Soviets to signal their displeasure with the course of developments in Czechoslovakia. Although technically these meetings involved only party and government leaders, in the broader sense the Pact did serve as a mechanism for policy coordination. Romania was not invited to participate in the meetings, however. Warsaw Pact maneuvers, involving East German and Polish troops, were also conducted along the Czechoslovak border in March, May, and June. In addition, the Soviets pressed for the holding of joint Soviet-Czech maneuvers on Czechoslovak soil, which finally began in June. These maneuvers served a dual purpose: to intimidate the Czech leadership and induce it to halt the reform movement, and to carry out preparations for a military invasion, if necessary.[21]

Military intervention, however, was regarded as a last resort. Throughout the summer, the Soviets engaged in an intensive search for a political solution. After the publication in June of the "Two Thousand Words" manifesto by leading Czechoslovak intellectuals, the Soviets intensified their war of nerves against the Czechoslovak leadership. In a move reminiscent of the tactics during the Hungarian crisis of 1956, for instance, the Soviets delayed the withdrawal of the troops that had been engaged in maneuvers on Czech soil agreed to by the Czechoslovak leadership in May.[22] Shortly thereafter, the Czech leadership received letters from the Polish, East German, Bulgarian, and Hungarian parties, expressing concern about developments in Czechoslovakia and calling for a conference of Warsaw Pact members to discuss the dangerous threat to socialism in Czechoslovakia.

This proposal, which was rejected by the Czechoslovak leadership, was followed by a new invitation for a joint meeting in Warsaw on 14–15 July. The Soviets used the meeting (which the Czechs did not attend) to draft a letter to the Prague leadership, expressing the "deep anxiety" of Pact members about developments in Czechoslovakia. It charged that "antisocialist and revisionist forces" were threatening to "sever Czechoslovakia from the socialist community" and warned that such a development was not simply an internal matter but jeopardized the common interests of all socialist countries.[23]

The Warsaw letter constituted a virtual ultimatum to the Prague leadership: either you take decisive action to halt the "counterrevolution" or we will do it for you. Its real significance, however, lay in its emphasis on collective security and the obligations that followed from

[123]

membership in the socialist community. Stressing that developments in Czechoslovakia were a source of legitimate concern to all members of the Pact, the letter enunciated the principle that became the basis of the doctrine of limited sovereignty (known in the West as the Brezhnev Doctrine), which was officially proclaimed a little more than a month after the invasion.[24]

In the weeks after the publication of the Warsaw letter, the Soviet leadership seemed to vacillate between intervention and seeking a political solution. The meeting at Cierna on the Soviet-Czechoslovak border, which was agreed to after the Czechoslovak leadership had refused a Soviet invitation to come to Moscow, represented a last-ditch effort by the Soviets to achieve a political solution. It was attended by virtually the entire Soviet Politburo, possibly because the Soviets hoped that such a show of political force would impress upon the Czechoslovak leadership the seriousness of the situation. (This attitude contrasted starkly with the pattern in Hungary in 1956, when only Mikoyan and Suslov had negotiated on behalf of the Politburo, and in Poland in 1956, when Khrushchev and two other Politburo members had represented the Soviet leadership.)

At the same time the Soviets conducted large-scale maneuvers in the USSR, calling up thousands of reservists and requisitioning civilian transports.[25] These maneuvers served as a means of intensifying the political pressure on the Czechoslovak leadership. But they were also a preparation for military invasion if a satisfactory political solution to the crisis could not be found.

The Cierna meeting was inconclusive and was followed by a second meeting at Bratislava a few days later, attended by all members of the Warsaw Pact except Romania. The communiqué issued at the end of the meeting made no mention of Czechoslovakia but committed all members to the defense of "socialist achievements." Perhaps more important, it called for cooperation on the basis of "fraternal mutual assistance and solidarity." Like the Warsaw letter, the significance of the Bratislava communiqué lay in its emphasis on collective responsibility "to preserve the achievements of socialism" and the obligation to provide "fraternal assistance" if these achievements were threatened. It explicitly acknowledged the right of the Soviet Union and its allies to provide "help and support" if the Dubcek leadership failed to carry out its obligations.[26]

In essence, the communiqué papered over differences. Each side maintained its position without visibly backing down. But each drew different conclusions from the meeting. The Czechoslovak leaders clearly left Bratislava thinking they had assuaged Soviet anxieties and could continue on their present course as long as they took care to keep the media in check. For their part, the Soviets felt they had made clear their dissatisfaction with the Czech leadership's handling of developments and had strengthened the ideological basis for military intervention, should it prove necessary.

The Prague leaders' belief that they had stood down the Soviets was probably buttressed by the withdrawal of Soviet troops from Czechoslovak soil on 3 August. The troops, however, were withdrawn only across the Soviet-Czech border and remained in a high state of readiness. As in Hungary in 1956, this withdrawal may have been an act of deliberate deception designed to lull the Czechs into a false belief that the crisis had abated. Certainly that was the effect if not the intent.

As in Hungary in 1956, the Soviet leadership seems to have been divided over the wisdom of intervention and decided in favor of using military force only after considerable debate.[27] Some members such as Ukrainian party leader Piotr Shelest appear to have been strong advocates of intervention, while others such as Mikhail Suslov, Vadim Zagladin, and Alexei Kosygin appear to have been among the skeptics.[28] There also appear to have been differences of view among the various Pact members. Ulbricht and Gomulka apparently strongly pushed for military action, while Kadar went along reluctantly.[29] Romania did not participate in the invasion.

The actual decision to invade was probably taken around 10 August. One of the key factors appears to have been the publication of the statute of the Czechoslovak party on 10 August, which was to be presented to the party congress, scheduled to be held in September. This new statute provided for the election of all party officials by secret ballot and permitted the continued advocacy of minority views after a policy decision had been taken. The Soviet leadership undoubtedly saw the statute as a dangerous departure from Leninist principles and further proof that Dubcek was incapable of halting the erosion of the party's monopoly of power.

Another important contributing factor was probably the approach of the party congress, which was widely expected to confirm Dubcek's reformist line and lead to a strengthening of the reformist element within the Central Committee. Once the congress had taken place and approved Dubcek's course, the Soviets knew it would be much more difficult to reverse the process of reform.

The Soviet decision was probably also influenced to some extent by estimates of the possible reaction of the United States to an invasion. The United States adopted an exceedingly cautious approach to the crisis in Czechoslovakia. At the height of the crisis in June and July it scrupulously avoided public criticism of Soviet behavior and had even withdrawn some of its forces from the vicinity of the Czech border so as to avoid any possible charges of inflaming the situation. At the same time it signaled a strong interest in the initiation of talks on strategic arms limitations.[30] These moves probably encouraged the Soviet leadership to believe that the United States was unlikely to take strong action if an invasion occurred.

Last, the Soviets probably calculated—again correctly—that they would face only minimal resistance and that an invasion could be carried out swiftly with little loss of life. Indeed, Dubcek's failure to prepare the Czechoslovak armed forces for armed resistance can be seen as a critical mistake. As Ivan Svitak has argued, had Dubcek prepared the army—even if he did not ultimately order it into battle— the Soviets would have been presented with a much more complicated political situation, and they might have been deterred from invading.[31] It was precisely because Gomulka mobilized the Polish army and the Soviets feared that the Poles would fight that they refrained from invading Poland in 1956. Similar fears were clearly operative in Poland in 1980–1981.

In carrying out the invasion, the Soviets had clearly learned from their experience in Hungary, where the first introduction of troops on 24 October had proved insufficient to crush the rebellion and had only exacerbated the situation. This time, they moved decisively and with overwhelming force, using four to five hundred thousand troops—nearly twice as many as were employed in Hungary in the second invasion on 4 November. As in Hungary, the Soviets moved quickly to seize the main airport, Ruzyne, outside of Prague. After capturing Ruzyne, they began a huge airlift of soldiers, armored cars, and tanks. Within several hours, an expeditionary force began to occupy the main streets and the principal buildings in Prague, such as the Central Committee building, the Parliament, and the Academy of Sciences. A parachute unit surrounded party headquarters and arrested the four party leaders who were inside, including Dubcek. Both resistance and casualties were light.

In contrast to the invasion of Hungary, however, which was primarily a Soviet operation, the invasion of Czechoslovakia was undertaken by the Warsaw Pact as a whole (with the exception of Romania). The East European military contribution was not particularly significant—indeed, many contingents were withdrawn a few days after the invasion. But their participation served an important political function: it underscored the collective nature of the action and shifted some of the opprobrium from the Soviet Union.

Politically if not legally, the invasion marked an important expansion of the Warsaw Pact's responsibilities. Whereas previously the primary functions of the Pact had been to combat external aggression, in the aftermath of the invasion, it assumed a new function: to combat "subversion" within the socialist community. In short, the invasion marked an important step in the expansion of Moscow's use of the Pact as an instrument for maintaining its hegemony in Eastern Europe as well as for coordinating policy within the bloc.

POLAND, 1980–1981

The crisis in Poland in 1980–1981 confronted the Soviet Union with the most serious challenge to its hegemony in the postwar period. The reform movement in Czechoslovakia in 1968 was essentially a revolution from above, initiated by the party with strong support from the intellectuals. The crisis in Poland, by contrast, was a genuine revolution from below, led by the workers with broad support from all segments of society. It was a mass popular revolt, which threatened to change the balance of political forces in Poland.

Solidarity challenged the very basis of the communist system: the primacy of the party. It represented a social force outside the control of the party and not subject to its dictates and thus posed not only an ideological challenge to Marxist-Leninist doctrine but a more fundamental political challenge to Soviet interests in Poland. If the Communist party were to lose its dominant role—if it were forced to share power with another social force, even covertly—Moscow could no longer be sure of Poland's loyalty and willingness to support Soviet foreign policy.

Moreover, Soviet security interests were more directly threatened than they had been in Czechoslovakia in 1968. Poland is the largest and most important country in the Eastern bloc. Traditionally it has acted as a buffer between the USSR and its Western neighbors, especially Germany. Any change in Poland's status would remove this buffer and leave the Soviet Union and the GDR more exposed. In particular, it would affect Soviet military strategy in any conflict in Europe. The Polish army is the largest and best-equipped non-Soviet military force in the Warsaw Pact. Polish forces have been earmarked for a rapid offensive role in any conflict in Europe. An erosion of cohesion and discipline within the Polish army—which contains a high proportion of conscripts—would have had a direct impact on Moscow's ability to conduct coalition warfare in any conflict in Europe.

There were also potential political repercussions for the rest of the bloc. As in Czechoslovakia in 1968 there was a danger that unrest would spill over and spark unrest in the other East European countries. This fear was undoubtedly accentuated in Soviet eyes by Solidarity's appeal at its first congress in September 1981 for other East European countries to establish trade unions. Although this appeal was not immediately answered anywhere in Eastern Europe, the general economic deterioration throughout the bloc and the fact that attempts had previously been made to set up trade unions in several bloc countries, including the Soviet Union itself,[32] undoubtedly increased Moscow's concern about the long-range implications of developments in Poland.

This concern was shared to an even greater degree by the GDR and Czechoslovakia. Both countries were harsh critics of the Polish party's handling of the situation. The East German leadership in particular manifested alarm over the possible repercussions of the turmoil for stability in the GDR and in the fall of 1980 took steps to prevent any spillover of the unrest including closing the Polish–East German border, expelling some twenty thousand Polish workers, and quadrupling the currency exchange requirements for Western visitors to the GDR.

Just as the dynamics of the crisis in Poland differed from those in Czechoslovakia in 1968, so too the problem of crisis management for the Soviet Union differed. In Czechoslovakia the Soviet Union had essentially been faced with a renegade party leadership unable to control the forces that it had unleashed and to a large degree sanctioned. Thus to contain the crisis the Soviets needed only to remove the top party leadership. The problem in Poland was far more complex. Stanislaw Kania, the party leader, remained loyal throughout; he was simply ineffectual. He seemed both unwilling and incapable of taking decisive action to halt the erosion of party authority.

For the first eight weeks or so after Party Secretary Edward Gierek's ouster (3 September 1980) an uneasy balance existed, and there seemed some hope that Kania might be able to bring the situation under control while avoiding bloodshed. After November 1980, however, events began to spiral out of control, taking on a dynamic of their own. The party seemed to lurch from crisis to crisis, with no sense of direction or control. Wildcat strikes erupted spontaneously.

No sooner was an incident in one area resolved than one would erupt in another area. To restore order, the party was continually forced to give ground and compromise. In the process Solidarity's strength grew and its demands escalated, taking on an increasingly political content.

The rapidity of the changes led to a serious weakening of the party's cohesion and authority. The problem was compounded by divisions within the Polish leadership. Although Kania had removed many of Gierek's closest associates, he never fully consolidated his hold on the party and had to balance competing pressures from several factions—the liberals centered around Mieczyslaw Rakowski and Kazimierz Barcikowski on the one hand and the hard-liners led by Stefan Olszowski and Tadeusz Grabski on the other. In addition, there also existed a conservative-nationalist faction led by General Mieczyslaw Moczar, the former head of the secret police, who once had been Gierek's main rival for power.

Crisis Management

As in Hungary and Czechoslovakia, Soviet policy toward Poland during the crisis was marked by vacillation and hesitation. The Soviet leaders were caught off guard by the outbreak of violence in August. Although obviously apprehensive about the potential repercussions of the unrest, they recognized that direct intervention could only exacerbate the delicate situation. Initially, therefore, they expressed cautious support for the new Polish leadership headed by Stanislaw Kania and gave it considerable leeway to deal with the situation as it saw fit.

As domestic tensions increased and Kania proved unable to quell the mounting unrest, Moscow adopted a more assertive policy. At the end of November and beginning of December it took several military actions designed to upgrade the preparedness and readiness of its forces: calling up reservists, deploying units out of garrison, providing refresher training, and bringing war reserve equipment up to readiness for use. As in Czechoslovakia in 1968, these maneuvers seem to have had a dual purpose: to intimidate Solidarity and increase the pressure on the Polish leadership to take a more resolute stand against Solidarity's demands and to bring Soviet troops up to a high state of readiness in case the crisis could not be resolved by political means.

Whether the Soviets really were on the brink of intervention and pulled back at the last second remains a moot point. Probably they regarded the maneuvers primarily as a means of political pressure and did not intend to invade at that time. One indication that this was their strategy is that on 5 December a special summit of the leaders of the Warsaw Pact nations was held in Moscow which was attended by all members including Romania. Ceausescu had made clear his firm opposition to military intervention shortly before the Pact meeting, and it is unlikely he would have consented to attend unless he had been assured in advance that invasion plans would not be discussed.[33]

The Pact meeting temporarily defused the tensions aroused by the Soviet military buildup. Kania apparently convinced the Soviets to give him more time to bring the situation under control. The communiqué issued at the end of the meeting expressed faith in the Polish leadership's ability to overcome its difficulties but noted that Poland could "firmly count on the fraternal solidarity and support" of the Warsaw Pact members—an oblique reference to the Brezhnev Doctrine.[34] Thus although military intervention was avoided, the meeting made clear that Kania and the rest of the leadership were still on probation.

The resurgence of instability in January and February intensified Soviet concern and led to renewed pressure on Kania to halt the erosion of the party's authority. At a special meeting at the conclusion of the Twenty-sixth Party Congress in March, Kania reportedly came under strong attack for his handling of the unrest in January and February.[35] The communiqué issued at the end of the meeting made an unmistakable reference to the Brezhnev Doctrine and called upon the Polish leadership to "reverse the course of events and to eliminate the peril looming over the socialist achievements of the nation."[36]

The crisis in Bydgoszcz in late March, which was sparked by an attack on several Solidarity representatives by the local police, can be seen as an important turning point in the Soviet approach to the Polish situation. Although Kania was eventually able to defuse the crisis and avert a nationwide strike, the party emerged seriously weakened and more divided than ever. During the Central Committee meeting of 29–30 March, which approved Kania's moderate approach, the hard-liners (notably Olszowski and Grabski), who had been pressing for a much tougher stance, came under strong attack and reportedly offered their resignations.[37] The acceptance of their resignations was reportedly prevented only by the personal intervention of Brezhnev.[38]

The strong pressures for reform manifested at the plenum and Kania's continued willingness to compromise appear to have seriously alarmed the Soviets and led to a shift in Moscow's policy. Before the plenum the Soviet media had avoided any criticism of the Polish United Workers' party (PUWP), concentrating its attacks on Solidarity and various elements allegedly seeking to undermine socialism in Poland. Over the next several months leading up the Fourteenth Party Congress in July, however, the Soviet media began openly attacking the PUWP and calling on the party to consolidate its ranks and take the ideological offensive. Charges of "revisionism" were also raised for the first time since the onset of the crisis in August 1980.[39]

In addition, the Soviets stepped up military pressure on Poland. During late March and early April the Soviets conducted another series of maneuvers under the code name Soyuz 81 under the direct command of Marshal Victor Kulikov, Soviet commander of the Warsaw Pact forces. During the maneuvers the Soviet, East German, and Czechoslovak Warsaw Pact forces simulated a landing on the Polish coast and a surprise night attack. These maneuvers, like the ones in December, probably were designed primarily to intimidate the Poles, but they also may have been intended as a rehearsal for an invasion.

Personal diplomacy was also used as an instrument of crisis management. At the end of April Mikhail Suslov, a member of the Politburo and Moscow's chief ideologist, made a hastily arranged visit to Warsaw. Suslov's visit, which was reminiscent of the intermediary role he had played with Mikoyan in the Hungarian crisis in 1956, appears to have had a twofold purpose: to give the Soviet leadership the opportunity to obtain a firsthand impression of the situation in the Polish party and to impress upon the Polish leadership the need to take more resolute action to reassert the party's leading role.

Finally, the Soviets forcefully reiterated their concern about the deterioration of the situation in Poland through a letter sent to the Polish leadership on 5 June. The letter was similar in tone and content to the Warsaw letter sent to the Czechoslovak leadership in July 1968. Singling out Kania and Jaruzelski, it bluntly accused the Polish leaders of pursuing a policy of retreat and compromise which could lead to the party's "liquidation" and called them to take more resolute action to eliminate the danger of "counterrevolution."[40] The letter also pointedly reminded the Polish leadership that the Soviet Union and its allies were determined to preserve the gains of socialism in Poland—thus once again raising the specter of intervention if the Polish leadership proved incapable of stabilizing the situation and halting the erosion of the party's authority.

One motivation behind the letter may have been to discredit Kania and encourage his replacement at the Tenth Plenum to be held several days later. At the plenum, Tadeusz Grabski, a noted hard-liner, openly attacked Kania's leadership in an apparent attempt to topple him. Kania successfully mounted a counteroffensive, however, and survived the challenge. In fact, the letter appears to have backfired. Rather than discrediting Kania, as the Soviets seem to have hoped, the letter actually strengthened his position. Many members of the party seem to have viewed Grabski as a stalking horse for Moscow and feared that Kania's removal would mean an end to the process of gradual reform. Thus rather than backing Grabski, they rallied behind Kania.

The Fourteenth Party Congress in July confirmed basic approval for Kania's leadership and moderate course. Although the Soviets appear to have been relatively satisifed with the outcome of the congress, they remained concerned about the inability of the Polish leadership, and Kania in particular, to arrest the growing strength of Solidarity. Matters came to a head with the convocation of Solidarity's congress in early September, which led to the adoption of a number of radical resolutions, including a call for free elections and an appeal for other East European countries to establish free trade unions along the Polish model.

The appeal to other East European countries clearly alarmed the Soviets. It raised the specter that the unrest in Poland might spread to other East European countries and provoked a second, even stronger letter from the Soviets to the Polish leadership, which was delivered by the Soviet ambassador in Warsaw, Boris Aristov. The Soviet statement constituted a virtual ultimatum. It sharply criticized the Polish leadership for allowing the emergence of "anti-Sovietism" and insisted that steps be taken to halt anti-Soviet manifestations, which it claimed aroused the "deep indignation of the Soviet people."[41] At the same time the Soviets indirectly threatened to employ economic leverage against Poland. At the end of September a hard-line member of the Polish Politburo with good ties to the Kremlin, Stefan Olszowski, warned in a nationwide television address that the Soviets might shut off economic assistance to Poland if there was not an end to anti-Soviet agitation.[42]

The second Soviet letter was a clear sign that Moscow had lost patience with Kania. On 18 October he stepped down as first secretary and was replaced by General Vojciech Jaruzelski, who already held the posts of defense minister and prime minister. The Soviets were clearly encouraged by Jaruzelski's selection, but they do not appear to have dictated his choice. Rather, his election was primarily influenced by domestic conditions in Poland at the time, particularly the situation in the Polish party. By the fall of 1981 the party was in acute disarray, too divided and demoralized to govern.[43] The army was the only force that still enjoyed the respect of the population and had the organizational cohesion to provide coherent leadership. Jaruzelski's selection as first secretary was tacit recognition of the army's position.

Kania's replacement by Jaruzelski on 18 October was an important turning point in the crisis. It resulted in a hardening of policy toward Solidarity and set the stage for the introduction of martial law on 13 December. The swiftness and precision with which the crackdown was carried out suggest that it had been planned well in advance, although the final preparations were probably not made until after Jaruzelski assumed the post of first secretary in October. The success of the military coup was facilitated by Solidarity's overconfidence and its failure to take minimal precautions against a crackdown and by the existence of an infrastructure for administering the country under martial law which had been set up by a secret law passed in November 1967.[44] This law established a hierarchical network of civilian and military cells throughout the country, headed by a Committee for Territorial Defense, which could be activated in case of a national emergency and transformed into an operational political-military, decision-making, and administrative apparatus with very little prior preparation.

The exact Soviet role in the crackdown remains murky and may never be known. The Soviets clearly exerted strong pressure on the Polish leadership to take a firmer line against Solidarity, and planning for the military intervention was almost certainly coordinated with Moscow. The timing of the crackdown, however, appears to have been a Polish decision and dictated by internal Polish events. This impression is reinforced by the fact that the coup took place on the last day of West German Chancellor Helmut Schmidt's visit to the GDR. Had the Soviets directed the coup, they almost certainly would have waited until Schmidt had returned to Bonn, thus sparing him the acute embarrassment of being caught in East Germany visiting Erich Honecker (who had been pressing for intervention) on the day that military law was introduced.

As in Czechoslovakia in 1968, meetings of the Warsaw Pact provided an important forum for policy discussion and coordination. Two meetings—of the Council of Foreign Ministers in Budapest (1–2 December) and of the Council of Defense Ministers in Moscow (1–4 December)—were held shortly before the crackdown. Although their main function was to coordinate policy on arms control, they also provided an opportunity to review the situation in Poland and discuss contingency plans. Moreover, as noted earlier, Marshal Kulikov, the commander in chief of the Warsaw Pact, was in Warsaw a few days before the coup, presumably to coordinate policy and review military planning for the crackdown.

SOVIET CRISIS MANAGEMENT: CONTINUITY AND CHANGE

Although the dynamics of the four crises discussed above differed, the Soviet response shared certain common elements. First, the Soviets were prompted to intervene in each case when they began to feel that the local party leadership had lost political control and could no longer manage the crisis. In each case it was a threat to the primacy of the party that prompted Moscow to take action. Although such a threat was less severe in Czechoslovakia in 1968, it is clear that the Soviet leadership believed it was only a matter of time before the party would be swept away by the forces unleashed by Dubcek.

Second, in each case the Soviet Union used force only as a last resort, after other efforts at a political resolution had failed. In Hungary, Suslov and Mikoyan tried to broker the crisis, but their efforts failed; in Czechoslovakia the decision to intervene came only after the Warsaw letter and the meetings at Cierna and Bratislava had failed to reverse Dubcek's course; and in Poland the Soviets opted for an "internal solution" only after repeated warnings and after Kania had failed to take strong action to restore the leading role of the party.

Third, in each case the Soviets relied on a combination of political and military pressure. In general, military pressure was used to reinforce political pressure and increase its credibility. At the same time, the Soviets took actions designed to prepare their military forces for intervention in case a political resolution of the crises proved impossible. The decision to intervene, however, was made only after efforts at a political solution had failed.

Fourth, there was a discrepancy between the Soviet perception of the threat and that of the local party leaderships. Nagy, Dubcek, and Kania all saw themselves as loyal Soviet allies and did not expect Moscow to use military force. Each in his own way underestimated the Soviet threshold for tolerance and at the same time overestimated his own freedom of maneuver.

Poland, of course, presents a special case. Here the Soviets chose an "internal solution" rather than direct intervention. There were several reasons for that decision.

In Poland there was an internal option such as had not been available in previous crises. In Hungary in 1956 there was no alternative leader such as General Jaruzelski who commanded popular respect and was also trusted by the Soviets. Nor could the Hungarian army be considered reliable. Part of it defected to the insurgents, and the majority remained neutral at best. Similarly, in Czechoslovakia in 1968, the pro-Soviet group around Vasil Bilak and Alois Indra had no popular support, and the Czech army fully backed Dubcek. Thus the Soviets had little choice but to use military force or else risk political changes that they regarded as unacceptable.

The cost of intervention in Poland would be high. In the case of Czechoslovakia in 1968 the Soviets could be relatively certain that they would face little, if any, resistance if they invaded and that a quick surgical strike, backed by overwhelming force, would succeed. The situation in 1980–1981 was quite different. Based on their experience in 1956[45] and their knowledge of the Poles generally, the Soviets had to assume that some units of the Polish armed forces would fight and that the Red Army might face large-scale popular resistance. Moreover, once active resistance had been eliminated, Moscow would have to occupy and garrison Poland indefinitely at a time when it was already bogged down in Afghanistan.

Indeed, Afghanistan may have acted as a restraining force in two senses. First, it is unlikely that the Soviet military was enthusiastic about becoming involved in a second armed conflict before the situation in Afghanistan was stabilized. Second, the Afghan invasion may have had a sobering impact on the Soviet leadership. Whatever their motivations for invading Afghanistan, the Soviets clearly miscalculated the depth and intensity of the resistance they would face. The Afghan experience therefore may have made the Soviet leadership more aware of the high costs of intervention and thus more reluctant to involve itself in a second military conflict unless it was absolutely unavoidable.

The general immobilism and drift that characterized Soviet policy during Brezhnev's latter years probably served to reinforce a tendency to temporize and seek a political solution. Moreover, Brezhnev had a strong personal stake in detente with the West—a policy with which he was closely associated—and he undoubtedly recognized that an invasion of Poland would drive the last nail in the coffin of this policy. Thus he had personal reasons for trying to avoid an invasion.[46]

The Western response in Poland was much stronger and less ambiguous than in previous crises. In the GDR in 1953 and Hungary in 1956 the Western reaction was extremely cautious. In 1956 Eisenhower went out of his way to signal the USSR that the United States did not intend to exploit the unrest or intervene. Similarly, the U.S. response during the Czechoslovak crisis was so timid as possibly to have led the Soviets to think that the United States was not particularly concerned about developments there.[47]

In Poland, by contrast, the United States and its Western allies made clear early in the crisis that any invasion would have serious consequences for East-West relations. President Jimmy Carter even used the "hot line" to communicate directly with President Brezhnev at one point in the crisis,[48] and the United States tried to warn Solidarity of the danger of invasion through both public and private communications. Although such warnings probably would not have deterred the Soviet Union from invading had it concluded that its vital interests were seriously imperiled, they did deprive the Soviets of the element of surprise and thus may have contributed in some degree to Soviet restraint. At a minimum, they made clear to Moscow that there would be a definite price to pay if it invaded.

Finally, by 1980–1981 the Soviet stake in maintaining good relations with the West, especially Western Europe, had increased visibly. The interventions in 1953 and 1956 occurred at the height of the Cold War, when relations with the West were tense and the political costs of direct military intervention in Eastern Europe were low. The Soviet stake in improved relations with the West had increased by 1968, when the Soviets invaded Czechoslovakia, but it was still relatively modest. Detente had not yet really begun. The Polish crisis, however, occurred after a decade of detente. Moreover, strains between the United States and its West European allies offered Moscow new opportunities to make inroads in Western Europe. These prospects would have been undermined by any invasion of Poland.

PROSPECTS FOR THE FUTURE

Although Moscow was able to resolve the Polish crisis without direct military intervention, the Soviets have little reason to be optimistic about Poland. The introduction of martial law was an admission of the party's political weakness. As a result, the military has supplanted the party as the real political power in Poland. The official lifting of martial law in July 1983 has done little to change this situation. The military continues to hold the key positions in the economy and the party. Given the potential for upheaval elsewhere in Eastern Europe, this must give the Soviets some cause for concern.

The Polish military's direct involvement in politics raises several other problems. Over the long run it risks growing politicization of the military. Studies of military intervention in many Third World countries suggest that when the army enters politics, politics enters the army.[49] There is no reason to think that Poland will be different. Thus the Polish army could find itself wracked by the same factionalism that has characterized the party, thereby weakening its organizational cohesion.

Perhaps more important from Moscow's point of view is the impact of continued military rule on Poland's contribution to the Warsaw Pact. The longer the army remains involved in security and administrative functions, the greater the deterioration of its military effectiveness is likely to be. Under present conditions it is highly questionable how effective the Polish army—70 percent of which is composed of conscripts—would be in any major conflict. Indeed, over the long run one of the major consequences of the Polish crisis could be its impact on the military effectiveness of the army. Such a situation, as A. Ross Johnson has suggested, could force Moscow to rethink its entire approach to coalition warfare.[50]

Moscow's problems in Eastern Europe are not limited to Poland, however. The countries of Eastern Europe are entering a period of austerity and economic stagnation that could have important political implications.[51] The 1976–1980 Five-Year Plan showed the lowest growth rates since the end of World War II, and even these relatively modest rates will be difficult to achieve in the new Five-Year Plans.

A gradual decline in living standards and the availability of consumer goods could have an impact on political stability in some countries, intensifying pressures for change and fueling political unrest. At the same time, economic decline could accentuate the "guns versus butter" dilemma and stimulate increased resistance to Soviet calls for higher defense spending. Romania, for instance, has openly rejected such calls—most dramatically at the 1978 Warsaw Pact meeting in Moscow—and in January 1983 it announced that it would not raise defense spending for the next three years above 1982 levels. Faced with growing economic constraints, other East European countries, particularly Hungary and Poland, might be tempted to follow suit, thus undercutting Moscow's efforts to carry out its modernization program within the Pact.

These problems will most likely occur against a background of a potential leadership change in the Soviet Union. The transition from

Brezhnev to Andropov was relatively smooth, but Andropov never consolidated his power. Konstantin Chernenko's age and poor health raise doubts whether he too will be anything more than a transitional leader. Thus the Soviet Union could be faced with a new succession problem in the not-too-distant future.

Traditionally the succession issue has had a major impact on Eastern Europe. East European elites have often sought to exploit the preoccupation of the Soviet leadership with internal consolidation either to experiment domestically or to increase their autonomy in foreign policy. This pattern was followed after Stalin's death, precipitating the upheavals in East Germany, Hungary, and Poland; it was followed after Khrushchev's fall and led to Albania's defection and Romania's first steps toward greater independence; and it could occur again.

All this suggests that new crises in Eastern Europe can by no means be excluded and that over the next decade Moscow is likely to face new threats to its hegemony in the area. How Moscow will manage these crises will depend on a combination of factors: the dynamics of the crisis, the Soviet perception of the stakes, the international situation at the time, the internal cohesion of the Soviet leadership, and last but not least, Western policy. The example of Poland, however, should not be construed to suggest that Moscow has necessarily forsworn the use of military force to preserve its interests. Military intervention remains—and is likely to remain for the foreseeable future—one of several options open to Moscow to maintain its hegemony in Eastern Europe, and it would be imprudent to assume that that option will not be used again under certain circumstances. Indeed, a continued deterioration of East-West relations may actually make the Soviet Union less reluctant to use military force to preserve its interests in the area because Moscow may conclude that it has less to lose vis-à-vis the West by such action.

PART III

PURSUIT OF
EAST EUROPEAN INTERESTS

[6]

Foreign Policy Goals

EDWINA MORETON

The members of the Warsaw Pact are not noted for their divergence in public on issues of foreign policy. With the exception of Romania, all the East European states make a habit of endorsing the Soviet foreign policy line, although with varying degrees of warmth. Nor are they any more receptive than the Soviet Union to the prying of Western scholars into their domestic decision processes, especially concerning their relations with the Soviet Union. Therefore, analysis of foreign policy divergence in Eastern Europe is difficult but not impossible. The trick is to approach the subject backwards. Instead of looking for clues in the public announcements of East European regimes, this chapter will look at the interests the individual East European states might seek to defend within the Warsaw alliance and the constraints upon their ability to do so.

DOMESTIC AND FOREIGN CONSTRAINTS

For the East European members of the Warsaw Pact limited sovereignty in domestic politics, meaning the obligatory retention of the basic structures of the Soviet model of socialism, has, because of the Soviet Union's enduring stake in Eastern Europe, always been matched by similar restrictions on the conduct of foreign policy. The region's acknowledged role as a physical security buffer along the Soviet Union's western borders has increased as the Soviet Union has made the postwar transition from diplomatic isolation to become a regional and then a global superpower. At each stage the importance of Eastern Europe to Soviet foreign policy has grown, both symbolically and ideologically.

In the early postwar years foreign policy was the effective monopoly of the four major powers in Europe—the United States, the Soviet Union, Britain, and France. Later the threat from the West—and in particular from a resurgent West Germany—cemented the Eastern bloc's solidarity in support of primarily Soviet foreign policy objectives.

West Germany's refusal to accept both the division of Germany and the postwar boundaries in Europe posed a direct challenge to the East German regime, whose existence West Germany officially ignored for thirty years, and to Poland, whose western boundary, the Oder-Neisse line, West Germany refused to recognize. For these two East European nations, the inclusion of a rearmed West Germany in NATO in 1955 added a military dimension to an already uncomfortable political problem. The other NATO governments did not wholly endorse the West German claim that the key to European security lay in the reunification of Germany (meaning the absorption of East Germany into West Germany) nor publicly contradict Eastern Europe's interpretation of West Germany's "revanchist" policy. The Soviet Union's primary concern was that West Germany would act as the spearhead of American power and influence. From the Soviet perspective, this threat played a major part in determining the early hostile relationship between East and West.

To the East Europeans, and particularly those states with a vested interest in resolving the German problem, a rearmed West Germany did pose a credible threat. As the only state in Europe actively working to change the political and territorial status quo, West Germany posed a direct challenge to East Germany (whose existence it ignored), to Poland (whose borders it refused to recognize), and to a lesser degree to Czechoslovakia. Until West Germany was prepared to modify its revanchist stance, any attempt by the West to expand political relations with Eastern Europe was destined to run into a Soviet veto.

The Soviet stake in Eastern Europe was enhanced when hostilities along the Sino-Soviet border in the 1960s reinforced the Soviet Union's need for security in the West. More recently, instability in Iran and Afghanistan has added to Soviet fears. But perhaps more important in the longer term, the growing attraction for the Third World in the 1970s of the Chinese and Eurocommunist models of development at the expense of the Soviet path has meant that Eastern Europe is now the only region where the Soviet model has taken root, however inadequately. Eastern Europe therefore provides not only the physical basis but also the ideological justification for the Soviet

Union's claim to superpower status toward both the West and the rest of the developing and Communist world. And as the most recent Soviet response to the Polish crisis has demonstrated, Leonid Brezhnev was no more inclined than was Stalin or Khrushchev to relax the Soviet Union's political and ideological grip on this strategically vital alliance.

The East European regimes have not, however, remained the quiescent satellites Stalin probably had in mind. Some thirty-five years after being installed in power by the Red Army, all these regimes have evolved their own separate identities. The image of a monolithic Soviet empire in Eastern Europe always lacked credibility, probably most of all in Moscow.[1] But the notion of a polycentric order in Eastern Europe, with individual states engaged in the pursuit of wholly independent policies, is equally absurd.

Although the history of Soviet–East European relations has been turbulent, when Communist party regimes have rebelled, as in Poland in 1956 and Czechoslovakia in 1968, they have done so primarily in support of domestic autonomy and the right to pursue their own paths to socialism. Whatever the propaganda justification used to defend Soviet actions—as, for example, the accusation in 1968 that Czechoslovakia was being subverted by Western influence—foreign policy has seldom been a crucial issue. It has generally been the Soviet response to domestic upheaval that has turned these challenges to political and economic orthodoxy into security issues for the entire bloc. Even the call for Hungary's withdrawal from the Warsaw Pact in 1956 was, for the Hungarian government at least, more a practical response to premature use of Soviet tanks than the unfolding of a premeditated grand strategy of realignment. Although throughout the Polish crisis of 1980 and 1981 all the protagonists were obliged to keep an eye firmly fixed on Moscow, they did so to stave off unwanted influence in a crisis with primarily domestic roots. As the series of upheavals in Eastern Europe over the past three decades suggests, this domestic challenge has proved extremely potent, and it will continue to be a primary preoccupation for Eastern Europe's ruling Communist parties.

Thus the second major constraint on the foreign policies of the Warsaw Pact states is the problem of maintaining domestic political and economic stability. The pervasive influence of Soviet power within the Warsaw Pact and CMEA—leaving aside any less formal channels of influence—is as much a domestic as a foreign policy issue in Eastern Europe. Increasingly, domestic pressures and Soviet constraints come together to pose problems for the security and stability of the regimes now in power. As the external threat from the West has receded, attention in Eastern Europe has focused on maintaining the ideological security and stability of the regimes placed in power after World War II. But whereas Soviet power was sufficient (and largely appreciated) in the early years as the guarantor of territorial and physical security, over the past two decades justifiable doubt has arisen as to whether Soviet military, economic, and political power is an equally reliable guarantor of regime security. Indeed, the events of 1968 in Czechoslovakia would suggest that Soviet doctrine and military power have become more of a threat to the security and stability of the East European regimes than is the West.[2] The Polish crisis since 1980 has been a dramatic example of how Soviet pressure to maintain the barriers to domestic political and economic change in Eastern Europe can undermine the credibility of civil authority. Should the Soviet Union, by accident or design, adopt policies likely to exacerbate domestic political tensions, it is uniquely placed to upset the underlying balance of interests to its own disadvantage in Soviet–East European relations. At times the East European regimes may be uncertain of the support of major segments of their population. Yet in dealings with the Soviet Union the interests of those regimes, in different combinations on different issues, are a vital element in the pattern of relations within the Warsaw alliance.

In sum, the major problem facing all the East European regimes during the 1960s and 1970s in the transition to "developed socialism" has not been the world outside but the adaptation of political structures and the maintenance of party authority and control in the face of increasingly complex economic tasks and in the light of the Soviet Union's self-appointed role as arbiter of bloc orthodoxy.[3] This aspect of regime security—the pressure of domestic issues and externally imposed constraints—provides the most fruitful avenue for analyzing the foreign policy perspectives of Eastern Europe.

Three underlying principles shape the foreign policy perspectives of the East European states. First, the present communist regimes will oppose any development—internal or external—which in their view threatens to jeopardize the leading role of the party. Second, decisions taken at the domestic level, attempting to resolve the pressures of modernization and adaptation, must not be allowed to threaten the continued existence of the wider ideological community, however loosely defined, of Warsaw Pact states. Finally, any foreign policy decisions by other states, including the Soviet Union, that threaten to undermine the pillars of regime security as defined by the indigenous regimes will be resisted.

At the same time the pressures for conformity are considerable. Although they may have differences with each other and with Moscow, both individually and collectively, all the current East European regimes share some common concerns. Ultimately, all claim to derive their legitimacy and authority to govern from their membership in the alliance of socialist states. Thus none is likely to kick too hard at the ideological traces. All share a common commitment to the Warsaw alliance, however loosely they might wish to define it.

Yet a discerning glance behind this public façade would reveal the parallel, by no means contradictory, and possibly more important conclusion, that each of the East European states has autonomously defined foreign policy interests based on nationally determined priorities and preoccupations which may or may not coincide with those of its allies in Moscow or of the other capitals in Eastern Europe. What has distinguished the different regimes from one another at different points in their postwar history has been the ability or inclination to pursue such interests and the degree of success achieved. Despite appearances to the contrary, there are good grounds for assuming that, although public foreign policy statements will continue to show remarkable coordination, national East European policy preferences and needs will in the future play an increasingly important part in the process of joint foreign policy formulation within the Warsaw alliance.

The View from Eastern Europe

The Soviet Union's military, economic, and political power far outweighs that of Eastern Europe. Yet a glance at the political development of the alliance over the past decade would suggest that the Soviet Union has found itself far from able to translate this military and economic advantage directly into corresponding political influence and control. This ambiguous relationship between Soviet power and influence on the one hand and the developing interests and capabilities of the various East European regimes on the other holds the key to an understanding of Soviet–East European relations in the 1980s.

The assumption of many analysts since the invasion of Czechoslovakia in 1968 has been that, faced with the choice between cohesion and viability of the bloc, the Soviet Union will always opt for cohesion and control and that consequently the last decade has witnessed a counterreformation in Eastern Europe designed to reinforce apparently shaky Soviet control.[4] The Soviet Union's reaction to the Solidarity challenge to Communist party rule in Poland confirms this thesis. On the other hand, exclusive focus on Soviet power reveals little either of the root causes that provoked this Soviet reaction or of the complexity of the Soviet–East European foreign policy environment that conditions Moscow's response.

The most obvious barrier to grasping the underlying complexity of the problem is the habit of equating "national" with "anti-Soviet" in Eastern Europe. The two are by no means synonymous. Nor are individual East European states above allowing subjective factors to enter into their relations with each other or the Soviet Union. From the earliest days, diversity in domestic political cultures and historical experience have helped to shape the divergent foreign policy perspectives of the East European states.

Cultural and national differences play a direct role in cross-border tension resulting from irredentist claims on the territory or national minorities of neighboring states. Despite many objective factors and shared interests, several states have longstanding border disputes, which periodically cloud their bilateral relations (for example, Romania's dispute with the Soviet Union over Bessarabia, the problem of the Hungarian minority in Romania, and Bulgaria's dispute with Yugoslavia over Macedonia). Though not a member of the Warsaw Pact, Yugoslavia shares some of the problems of its neighbors that are members. Indeed, for Yugoslavia nationality problems have become security problems and pose a particularly grave threat to the stability of southeastern Europe. Other East European regimes have tended to see interstate border tensions as a barometer of relations in other spheres rather than as contentious issues in their own right. At the same time, however, as the Yugoslav example suggests, a threat to national cohesion must affect the ability of individual East European regimes to pursue their own foreign policy interests within the bloc.

The exclusive focus on Soviet power as an arbiter of the foreign policy process blocks consideration of issues. It makes obvious foreign policy deviancy and its corollary, Soviet inability to control divergence from its prescribed policy, the sole yardstick of foreign policy autonomy in Eastern Europe. Not only does this bias ignore the possibility of large areas of foreign policy on which the interests of the Soviet Union and its allies might naturally converge, but it also excludes any chance that the individual East European states might be able to defend their own interests through bargaining within the alliance. Conflict is always assumed to be resolved on Soviet terms. Yet the recent history of both the Warsaw Pact and the CMEA would suggest that foreign policy is of necessity the result of compromise rather than simple Soviet fiat. Although each of the East European regimes would claim to be pursuing the same long-term ideological goals—creating international conditions favorable to the development of socialism and strengthening the socialist alliance—there is far less inclination to agree, either among themselves or with the Soviet Union, on specific short- and medium-term objectives or the strategies designed to secure them.

The traditional focus on Soviet power not only understates the complexity of Soviet–East European relations on a broad scale, it also excludes the possibility that events and policy concerns in Eastern Europe might have a reciprocal modifying impact on Soviet policy. Yet the argument is compelling that Moscow's insistence on a close and interdependent relationship between the East European regimes and the Soviet Union helps forge a close link in Eastern Europe between domestic and foreign policy. Unless the Soviet Union is prepared on occasion to modify its own peculiarly national foreign policy perspectives, over the coming decade this close interrelationship between domestic and foreign policy will ultimately reinforce the potential for conflict over a wide range of issues within the alliance.

THE GERMAN PROBLEM

Hard to trace but of great importance for the conduct of alliance politics are issues that directly affect a particular regime's perceptions of its own security and stability. Here a number of general concerns can be identified, including the continued threat to the security of individual East European regimes created by the failure to find a solution to the German problem. For East European governments their membership in the Eastern bloc, and since 1955 in the Warsaw alliance, increased and reinforced the threat from the West. Yet clearly the credibility of this threat has declined over the years, and its impact on foreign policy has varied from state to state. East Germany and Poland in particular had vital interests to defend: continued existence and recognition of national sovereignty and international recognition of the Oder-Neisse border as Poland's western frontier, respectively.

West Germany's refusal, until the Brandt government's initiative in 1969, to recognize postwar boundaries in Eastern Europe or the separate existence of an East German state continued to sour political relations, even if the military threat from West Germany seemed hardly credible. In particular, West German adoption of the Hallstein Doctrine, putting pressure on third states not to recognize the separate existence of East Germany, almost completely preoccupied the East German regime. In many cases the success of West German pressure over recognition of East Germany left the East German regime with no diplomatic contact with the outside world other than through the good offices of its Warsaw Pact allies, especially the Soviet Union. Yet whatever the shortcomings of their fraternal Soviet allies—and the East Germans were particularly nervous on this score—no alternative source of support was available.

From the point of view of the alliance as a whole, despite the declining credibility of the West German military threat, the issues involved in the German problem were sufficiently important in principle to hamper relations between East and West until 1969. West German modifications to its own *Ostpolitik* proved persuasive to the GDR's allies, Poland and the Soviet Union, if not to the GDR itself. For those East European states not directly threatened by an unresolved German problem, frustration at being forced to decline West German offers of improved trade relations in the interest of alliance solidarity had already become increasingly apparent. Romania broke ranks in 1967 and exchanged diplomatic recognition with the Federal Republic; Hungary and Czechoslovakia were apparently ready to follow suit but were obliged to await a settlement of the central issues. As soon as West Germany and the Soviet Union had settled the framework of the new relationship in the Moscow treaty of 1970, the others lost little time in falling into line.

For the GDR the issue was more complex, and the ideological threat from a socially acceptable West Germany loomed large. For much of its thirty-year history the prime concern of GDR foreign policy was to ensure that West Germany gained no political influence in Moscow or Eastern Europe at its expense. Therefore, no improvement in either political or economic relations with West Germany could take place until Bonn acknowledged the existence of a separate and fully sovereign East German state. Consequently, GDR foreign policy, such as it was, aimed at maintaining alliance discipline in support of GDR national policy. By the end of the 1960s, however, the political barometer in Europe was set for rapid change.

As long as Moscow saw its immediate interests in the German problem as coinciding with those of East Berlin, the GDR leadership appeared to wield considerable political influence in Eastern Europe. Once Soviet policy began to respond to a change in signals from Bonn, the GDR could only block Soviet initiatives. Much to Soviet annoyance, the GDR did so repeatedly during the course of 1970 and early 1971. The issues at stake were fundamental. The first concerned East German sovereignty. Although the Soviet Union would not have countenanced a threat to the existence of the GDR and gave strong verbal support to East Germany's claim to full diplomatic status, it was not willing to allow the issue of diplomatic relations between the two German states to hold up progress in Soviet relations with West Germany. The West German chancellor, Willy Brandt, had already made the important concession and accepted that East Germany existed as a separate state—a reversal of twenty years of West German policy.

The second bone of contention between East Germany and the Soviet Union was Berlin. The Four Power Agreement on Berlin, signed in 1971, acknowledged legitimate ties between West Berlin and West Germany and reaffirmed Berlin's status under four-power administration. To West Germany that agreement assured West Berlin's existence. To East Germany it was a continuing thorn in the side of the regime, a further diminution of its claims to GDR sovereignty by an affirmation of formal Soviet rights (as one of the four powers) to overrule East Germany's claim to sovereignty over its own capital.

Although ultimately the GDR was unable to deflect Moscow from its chosen course, the German problem was an area in which the GDR leadership had clearly defined interests, considered vital to its security. It had been prepared to defend these interests before the conclusion of the treaties between East and West in the early 1970s; it has consistently done so since.[5]

The German problem has now been partially resolved both in Eastern Europe and between East and West. But the GDR has shown over the past decade that it remains sensitive to any move on the part of its allies toward acceptance of West Germany's definition of a special relationship with the GDR or Berlin. At the same time, to the extent that the unresolved German problem gave Moscow additional leverage over the foreign policy of its allies, the future may conceivably see an increased potential for autonomous foreign policy activity, particularly on the part of the GDR and Poland.[6] East German autonomy, however, will always be subject to special constraints.

ROMANIA'S DEFIANCE

Membership in any political or economic alliance is likely to generate conflict between primarily national concerns and the wider interests of the alliance as a whole. If member states are at widely divergent levels of socioeconomic development such conflicts can become acute. Romania's relations with the Soviet Union in the CMEA have followed this pattern, with differences in policy on nominally economic issues souring relations across the board. As early as the mid-1950s Romania first caused friction within the alliance by its attempt to avoid becoming the market garden and raw materials supplier to the more developed CMEA economies. And there is at least circumstantial evidence to suggest that from the earliest stages in 1956 Romania successfully used the bargaining chip of its support for Moscow in the emerging Sino-Soviet dispute to head off unwelcome Soviet political and economic pressure and in particular to induce Khrushchev in 1958 to water down his proposals for the supranational integration of the CMEA.[7] Romania also took advantage of Khrushchev's new mood of reconciliation following the revelations of the secret speech in 1956 to obtain withdrawal of Soviet troops from Romanian territory. And later the Romanian Communist party (RCP) sought to bolster its national autonomy still further by mediating directly in the Sino-Soviet dispute—although probably less in the expectation of resolving the dispute than in the hope that the rift could be somehow contained within the world communist movement. The attempt failed, leaving the RCP out on a limb in the Eastern bloc.

It was largely to defend this exposed position and maintain Romanian policy autonomy that in 1964 Ceausescu enunciated the Romanian party's "declaration of independence," emphasizing national autonomy and party sovereignty. These principles have since consistently guided Romanian policy both within the alliance and beyond. In 1968, although the RCP had little sympathy for the reform program contemplated by Dubcek in Czechoslovakia, Ceausescu went to considerable lengths publicly to defend the Czechoslovak party's right to determine its own internal course. The RCP took a similar line during the Polish crisis in 1980 and 1981, despite a total lack of sympathy for the political goals of Solidarity and mounting concern at the Polish Communist party's rapid disintegration.

On a wider plane the RCP's insistence on foreign policy autonomy has led to differences with Moscow over policy toward West Germany, the Middle East, arms control (the Romanians are the only members of the Warsaw Pact to have called for the dismantling of Soviet SS-20 missiles), and so on. This independent stance within the alliance has been given practical assistance by strenuous efforts on the part of the regime to diversify Romania's foreign economic ties

[150]

outside the CMEA such as contacts with the European Economic Community (EEC) and membership in the General Agreement on Trade and Tariffs (GATT), the International Monetary Fund (IMF), and the Group of 77.

Until recently Romania has been relatively successful in all these areas. Economic considerations and the consequent need to defend national integrity as defined by the leadership of the RCP were the original catalysts to Romania's pursuit of an autonomous foreign policy. But the international climate today is far less hospitable to Romania's course. Western interest in a maverick East European state declined as relations with Moscow improved in the 1970s.

In recent years the limits of Romania's semiautarkic industrial development policy have become increasingly apparent. Even before the Polish crisis put a squeeze on all the CMEA economies there was a need for an external policy better suited to Romania's new economic needs. Political and economic developments have led to the elaboration of a policy of selective economic cooperation both in the socialist (CMEA) and world capitalist economies.[8] So far the RCP's policy shifts—initially away from entanglement in CMEA integration and the more recent moves toward selective economic cooperation with Romania's East European and Soviet allies—have been inspired by domestically determined priorities. During the 1980s Romania's deepening economic crisis and fears of social unrest could propel the RCP even closer into the Soviet orbit, particularly if Western trade and credits dry up.

The China Factor

The prolonged Sino-Soviet dispute in the 1970s enhanced still further the political, ideological, and even military value of Eastern Europe to the Soviet Union. Yet the seriousness of the dispute diminished the ability of the East European states to use it as a lever in their relations with Moscow.[9] Thus all the East European states, including Romania, which is thought to have attempted to gain most from its mediation attempts, have for one reason or another sided firmly with the Soviet Union against the Chinese in the past. Indeed, on occasion the Chinese Communist party has proved more of an irritant than an ally to the East Europeans. For example, Romania, which has been more successful than the other East European states in balancing relations with both China and the Soviet Union, has resented Chinese leaders' use of their trips to Bucharest to take pot shots at the Soviet

Union.[10] The East Germans occasionally have been embarrassed to find their problems over recognition used by China as ammunition to fire at Moscow. Chinese criticism of halfhearted Soviet support of East Germany in the national question has similarly provided opportunities for the East Germans to voice muted criticism of the Soviet Union by reproducing without comment the Chinese attacks.[11]

Although China has provided no practical or ideological alternative to alliance with the Soviet Union, the 1980s are likely to see continued debate within the Warsaw alliance over the issue of the correct relationship to China despite the beginnings of a thaw in Sino-Soviet relations in 1982. Since 1969 and much publicized clashes on the Ussuri River the Soviet Union has evidently put considerable pressure on its allies, not only to join in an attempt to excommunicate China from the world communist movement but also to extend the commitments of the Warsaw alliance to the defense of the borders of socialism outside Europe in particular, to defense of the Sino-Soviet border. It remains to be seen whether the improvement in Sino-Soviet relations in the 1980s will remove this pressure entirely. Although all the East European states have bilateral treaties with the Soviet Union committing them to mutual defense without specific territorial restriction, all, including the GDR as the most actively loyal to the Soviet foreign policy line, have declined to support the Soviet position. To date, this refusal has had only symbolic importance, but it should not be underrated.

DIVERGENCE WITHIN CMEA AND WTO

Economic issues are likely to loom large in the 1980s. Perhaps more than in the 1970s, foreign economic policy and, above all, the intricacies of CMEA energy policy will have a direct impact on the political stability of the East European states and hence on the security concerns of the Soviet regime. Although the Soviet Union will hope to rely on its oil exports to Eastern Europe as a potential lever, the serious political repercussions of any drastic Soviet interference with the flow of oil to its allies limits Soviet ability to use this weapon in a blunt but effective manner.[12]

The pressing need for economic cooperation in many areas gives the East European regimes a greater opportunity and incentive to make their voices heard in the formulation of joint CMEA strategy. Their inclination to press autonomous policy concerns and make use of any additional room for maneuver is also likely to be reinforced by the undiminished seriousness of the threat posed by the prospect of economic discontent throughout the region. For many sound economic and technical reasons, states with more highly developed economies, such as the GDR, Czechoslovakia, and Poland, are likely to be increasingly attracted by the international socialist division of labor within the CMEA.

Already it is clear that despite the expansion of the CMEA to include Cuba, Mongolia, and most recently Vietnam, a two-tier integration policy has developed. The more advanced yet resource-dependent economies of the European CMEA states benefit considerably from access to Soviet raw materials. They also cooperate with each other in energy production and in extractive and manufacturing industries and provide markets for each other's goods. In particular, East Germany, Czechoslovakia, and Poland seemed in the second half of the 1970s to be developing into a small but intensive trading bloc within the European CMEA. At the same time, however, each of these states may have legitimate reservations on economic issues in its dealings with the Soviet Union. These are likely to be articulated and perhaps listened to.

But aside from their direct implications for bloc policy, economic issues also play an indirect but major role in other spheres of foreign policy. One recent example has been the East European reaction to Soviet pressure for defense commitments on the part of its allies in the Warsaw Pact. Over the past decade, but most notably since the November 1978 Political Consultative Committee meeting in Moscow, the Soviet Union has been pressuring its allies on a number of issues. Debates focused on the familiar issues of burden-sharing, the integration of military establishments within the Warsaw Pact, and the modernization of national armed forces and have intensified recently as the Soviet Union has been pressing its allies to respond directly to recent NATO decisions concerning increased national defense budgets and the deployment of new weaponry.

The financial commitment of the individual East European states varies considerably.[13] At the meeting of the Political Consultative Committee in November 1978, the Soviet Union called for a 5 percent increase in military expenditure by the smaller Warsaw Pact states. Yet whatever the internal logic of the Soviet argument, the deteriorating economic situation throughout Eastern Europe makes it both politically and economically difficult for the East Europeans to undertake such increased commitments, even were they inclined to do so. Undoubtedly in such circumstances military coordination and integration could make greater economic sense.[14] But with the exception of the GDR, whose entire armed forces are subject to Warsaw Pact (Soviet) command, there has been little enthusiasm for such a move. Romania effectively walked out of the November 1978 PCC meeting. On his return home, Ceausescu rejected both further multilateral integration within a Soviet-dominated command structure and the need for increased budget allocations for defense. In the latter case, he drew public attention prophetically to the question of much concern in Warsaw Pact capitals in private that in Eastern Europe popular contentment, or at least the absence of unrest, is a primary strategic resource.

It is clear from the current drift of Soviet policy and East-West relations in general that the 1980s are likely to see increasing focus on these organizational aspects of the Warsaw alliance. Yet it is equally clear that if it is to be successful Soviet pressure for greater coordination, integration, and commitment on the part of its allies will entail greater need for effective consultation, reasoned argument, and flexibility.

EAST-WEST RELATIONS

After the Helsinki agreements and the wave of dissent throughout Eastern Europe which followed, concern for regime security resulted in considerable policy coordination both domestically and with respect to the outside world. Even Romania, the most resolute in defending national autonomy and rejecting Soviet overtures for enhanced ideological and political coordination, actively participated in formulating joint strategies—including the arrest and possible deportation of dissidents—aimed at ideological cooperation to stamp out the growing tensions. In this respect, the Helsinki accords have probably proved disappointing to Western governments. East European participation in East-West relations has been institutionalized; it is not clear that it has been significantly expanded.

Although Romania has made much of the nonbloc nature of the Helsinki process, in fact on all major issues except perhaps the importance of East-West trade the East Europeans have not taken bold, independent initiatives. The exception, perhaps, is Romania's acceptance of an East-West compromise at the Madrid CSCE review conference after the Soviets had rejected it. The Russians later changed their minds and accepted a deal. At the MBFR talks in Vienna individual East European delegates have on occasion expressed concern over issues in dispute in the negotiations. Such contacts have remained informal, however, and proposals raised by East Europeans at the talks have been formally set within an agreed Warsaw Pact framework.

On the other hand, several East European states have voiced alarm over the recent deterioration in East-West relations. Polish, Hungarian, and East German nervousness over the health of East-West detente in the post-Afghanistan era was obvious. In the case of Poland and Hungary the causes are clear. Both states had allowed their economies to become increasingly outward-oriented and intertwined with those of the capitalist West. Both would suffer serious damage were East-West relations to sour dramatically. Hence they had a vested interest in arguing for moderation in Moscow—albeit after the main event. And following the coup in Poland, the Hungarians spoke publicly of the serious damage their economy would suffer if Western banks and governments allowed the Polish crisis to color their trade and lending policies to all CMEA states. The Poles may be loath to admit it, but they would prefer to see East-West trade continue.

The possible repercussions on Eastern Europe of President Ronald Reagan's policy of economic sanctions on the Soviet Union also caused concern. The Hungarians in particular, whose per capita debt is higher than that of Poland, worried that a credit embargo or a serious downturn in their trade with the West could seriously undermine their international trading position and their domestic economy. Talk of "economic warfare" against the Soviet Union causes acute concern in Eastern Europe.

For the GDR, the case is more complex. It is unlikely that even a right of center West German government will seriously disrupt intra-German trade relations. The GDR was among the first to support publicly the Soviet action in Afghanistan and welcome the Karmal regime. Throughout the Polish crisis it kept up a particularly bitter propaganda barrage against Solidarity and its demands for reform. During 1980 and 1981 the East German regime was obviously determined to halt any spread of the Polish virus to its own territory. But the Honecker regime may have even more cause for concern. The Soviet Union has a clear interest in maintaining open channels to at least one key Western power. West Germany is an obvious target, and the GDR is uniquely placed to further Soviet foreign policy goals. It remains to be seen how the GDR would respond to overwhelming Soviet pressure for concessions at the intra-German level, designed to woo West Germany to a midstream position in central Europe. Again, the degree of conflict over this issue in GDR-Soviet relations depends much on the Soviet Union. This is a sensitive issue for the GDR and one on which it has been prepared to stand and fight, even if the political battles have eventually been lost.

Each of these three states, therefore, has a different political stake in the future of East-West relations. All have a strong incentive to prevent any further disturbance of the political climate in Europe. The calculation of the benefits versus the costs of future Soviet foreign policy actions will be different for Warsaw, Budapest, and East Berlin than for Moscow.

RELATIONS WITH THE DEVELOPING WORLD

Another problem for all the East European states has been the recent Soviet practice of using the CMEA as a tool in its global foreign policy. Mongolia, Cuba, and most recently Vietnam are now full members. Even if a two-tier system is put into operation, leaving the non-European members out of the process of economic integration, these much poorer and less developed states will undoubtedly lay some claim to a share in the economic resources of their richer fraternal allies. Czechoslovakia has already registered a clear objection to underwriting the economic reconstruction of the new Vietnam.[15] Romania refused to participate in the venture. Since the 1950s several of the East European states have contributed economic resources and manpower to Third World countries. Thus the policy is not new, but the scale and pattern have changed. So far there is no indication that the CMEA as a whole will concede to what appears to be strong Soviet pressure to induce its East European allies to share the financial burden of Soviet foreign policy commitments.

A similar pattern has emerged in respect to military aid. Although decisions to dispatch military equipment and personnel from the East European states to such countries as South Yemen, Ethiopia, and Angola may be discussed in general terms in multilateral Warsaw Pact meetings, the impression so far is that participation in such activity is on a bilateral rather than a multilateral basis. Since East European involvement in the Third World was stepped up in the 1970s, the GDR and to a lesser extent Bulgaria and Czechoslovakia have been more willing to commit their nationals to military activity there than either Poland or Hungary. Romania has often been actively involved politically, but not necessarily on the same side or the same terms as the others, for example, in Angola.

As the most actively involved, the East Germans have been dubbed "Europe's Cubans." Their technical expertise has been successfully harnessed to Soviet logistics and Cuban troops in support of primarily Soviet foreign policy objectives. On the other hand, the GDR has a long history of bilateral political and economic contacts with a number of African and Middle Eastern states. Partly because normal state-to-state contacts were hard to establish, the GDR has since the early 1960s concentrated its attention to cultivating ties with national liberation movements. These early contacts included such later successes as Frelimo in Mozambique and the Popular Liberation Movement in Angola. Since the early 1970s the GDR has assiduously cultivated close contacts with the Palestine Liberation Organization (PLO).[16] This policy both furthers the interest of the socialist community at large and provides East Germany with a foreign policy platform not readily available elsewhere, access to much needed raw materials, and a useful trading relationship to dispose of goods not easily marketable either in the CMEA or the West.

The policy also entails some risk. When Soviet relations with a particular state or region turn sour, East German ties tend to be affected. For example, condemnation of the Soviet invasion of Afghanistan by Third World and nonaligned states reflected badly on East Germany, which had publicly supported the Soviet move, rather than on East Germany's neighbors in Eastern Europe that did not.[17]

Commercial and formal ideological considerations aside, the GDR has always been a more acceptable ambassador of socialism to the developing world than the less tactful Soviet Union. Its aid programs are well organized, offering specific expertise from highly trained professionals in key areas such as medicine, engineering, and communications. In some cases such aid programs have suffered as a result of sudden changes in or sudden reversals of Soviet foreign policy. In Somalia, for example, the GDR still maintains its aid projects despite Somalia's abrogation of its treaty with the Soviet Union and the expulsion of all Soviet personnel from the country.

It remains to be seen whether possible future Soviet blunders in foreign parts which undermine this painstaking and long-term GDR strategy will be accepted unblinkingly in East Berlin. Involvement in shifting Third World politics has already led East Germany into some strange alliances. Its involvement with Libya, for example, reportedly led to active support of the Libyan incursion into Chad and, by offending the Organization of African Unity, put a slight dent in the shiny internationalist image the GDR had earned for itself. Rather, as in the case of Cuba, where Castro had the rug pulled from under his feet in the nonaligned movement by the Soviet invasion of Afghanistan, this close tie to Soviet foreign policy in Africa and Asia may at some point prove dysfunctional.

CONCLUSIONS

A glance back over the 1960s and 1970s and forward to the end of the 1980s would suggest that there are a number of contentious issues in Soviet–East European relations. To judge by past experience, all the East European states are capable of defining their national priorities within the context of the multilateral alliance. What has often been lacking is the inclination or ability to pursue them to a successful conclusion. The reasons are basically twofold. First, with the exception of the very early days of the Sino-Soviet dispute, for most of the East European states—Romania being the most obvious exception—the Warsaw alliance still represents the sole platform for foreign policy initiative. As a result, the pressure to coordinate policy under the Soviet umbrella is often intense.

Second, short of threatening to collapse, the individual East European regimes often lack direct and positive leverage over much of the foreign policy of their major ally. Unless their direct participation or acquiescence is required in the practical conduct of Soviet foreign policy (for example, GDR participation in a negotiated settlement with West Germany and Romanian participation in CMEA or Warsaw Pact initiatives) the Soviet Union can normally proceed quite happily despite them. And when the Soviet Union considers it has vital foreign policy goals at stake and turns on the pressure, more often than not the East Europeans can at best drag their feet, rather than change the foreign policy course. The Strategic Arms Limitation Talks (SALT), Sino-Soviet relations, superpower relations in general, and the Soviet invasion of Afghanistan are all examples of the ability of the USSR to conduct a global foreign policy without reference to its allies, even when the repercussions of its actions have a direct impact on East European security concerns.

Yet acceptance that the Soviet Union remains the dominant power within the Warsaw Pact and the CMEA need not exclude consideration of the view from Eastern Europe. The more the Soviet Union tries to encourage greater coordination of policy, particularly economic policy, the more it will have to listen to East European complaints and ideas. Because the 1980s seem to be an uncertain decade for almost all the East European economies, these countries can be expected to lobby hard in Moscow in defense of their own particular interests. In this area Soviet decisions affecting its close allies will be forced to take greater account of those allies' anxieties and the need to maintain domestic political and economic stability.

The Soviet Union remains the single most important determining factor in the formulation and conduct of East European policy. What has changed is the East European regimes' expectations of their Soviet ally. In each case the external (Soviet) environment remains a recognized input in the foreign policy process. Yet, just as clearly, its impact has varied considerably. For example, whereas the East German regime in particular has in the past consciously emphasized legitimate Soviet involvement in, indeed responsibility for, East German domestic stability, it has done so in support of national goals. Conflict has arisen in East German–Soviet relations nonetheless. By contrast, Romania has skillfully manipulated its relations with the Soviet Union to produce a strikingly independent foreign policy. With perhaps the exception of post-1968 Czechoslovakia, the remaining East European states, although subject to absolute if dangerously undefinable Soviet limits, enjoy more room for maneuver than they have thus far attempted (Poland and Hungary are two candidates here).

One way for individual East European states to counter such problems and take advantage of any room for maneuver over the long term would be to diversify as far as possible their foreign policy commitments and memberships in international organizations not directly subject to Soviet control. Romania has made this practice a consistent plank in her foreign policy. Poland, Czechoslovakia, Romania, and Hungary are members of GATT; in 1981 Poland and Hungary applied for membership in the IMF; and several East European states have become heavily involved in trade and credit relations with the West. Although the Soviet invasion of Afghanistan may initially have caused nervousness in some East European countries because of their economic vulnerability to Western displeasure, over the longer term this interlacing and overlapping of interests may equally encourage the East European leaders concerned to argue the case for restraint and caution in Moscow over a wide range of issues. This was at least part of the reason why the Hungarians sought to diffuse tensions over the Polish crisis. A Western backlash against trade and credit facilities for the CMEA would have a disastrous impact on Hungary's balance of payments. If starved of Western finance, the Hungarian economy, although far healthier now than that of Poland, could easily be pushed into crisis. The Hungarians can be expected to put their point across clearly to their CMEA partners, not just to their Western creditors and customers.

The increasing complexity of the international environment, ensuring that no single area of foreign policy can be effectively isolated from the rest, offers some prospect that issues nominally the exclusive concern of the Soviet Union will be subject to increasing East European comment and criticism. Such changes in Soviet–East European relations as a result of long-term processes may be relatively slow and incremental rather than immediate and spectacular. Yet by downplaying the complexity of the policy environment of the 1980s within the Warsaw alliance, the more traditional focus on the primacy of Soviet power can easily miss the important nuances and understate the ability of the East European states to make their voices heard. Short of the sealing off of Eastern Europe from all contact with the world outside, the process of integration, coordination, and interdependence which the Soviet Union encourages is increasingly likely to subject Soviet foreign policy to influence and modification by its East European allies—and not simply at the margins.

Unless the Soviet Union chooses deliberately to ignore some vital security interest of its allies, the coming years will see considerable coordination in public foreign policy statements by the members of the Warsaw alliance. Yet this need not reflect increasing Soviet domination, whatever the Soviet leadership's basest intentions. A more realistic assessment would be that such coordination will be the result of three developments: the partial resolution of some of the long-standing and highly contentious issues that have clouded alliance politics in the past such as the German problem; greater consultation and mutual influence within bloc councils because of the complex nature of the issues at stake and the potential repercussions on political stability of the policies adopted; and possibly a greater division of labor within the alliance, allowing individual states to press particular interests and concerns but within a coordinated framework.

At the same time, however, there is no guarantee that behind the scenes the process of foreign policy formulation will be any smoother in the future than it has been in the past. There are many issues to be resolved, and it is unlikely that the Soviet Union and its allies will all see eye to eye on any one of them.

[7]

Security through Detente and Arms Control

Jane M. O. Sharp

East European governments face threats from three different sources: political challenges to the ruling Communist parties; Soviet military intervention such as occurred in East Germany in 1953, Hungary in 1956, and Cezchoslovakia in 1968; and external threats to the physical security of their states stemming from involvement in an East-West military conflict.[1] These categories cannot be strictly compartmentalized because the degree of confidence each East European government has in its own brand of communism affects its attitudes toward domestic, intrabloc, and international relations. Nevertheless, this chapter focuses primarily on external threats to state security and East European attitudes to East-West arms control.

East European elites learned three lessons from World War II: Germany posed the most likely danger to their national security; little or no support to meet this threat was likely from Western Europe; therefore, protection from and accommodation with the Soviet Union was essential for regime survival.[2] Dependent on the Red Army for their existence, these governments had little choice but to sign the bilateral treaties to meet the German threat demanded by the Soviets in the late 1940s and the multilateral Warsaw Treaty in 1955; the latter especially was portrayed as a response to West Germany's rearmament and adherence to the North Atlantic Treaty Organization. For the first decade after the establishment of the WTO, the three lessons of World War II remained valid.

The Soviets could still present West Germany as the spearhead of the Western threat because, until the late 1960s, the Federal Republic actively sought to change the post-1945 status quo by seeking the reunification of Germany and refusing to recognize East Germany as a separate state or the Oder-Neisse line as the German-Polish border. In addition, successive West German governments firmly resisted any attempts to establish nuclear-free zones or to disengage forces from central Europe and, until the 1966 "Peace Note," did not even repudiate the infamous Munich Agreement of 1938, which laid claim to the Sudetenland.

Even though Germany could still be invoked as the primary threat, Soviet "protection" proved a mixed blessing when military force was repeatedly used to shore up Communist party control, thereby underscoring the third lesson from the war: that no relief could be expected from the West. Despite the rhetoric of John Foster Dulles and the encouragement of East European dissidents by some Western radio stations, it remained painfully clear that no outside assistance would be offered to resist Soviet force.

Under these conditions, the security interests of East European regimes were generally well served by Soviet arms-control diplomacy in Europe, which focused on three main objectives: to codify the political and territorial status quo in Europe; to limit the military potential of NATO in general and of West Germany in particular; and to limit American forward-based nuclear weapons, especially to prevent nuclear control-sharing with West Germany.

Moreover, the Soviets packaged their European security and arms-control objectives as coordinated WTO policy. Parallel to the efforts to improve economic and military integration in the bloc since the early 1960s, the Soviets sought to enhance the machinery of WTO cooperation on the development and conduct of European security policy on both the academic and the intergovernmental levels.[3]

Through the 1970s more opportunities were provided for East European leaders to present their views to the Soviet leadership, including meetings with President Brezhnev in the Crimea each August. In 1976, the Political Consultative Committee set up a formal Council of Foreign Ministers with its own secretariat the better to coordinate policy. These high-level meetings are used both to launch new Soviet arms-control initiatives with WTO backing and to respond to Western proposals. The meetings usually endorse a litany of proposals embracing the principal longstanding Soviet security objectives outlined earlier. Among the standard themes since the mid-1950s are the following: recognition of the inviolability of post-1945 territorial borders in Europe; the need to improve East-West economic, scientific, and technological relations; conclusion of a nonaggression pact between NATO and the WTO; abolition of foreign military bases and return of foreign-based troops to their national territories; replacement of the two opposing military alliances with a pan-European security system and, pending such a system, the dismantling of the integrated military command organizations in NATO and WTO; establishment of nuclear-free zones in Europe and the mutual renunciation of nuclear weapons by both German states; outlawing of new weapons of mass destruction; and setting ceilings on the military expenditures of NATO and WTO countries.

Variations are added when necessary to address innovations in NATO military doctrine, to curb the latest round of NATO weapons modernization, or to counter unwelcome political developments. Thus NATO's various schemes for nuclear control-sharing with the allies in the late 1950s and early 1960s, Defense Secretary James Schlesinger's enthusiasm for limited nuclear options in the mid-1970s, and the December 1979 "double track decision" to deploy longer range weapons in Western Europe all generated new WTO proposals for nuclear-free zones and agreements pledging no-first-use of nuclear weapons. The news that Spain was planning to join NATO generated a WTO proposal to freeze the current membership of both alliances. Unrest in Eastern Europe usually brings renewed emphasis on the need for a nonaggression pact between NATO and the WTO, presumably to dissuade East European dissidents from reliance on possible support from the West in the event of a Soviet crackdown. Indeed, this message is explicit in the Prague Declaration of 5 January 1983.[4]

It would be a mistake, however, to dismiss WTO arms-control policy as purely reactive and propagandistic. Communiqués also reveal important shifts in priorities and intraalliance differences. Among the standard bromides issued from Iuryi Andropov's first Political Consultative Committee meeting in Prague in January 1983, for example, were an appeal to reopen the bilateral arms-control forums cut off by President Carter after the invasion of Afghanistan; a strong indication, consistent with earlier speeches by Foreign Minister Andrei Gromyko, that the Soviets were now ready to accept more cooperative monitoring of arms-control treaties; and a suggestion that one way to shift MBFR into a higher gear would be mutual Soviet and American troop withdrawals outside the framework of a formal agreement. The most interesting omission was any commendation of the Soviets' latest public proposals made in connection with the Geneva talks on intermediate-range nuclear forces, suggesting that perhaps not all the East European leaders agreed with Andropov's handling of the INF issue.

Just as in NATO, West European interests often diverge from those of the United States, so in the WTO East European security interests are not always identical with those of the Soviet Union. But although East European influence on Soviet policy is obviously limited, it is not negligible. To a degree perhaps not fully anticipated by the Soviets nor fully appreciated by the West, East European leaders have used the increased contact with Moscow not only to present but actively to press their own national interests. This chapter seeks to assess how well East European security objectives have been met at a number of East-West negotiating forums: the multilateral Conference on Security and Cooperation in Europe, the interalliance Mutual and Balanced Force Reductions talks, and various efforts to control nuclear weapons in Europe, including the talks on intermediate nuclear forces in Geneva.

THE CONFERENCE FOR SECURITY AND COOPERATION IN EUROPE

The main vehicle by which the Soviet Union has sought to codify the post-1945 political and territorial status quo in Europe is the Conference for Security and Cooperation in Europe. First formally proposed at the Berlin Foreign Ministers' Meeting on 10 February 1954 by Soviet Foreign Minister Molotov as a pan-European Security Conference (ESC) designed to prevent West Germany from joining the European Defense Community, the ESC concept was reiterated through the late 1950s and the 1960s and finally convened in Helsinki as the CSCE in November 1972.[5] Initially, all the Warsaw Pact elites supported the ESC but with varying degrees of warmth, East Germany being the most apprehensive and Poland the most enthusiastic.

As the only Warsaw Treaty country whose survival as a separate state depends on the division of Germany and the codification of post-1945 borders, East Germany supported the broadest possible acceptance of the postwar political and territorial status quo in Europe. The East German leaders did not want to venture very far into an East-West rapprochement, however, because any warming up of Bonn-Moscow relations was likely to be at the expense of Soviet support for the consolidation of the GDR.[6]

By contrast, Poland has actively pursued East-West detente since the late 1950s, when the Polish Foreign Ministry was advocating "constructive coexistence" with the West, a concept akin to the "active coexistence" sought by Yugoslavia and more dynamic than the "peaceful coexistence" decreed by the Soviet Union.[7] Constructive coexistence was initially formulated by Deputy Foreign Minister Jozef Winiewicz and Professor Manfred Lachs, who believed that Poland could, and should, act as a bridge between the two halves of Europe. They advocated a divided Germany but also believed Poland's interests would be best served by a Bonn-Warsaw detente. Polish support for the ESC was thus more than merely toeing the Soviet foreign policy line and reflected genuine interest in playing a central role in any solution to the German problem and gaining the widest possible acceptance in the West of the Oder-Neisse line as the German-Polish border.

After Khrushchev's fall from power in 1964, Poland took the initiative in resurrecting the proposal for an ESC, specifically for "a conference of all-European states with the participation, of course, of both the United States and the Soviet Union."[8] The inclusion of the United States went beyond the Soviet position at the time. Until late 1966, Foreign Minister Gromyko was unwilling to include the Americans, urging, for example, in April 1966 "settlement of European security problems by the Europeans themselves" and complaining that the U.S. military presence in Western Europe hindered efforts to reduce East-West tension.[9]

BACKGROUND OF THE CSCE

The Soviets intensified the campaign to convene a European security conference at the time NATO suffered the combined strain of French defection from the integrated military command and West Germany's growing resentment at superpower complicity in the negotiations toward a Non Proliferation Treaty. In July 1966, the WTO Political Consultative Committee meeting in Bucharest endorsed Soviet objectives for such a conference, which were to ratify post-1945 borders and the existence of two separate German states; to dissolve at least the military organizations, if not abrogate the treaties of NATO and the Warsaw Pact; to replace the European Economic Community and the Council for Mutual Economic Aid with all-European trade organizations; and to increase scientific and technical cooperation between East and West. In April 1967, at a meeting of European Communist parties in Karlovy Vary, Czechoslovakia, the rhetoric about dissolving NATO was more aggressive. Leonid Brezhnev suggested that NATO's twentieth anniversary in 1969 provided a special opportunity in the struggle against the Western bloc because the NATO treaty called for a review at that time: "In our opinion it is very right that Communists and all progressive forces are endeavoring to make use of this circumstance in order to develop on an ever wider scale the struggle against preserving this aggressive bloc."[10]

The invective against NATO continued through 1967 but faded as the Soviet Union faced disintegrative forces in its own sphere. After invading Czechoslovakia in the summer of 1968, the Soviet Union suffered severe political setbacks not only in East-West relations but also within the bloc. Albania, which had not participated de facto in WTO affairs since the Sino-Soviet split, now formally withdrew in protest.[11] Yugoslavia and Romania also denounced the invasion, and President Ceausescu, who since the early 1960s had refused to participate in joint Warsaw Pact exercises or to allow Soviet troops on Romanian territory, intensified his efforts to establish a national defense doctrine for the Romanian armed forces.

The result, in the late 1960s at least, was a more conciliatory Soviet policy both within the bloc and toward the West. The Warsaw Pact PCC meeting in Budapest in March 1969 invited the Western nations to participate in an ESC and emphasized the need to preserve Europe "as it emerged from the second world war" rather than the dissolution of NATO and the EEC. Soviet goals, which had earlier been portrayed as preconditions to the conference, now became items for discussion on the agenda, and the Soviets seemed less inclined to press for a reduction of American forces in Europe and more ready to embrace the military status quo.

Before the CSCE was convened, however, most of what the Soviets had sought at the conference had already been achieved through the *Ostpolitik* of Chancellor Willy Brandt, the essential feature of which was recognition of the political and territorial realities in Europe, however painful these were in perpetuating the division of Germany. A series of concessions by West Germany made possible a set of treaties which resolved a number of formerly contentious issues. The Federal Republic abandoned the insistence on progress toward German reunification as a precondition for East-West detente; accepted the Oder-Neisse line which explicitly recognized the postwar transfer of territory from Germany to Poland; acknowledged the invalidity of the 1938 Munich Agreement; and embraced Brandt's concept of two states within one nation which made possible the Basic Treaty accepting both halves of Germany. These concessions were balanced by a more secure Western position on Berlin in the Four-Power Agreement, conclusion of the final protocol of which in June 1972 was one of the conditions for Western participation in the CSCE. Another condition was WTO willingness to participate in interalliance talks on mutual and balanced force reductions in central Europe.

East European Goals at the CSCE

If the initial Soviet objectives for a pan-European security conference had been met via the *Ostpolitik,* what more did the other WTO countries hope to achieve at the CSCE? At least four goals were discernible in the early 1970s. One was obviously to gain multilateral acceptance of the principles embodied in the series of bilateral treaties between the Federal Republic and the Eastern bloc, especially that of the inviolability of borders. Second, East European countries, together with many of the West European and nonaligned states, shared the hope that the CSCE would further the interests of small states in general. Unlike the bloc-to-bloc format at the MBFR talks in Vienna, which was dominated by superpower interests and distinguished between central and peripheral participants, all thirty-five states participated at CSCE on equal terms, at least theoretically. Third, all the WTO countries (with the possible exception of the GDR, which profits most from intrabloc trade) hoped the conference would bring healthier conditions for East-West commerce and make available substantial Western scientific and technical expertise, thereby easing their dependence on the CMEA.[12] Finally, to the extent that the CSCE might further consolidate East-West detente, the East European leaders also hoped it would reduce Soviet pressure on them to accept a greater share of the financial burden of the WTO military effort.[13]

Three baskets of issues made up the CSCE agenda and the Helsinki Final Act signed by all thirty-five participating states in July 1975. Basket I deals with questions relating to security in Europe in two parts. The first is a set of ten principles to guide relations among states; the seventh of these principles calls on the signatory states to respect human rights and fundamental freedoms, including the freedom of speech, thought, religion, and belief. The second part of Basket I relates to specifically military security issues—the so-called confidence-building measures (CBMs)—which require signatories to give advance notice and invite observers to military maneuvers involving more than twenty-five thousand men. Basket II deals with economic relations between participating states and calls for expanded commerce and increased cooperation in science and technology, and Basket III concerns humanitarian cooperation and the exchange of information.[14] Thus, although the CSCE provided a forum for the discussion of military security and economic relations, both high priorities for the East European states, the conference, and particularly the review process, gave the Western and nonaligned states an opportunity to call the Soviet bloc states to account for their domestic practices in the areas of human rights and individual freedoms. Ironically then, though the CSCE was a WTO initiative in which the NATO governments originally agreed to participate with reluctance, the Soviet and East European governments were most on the defensive in this forum.[15]

HUMAN RIGHTS AS AN ISSUE AT CSCE

Not only did the expected economic benefits not materialize because of a combination of Western protectionism and political sanctions imposed in the wake of Afghanistan and Poland, but the Helsinki Final Act brought unforeseen threats to regime security throughout the Eastern bloc, as small but courageous groups of free spirits formed Helsinki watch committees to monitor their governments' compliance with the CSCE provisions. Whereas protests in the Eastern bloc through the early 1970s were usually conducted by lone dissidents crying in the wilderness, post-CSCE protests were organized on firm legal grounds, focusing on specific violations of human rights, which, though always theoretically guaranteed by national constitutions, were now backed up by an international legal document.

Soviet authorities faced Helsinki monitoring groups in Leningrad, Moscow, Armenia, Georgia, Lithuania, and the Ukraine, but the most active groups were in Poland and Czechoslovakia. The earliest CSCE-related protests occurred in Poland in December 1975, when intellectuals and members of the Catholic hierarchy invoked the Final Act to block proposed amendments to the Constitution which would have proclaimed Poland's ties to the Soviet Union "unbreakable" and made citizens' rights dependent on fulfillment of their duties to the state. In September 1976, following government harassment of workers who in June had protested rising food prices, a group of intellectuals formed the Committee for the Defense of the Workers, which became influential in the Solidarity movement in 1980. In early 1977, the Movement for the Defense of Human Rights was formed with the objective of bringing Polish law into conformity with international human rights legislation.

Although there were no organized Helsinki monitoring groups in East Germany, the impact of the CSCE was dramatically demonstrated there by the one hundred thousand GDR citizens who applied to emigrate in 1976, citing the Helsinki Final Act and the United

Nations Declaration on Human Rights as the basis for their appeals. Not surprisingly, a communiqué issued by the WTO Political Consultative Committee in late 1976 reflected concern that the CSCE process might be getting out of hand, noting:

> The 1975 Helsinki Accords had made a positive contribution to East-West detente in Europe, but the West was exploiting human rights issues in Basket III at the expense of security and cooperation in Baskets I and II; East-West cooperation in humanitarian and cultural fields must not be confused with ideological capitulation by the socialist states to capitalist values; if the East is to fulfill its CSCE obligations to promote further East-West cooperation it must consolidate its unity both in foreign policy and ideological cooperation.[16]

Undeterred, a group of intellectuals in Czechoslovakia in January 1977 formed Charter 77 expressly to "enter into a dialogue with political and state authorities on the observance of the Final Act and the human rights conventions which have been incorporated into Czechoslovakia's legal system."[17]

MILITARY SECURITY ISSUES AT THE CSCE

Military confidence-building measures in the CSCE context stem from the Western preference for controlling the use rather than the level of forces and focused primarily on prior notification of military movements and maneuvers designed to reduce the risk of surprise attack in Europe. At first the Soviets were reluctant even to discuss notification requirements but eventually came to accept the validity of CBMs and even to fashion them to serve their own needs.

For the neutral and nonaligned states (NNAs) who played no role in MBFR, and for the flank states of NATO and the WTO who were not full participants in the Vienna talks, the CSCE was an important forum in which to raise their security concerns. Romania was the most active Pact state in the formulation of CBMs and worked with an informal coalition, which included the British and the NNAs, to devise more stringent reporting requirements to cover smaller military movements, further from other states' borders than the Soviets were originally willing to consider. Romania was also instrumental in inserting language into the ten Principles of the Questions Relating to Security in Europe which would remove any justification for a repeat

of the 1956 and 1968 Warsaw Pact invasions of Hungary and Czechoslovakia, for example:

> Each nation has the right to belong to, or not belong to international
> organizations . . . including the right to be or not to be parties to an
> alliance. . . . No consideration may be invoked to serve to warrant resort
> to the threat or use of force. . . . Participating states will refrain from
> making each other the object of military occupation. . . . Participating
> states will refrain from intervention, direct or indirect, individual or col-
> lective in the internal or external affairs falling within the domestic juris-
> diction of another participating state regardless of their mutual rela-
> tions.[18]

THE CSCE REVIEW PROCESS

Given its poor record of compliance with the human rights provisions of the Helsinki Final Act, the Soviet Union prepared for the
Belgrade CSCE review conference in late 1977 with a damage-limiting
approach. Armed with criticism of Western compliance of the Basket
II provisions on economic relations and with proposals for a new
conference on military detente and disarmament in Europe, the Soviets hoped to transfer the pan-European security dialogue to a new
forum isolated from the human rights portion of the CSCE agenda.
The East Europeans approached Belgrade hoping that the CSCE format could still yield political and economic benefits and consolidate
detente. They, too, however, supported the call for a new conference;
indeed, the Romanians would later claim to have initiated the idea.[19]

During the debate on military security issues, the Western states
proposed extending the geographical scope of the CSCE/CBMs to put
more Soviet territory under surveillance than the 250km strip in the
1975 provisions. For their part, the Soviets proposed that the CBMs
should cover air and naval maneuvers as well as ground movements,
in an obvious effort to hinder the reinforcement of NATO with troops
from North America, and also tried to impose a ceiling of fifty to sixty
thousand men for maneuvers to curb the NATO practice of holding
large multilateral exercises in Europe each autumn. Predictably, the
Romanians went one better, proposing the abolition of maneuvers
near the borders of another state. All these views were debated in
Belgrade, but nothing was achieved there except to publicize the poor
record of the WTO states on human rights. Poland and Hungary
came out of the barrage of criticism relatively unscathed, but in gener-

al the East Europeans found themselves grouped with the Russians when repressive treatment of the Helsinki watch groups came under public scrutiny. Not only the Socialist International but West European Communist parties also joined in the chorus of condemnation, thereby further undermining Moscow's role as leader of the international communist movement.

Between the Belgrade and Madrid review conferences superpower relations deteriorated for a combination of reasons, including the NATO decision to introduce new longer range nuclear weapons into Western Europe and the Soviet invasion of Afghanistan. Many WTO leaders were concerned about the undermining of East-West detente in this period. Romanian spokesmen overtly, Poles and Hungarians more discreetly, voiced their opposition to the invasion of Afghanistan and to the buildup of nuclear weapons in Europe by both sides.[20] Leaders from these three East European countries also worked hard within the bloc to improve the East-West atmosphere. At a time when the rhetoric between the United States and the Soviet Union was particularly tense, the relatively conciliatory tone of the communiqué issued by the Pact Political Consultative Committee meeting in Warsaw in mid-May 1980 suggests substantial input by the East Europeans.[21]

Nevertheless, when the Madrid CSCE review conference opened in September 1980, the Soviets faced another barrage of criticism, this time over the invasion and occupation of Afghanistan. The Soviets again sought to divert attention by focusing on the proposal for a new European disarmament conference, and Warsaw was now offered as the site for such a gathering. Meanwhile, President Giscard d'Estaing of France had also proposed a new pan-European disarmament conference. Tailored to French defense plans, which called for more nuclear weapons at the expense of conventional forces, the Conférence Désarmement Européen (CDE) explicitly excluded nuclear weapons from consideration. The French emphasis was on a first-stage agreement imposing mandatory, verifiable, and militarily significant CBMs, as distinct from the modest, voluntary CBMs in the CSCE, and aimed to curb the geographical advantage enjoyed by the Soviet Union at CSCE and MBFR by extending the zone of CBM surveillance to the Ural Mountains. Thus whereas the CBMs proposed by the WTO would apply only to a narrow 250km strip inside the Soviet border, the French CBMs would include all the Soviet western military districts, a provision with obvious attractions for East Europeans.

At the twenty-sixth CPSU congress in February 1981 Brezhnev said he would accept a CBM zone stretching as far east as the Urals as long as there was a corresponding expansion of the western zone to include, for example, air and naval activities in the Atlantic and possibly even cover activities off the eastern seaboard of North America. At Madrid in 1981, Western delegates agreed to include military activities in contiguous sea and air space which were "integral to operations on the continent," but this concession did not, at least initially, appear to satisfy the Soviets, who suggested that the maritime portion of the CBM zone should be as wide as the continental portion. In an interview with *Der Spiegel* in November, Brezhnev modified the Soviet position to suggest that the zone should include "island territories adjacent to Europe, respective sea and ocean areas and the air space over them."[22] This formulation, however, would include islands such as the Portuguese Azores, designated as fueling stations for the new United States rapid deployment force, and so was unacceptable to the Reagan administration.

The imposition of martial law in Poland in December 1981, however, put a damper on all CSCE activities through most of 1982, and the Reagan administration in particular, but with the concurrence of the Western states, used the Madrid forum to castigate the Soviets for their menacing military maneuvers on the Polish border and the Jaruzelski regime for harassment and repression of the Solidarity trade union movement. In November, however, President Brezhnev died and was replaced as general secretary of the CPSU by Iuryi Andropov; Lech Walesa was released from custody along with several hundred other Solidarity detainees; and the Polish government was promising to ease martial law. Through late 1982 and 1983, the relatively stable situation in Poland combined with new leadership in Moscow and the highly charged Soviet-American atmosphere surrounding the mutual recrimination about who was to blame for the slow progress in arms control, particularly at the Geneva INF talks, made the smaller states more anxious than ever for a new conference to deal seriously with European security issues. This sense of urgency made the Madrid conference more businesslike and less confrontational because both superpowers were pressured by their allies and by the NNAs to resolve their differences on the format for the proposed new conference. The Soviets now seemed more inclined to accept the Western formula for CBMs in order to escape the human rights pressures of CSCE. The delegates negotiated a final document in the summer of 1983, which tightened up the code of conduct on human rights and scheduled six new meetings: a conference on security and confidence-building measures and disarmament in Stockholm in January 1984; to settle international disputes in Athens in

[172]

March 1984; on economic cooperation in Venice in October 1984; on human rights in Ottawa in May 1985; on human contacts in Berne in April 1986; and another full-scale CSCE review conference in Vienna in November 1986.

MBFR AND WARSAW PACT SECURITY INTERESTS

The Vienna negotiations on mutual and balanced force reductions stemmed from a NATO initiative but in some respects provided a more comfortable forum for East European states to pursue their security interests than the CSCE.[23]

In the mid-1960s the Soviet threat to Western Europe no longer loomed large, and there was a steady trickle of NATO forces away from central Europe to deal with the allies' extra-European commitments. Former Great Powers were tidying up various remnants of empire, and the United States was becoming increasingly involved militarily in Southeast Asia. Initially, what might otherwise have been troublesome shortfalls in NATO manpower were offset by the steady buildup of the Bundeswehr in this period. When even West Germany began to contemplate force reductions, however, NATO leaders proposed negotiating mutual and balanced force reductions with the Warsaw Pact, primarily as a damage-limiting exercise to stem the flow of unilateral withdrawals or at least to gain reciprocal Soviet reductions from Eastern Europe. Many West Europeans also welcomed the MBFR proposal as a pragmatic counterproposal to the repeated Warsaw Pact proposals for a pan-European security conference.

The first sign of Soviet interest in MBFR came at a meeting of the Warsaw Pact foreign ministers in Budapest in June 1970. A second signal emerged at the CPSU conference in Moscow in March 1971, when President Brezhnev tied force reductions in Europe to the long-standing Soviet campaign to abolish foreign military bases. Six weeks later, speaking in Tbilisi on the fiftieth anniversary of the Georgian Republic, the Soviet leader called explicitly for negotiations on force reductions, chastising the NATO countries for their lack of resolve "to taste proposals that interest you."[24] Whether intended or not, Brezhnev's speech effectively defeated an amendment before the United States Senate aimed at further reducing the number of American troops in Europe. This result may seem paradoxical, since Soviet writings had previously often stressed the pernicious effects of the American military presence on the Continent and especially of the threat posed by the Bonn-Washington axis. After the turbulence in Czechoslovakia in 1967 and 1968 and the Sino-Soviet clashes along the Ussuri River in 1969, however, the Soviets showed more interest in preserving the military status quo in Europe than in ridding the Continent of American troops.

Despite their declared interest in MBFR, the Soviets would not commit themselves to a firm date for negotiations until the Western powers agreed to participate in a European security conference and West Germany accepted East Germany as a separate state, nullified the 1938 Munich Agreement, and recognized the Oder-Neisse line as the German-Polish border. Later, the Soviets embraced the initiative as their own, claiming that the negotiations stemmed from repeated Soviet proposals for force reductions since 1946.

In October 1972, President Brezhnev outlined three principles that should govern the negotiations.[25] Reductions should apply to stationed and indigenous troops, land and air forces, and nuclear weapons; an MBFR agreement should not disturb the existing East-West military balance in Europe; and reductions should therefore be addressed either by equal percentage or equal numerical cuts. Soviet tactics since the opening of talks suggest that rather than seeking radical reductions the Soviets hoped to use MBFR primarily to impose limits on the West German Bundeswehr but also to maintain a *droit de regard* over NATO force planning, to prevent the emergence of an integrated West European defense community led by a stronger, more independent West Germany, and as explicitly declared, to preserve the equilibrium of military force which has not only kept the peace between East and West in Europe since 1945 but also maintained Soviet control over a sometimes restive Eastern Europe.

The Soviets saw at least four interlocking balances in need of maintenance. First, a rough parity was needed between NATO and the WTO to deter NATO from attempting to interfere with any police action the Soviets might need to undertake in Eastern Europe. Second, to ensure that West Germany would not be tempted to intervene in support of any future uprising in East Germany, a balance was necessary between Soviet forces in East Germany and the Bundeswehr in West Germany. Third, as Brezhnev's helping hand to the Nixon administration in dealing with the 1971 Mansfield amendment suggested, the Soviets wanted to retain American troops in Western Europe and a certain ratio of stationed to indigenous forces in West Germany as a constraint on the Bundeswehr. Retaining American troops on the Continent obviously helped to rationalize the presence of Soviet forces in Eastern Europe. The fourth essential component of the balance, from the Soviet perspective, was the equilibrium between stationed Soviet and indigenous East European forces to prevent any individual East European country from acquiring the capability to resist Warsaw Pact military action such as subdued Czechoslovakia in 1968.

East European members of the Warsaw Pact shared some of the Soviet Union's attitudes and goals at MBFR through the 1970s, in particular the effort to impose limits on NATO's nuclear forces and to curb the Bundeswehr.[26] The Northern Tier countries—East Germany, Poland, and Czechoslovakia—were also well served by the linkage politics and the delaying tactics employed by the Soviets in setting the date for formal MBFR talks. The East Germans wanted West German acceptance of their separate status, the Poles needed reassurance on international recognition of post-1945 borders, and the Husak government in Czechoslovakia wanted prior resolution of the issue of the Sudetenland Germans, which was finally put to rest when a 1973 agreement with West Germany nullified the 1938 Munich Agreement.

As citizens of small states, however, East Europeans were sometimes apprehensive about superpower condominium over European affairs and uncomfortable with the discriminatory and hierarchical aspects of the MBFR process. In addition, not all East European states were as enthusiastic about preserving the current equilibrium of military forces in Europe as the Soviets, particularly with respect to the intra-Pact balance.

THE DISCRIMINATORY ASPECTS OF MBFR

A recurrent problem in East-West arms control is European anxiety that the nuclear superpowers, preoccupied with limiting threats to each other, will neglect the security interests of the smaller states, including their allies. Thus in early 1972 West German analysts speculated that the proposed MBFR negotiations might impose reduction and inspection requirements that would create several classes of European states.[27] When NATO ministers issued the original MBFR declaration from Reykjavik in June 1968, they did not exclude any members of NATO or the WTO, but the invitation to conduct exploratory talks, issued in November 1972, separated participants from both alliances into categories of full and observer status. NATO assumed central Europe would constitute the MBFR reduction zone and that only states with troops stationed there would participate in the negotiations. Initial plans envisaged that NATO participants would be the United States, Canada, Britain, France, West Germany, Belgium, the Netherlands, and Luxembourg. For the Warsaw Pact, NATO assumed that in addition to the Soviet Union, East Germany, Poland, Czechoslovakia, and Hungary would participate and that these four East European states would make up the WTO reduction zone.

This plan implied that Iceland and the states on both the northern and southern flanks of NATO as well as Romania and Bulgaria on the southern tier of the WTO would be accorded observer status, a situation unpopular in both alliances. In NATO, only Iceland raised no objections. Of the rest, Turkey and Italy objected most strongly, but Norway, Denmark, Greece, and Portugal in varying degrees insisted on being included, and all sent representatives to Vienna when preliminary talks opened in late January 1973. France, by contrast, refused to participate—despite pressure from both the United States and the Soviet Union—on the grounds that superpower interests would dominate any bloc-to-bloc forum. The West Germans did not want East Germany listed in the official invitation because they were in the midst of delicate negotiations to normalize relations and had not yet formally accepted the German Democratic Republic as a separate state.[28]

The United States suggested that indirect participation could be arranged for NATO flank countries and for Romania and Bulgaria. The official WTO response did not come until mid-January 1973, but in December President Ceausescu of Romania was already echoing France's objections that the MBFR talks should not be in a bloc-to-bloc format dominated by the superpowers but in a pan-European framework and preferably as part of the CSCE just getting under way in Helsinki; European neutrals also favored this position. Romania pressed for a wider forum to include, as Ceausescu put it, "all nations which may have influenced Moscow's thinking," then later for the inclusion of Romania and Bulgaria in the NATO-WTO format. This proposal presented NATO with a dilemma because admitting the two southern WTO states could have reopened the issue of the NATO flank countries' participation.

In the end, there was little debate over Romanian and Bulgarian participation because the Soviets not only acquiesced in their exclusion from direct participation but insisted on excluding Hungary as well. Otherwise, as the Soviet delegate, Oleg Khlestov, argued, all Soviet troops stationed in Eastern Europe would be subject to MBFR limits whereas American troops at European bases outside the narrow MBFR zone would be unconstrained. Khlestov argued successfully that, at a minimum, Hungary should be accorded the same status as Italy; either both should be included or both excluded. NATO reluctantly agreed to exclude both but reserved the right to raise the issue of Hungarian participation at a later date. The Hungarian delegate, Endre Ustor expressed official satisfaction with the decision but admitted later that he would have preferred including both Italy and Hungary as direct participants. The same view was expressed by Romania and Yugoslavia, which both share a border with Hungary and obviously hoped MBFR would impose limits on all Soviet troops in Eastern Europe. A common concern of all the flank states in both alliances in the early 1970s was that an MBFR agreement could simply withdraw Soviet troops from central Europe to be redeployed near their borders.

EAST EUROPEAN ATTITUDES TOWARD THE MILITARY BALANCE

The Soviets claim that NATO and WTO weapons and manpower are essentially balanced, both globally and regionally in the narrower MBFR guidelines area, which includes East Germany, Poland, and Czechoslovakia for WTO and West Germany and the three Benelux countries for NATO. NATO, by contrast, asserts that WTO enjoys superiority in manpower in the MBFR zone. The proposals each side has made in Vienna reflect these different perceptions, with NATO proposing unequal reductions and the Soviets claiming that equal cuts will produce common alliance ceilings.

Manpower estimates are more complicated than assessments of military hardware and doubly hard when negotiations are anticipated. WTO troop strengths would be difficult to estimate under the best of circumstances because the Soviet Union rotates hundreds of thousands of conscripts in and out of Eastern Europe every six months and because many of the tasks performed by uniformed personnel in the WTO armies are taken care of by civilians in NATO. Thus before MBFR, intelligence analysts calculated WTO strength on order of battle lines in terms of military units. On this basis at the beginning of the 1970s the Central Intelligence Agency estimated that WTO and NATO manpower were essentially balanced with WTO perhaps enjoying a superiority of between 10,000 and 20,000 men.[29] Once MBFR talks were formally scheduled, however, and numerical balances took on diplomatic importance, all uniformed manpower was included whether assigned to combat duty or to clerical, construction, catering, or medical support functions. WTO ground force strength then jumped from near parity with NATO to a superiority of some 150,000 men.

Even more troublesome is the tendency, when a contractual agreement is in prospect, for estimates of the adversary's strength to be tailored to fit preconceptions of the balance or preferred negotiating options. An example of this phenomenon on the Western side is the recurrent lobbying of the International Institute for Strategic Studies by NATO officials when the East-West balance as portrayed in the annual *Military Balance* proves inconvenient.[30]

WTO estimates of NATO strength are presumably at least as subjective. In their public statements East European spokesmen toe the Soviet line about East-West parity without specifying any numerical comparisons. Judging from the parsimonious way in which the Soviets released data at MBFR, we can assume that information on force structures is released on a strictly "need to know" basis within the WTO so that even military leaders may be unaware of the strengths of the other national armies in Eastern Europe quite apart from the NATO-WTO balance. Those East European leaders who see as serious a threat from the East as from the West tend to view NATO as a stabilizing influence on the Continent, not only by containing West German military and political power but also in the sense that American troops in Western Europe provide a counterweight to Soviet troops in the East.

Poland, for example, saw resolution of the data discrepancy as more important than correcting any possible WTO inadequacies at MBFR and from the outset of the negotiations urged compromise between East and West. While not explicitly admitting a double system of manpower bookkeeping, Polish delegates indicated in the late 1970s that there was room for adjustment if and when the political climate warranted more cooperative behavior from the East. In June 1980, for example, the Poles "found" 13,200 men in amphibious units that had not previously been included in WTO data.

East German delegates in Vienna, by contrast, adopted the view that American military power and the Bonn-Washington axis remained a serious threat, and nothing in East German rhetoric suggested any value in East-West parity or in retaining the American military presence in Western Europe. One emigré interviewed in 1977 claimed that at least through the mid-1970s East German officers taught new recruits that the concept of a military balance in central Europe was "a deception of the imperialists for obscuring the real relationship of forces" and insisted that WTO was, and must remain, numerically superior in order to deter an attack from better equipped

NATO forces.[31] Given the data dispute in Vienna, it is difficult to judge whether the East Germans were substituting rhetoric for reality in asserting WTO superiority—a time-honored practice both in pre-revolutionary Russia and in the Soviet Union—or whether they actually believed superiority existed and must be maintained. Of all the WTO elites, the East Germans are the most paranoid about the military balance. They are the only East Europeans to express anxiety about Spain joining NATO because of the extra 350,000 troops thereby available for any NATO engagement against the WTO. East German military journals also warn of the deleterious effects of detente on the morale of the fighting man and emphasize that the Vienna talks have not reduced the menacing threat of the Bundeswehr.[32]

If attitudes about the ideal and the actual East-West military balance vary, one MBFR objective to which all WTO member countries subscribed was the need to impose a ceiling on the Bundeswehr to prevent West Germany from becoming topheavy in NATO. At MBFR the WTO initially sought to do this by imposing national subceilings on all participants with forces in the guidelines area. As the Soviets were well aware, the national subceiling issue was potentially divisive in NATO because it recalled Germany's defeat in World War II and emphasized existing limits imposed on the Bundeswehr by the Western powers in the mid-1950s. The European Defense Community Treaty of 1952, which the French refused to ratify, imposed a ceiling of five hundred thousand men on the air, land, and naval forces of West Germany as well as prohibiting the manufacture of chemical, biological, or nuclear weapons. These provisions were carried over in an unpublished protocol to the 1954 Paris agreements which set the conditions for West Germany's rearmament and membership in NATO.

As part of its June 1978 package of proposals in Vienna, WTO accepted NATO's goal of common alliance ceilings of seven hundred thousand ground troops and nine hundred thousand ground plus air forces and offered a compromise to its earlier insistence on national subceilings. Under this scheme participating countries could increase their forces by no more than half any unilateral reductions made by another country in the same alliance. This formula was consistent with the WTO goal of not permitting the Bundeswehr to make up any shortfall in NATO forces. It would also have ensured that the ratio of Soviet to East European forces would not change drastically, in the event of an MBFR agreement requiring substantial reductions of stationed Soviet forces from Eastern Europe, further indication that maintaining the intra-WTO military balance is an important Soviet

objective. Many East European elites, however, are as apprehensive
about unconstrained East German forces as they are about the Bundeswehr and enthusiastically endorsed national subceilings because
they would impose limits on both German armies as well as on the
Soviets. Most East European governments would also welcome contractual limits on their own armed forces. Thus modifying the national subceiling position was more than merely a Soviet concession
to NATO; it was an issue requiring delicate intra-WTO bargaining to
bring the East Europeans on board.

Eventually, the WTO embraced a simpler compromise which was
first floated informally by British and American delegates to MBFR.
This was the so-called 50 percent solution whereby no individual
country could contribute more than 50 percent of the manpower in its
MBFR guidelines area. As originally conceived in the West, this plan
was designed to meet the explicit concern of the WTO countries,
which were also implicit concerns of many West Europeans, namely,
to reaffirm the EDC limits on the Bundeswehr, and the explicit concern of NATO, which is shared by the majority of East European
governments and populations, namely, to limit the size of Soviet
forces in Eastern Europe. It did not, of course, meet the concern of
East European governments to impose limits on East German or their
own forces, but it was eminently practical because it would have
codified the status quo on both sides. The Bundeswehr contributes
approximately half the NATO manpower in the western MBFR zone,
as do Soviet forces in the Warsaw Pact Northern Tier, which com-
prises the eastern MBFR zone. The proposal clearly made sense to
Chancellor Schmidt, who informally endorsed it on two occasions in
1979.[33] Nevertheless, when the 50 percent solution appeared as a
provision in the WTO proposal of February 1982, it was still considered too discriminatory by the West German Foreign Minister Hans
Dietrich Genscher and was formally rejected by NATO.

EAST EUROPEAN ATTITUDES TO NUCLEAR ARMS CONTROL

Some Western analysts suggest that East Europeans see protection
under the Soviet nuclear umbrella as one advantage of membership
in the WTO.[34] But East Europeans seem at least as uncomfortable
with their dependence on Soviet nuclear weapons as West Europeans
are about the American nuclear "guarantee." Debates about nuclear
policy in the WTO may be more muted than those in NATO, but in
both cases nuclear weapons tend to emphasize the hierarchical struc-

ture of the alliance and the uncomfortable dependence of nonnuclear states on a nuclear defense policy.[35] Concern about Soviet nuclear doctrine has been articulated with varying degrees of resentment by government and military spokesmen in Poland, Czechoslovakia, and Romania since the 1950s and more recently by unofficial peace groups in Hungary and East Germany.

One obvious problem is that the risks posed by NATO's nuclear arsenal are not identical for the Soviets and the East Europeans. The latter are threatened by all nuclear weapons deployed in Western Europe, whereas the Soviets are directly threatened only by longer range systems. For a brief period in the 1960s Soviet territory was threatened by long-range missiles deployed in Western Europe— Thor and Jupiter missiles in Britain, Italy, and Turkey and Mace and Matador missiles in West Germany—but the consistent threat to Soviet territory has come from American forward-based nuclear-capable aircraft first deployed to Western Europe during the Berlin blockade in the late 1940s.

It follows that although all the WTO states share a common interest in reducing NATO's nuclear capability, the most energetic Soviet efforts have concentrated on limiting American forward-based nuclear-capable aircraft, while East European concerns and initiatives have focused on attempts to establish nuclear-free zones which would also remove both Soviet and American shorter range land-based nuclear missiles from the Continent. The Soviets have not been slow to reap the political benefits of opposing the shorter range systems. They pay lip service to all the East European proposals for nuclear-free zones and waged a particularly energetic propaganda campaign against the neutron bomb in the late 1970s, but they reserved their most pragmatic and sophisticated diplomatic effort—at SALT I and SALT II and the INF talks—to limiting the European systems that threaten them directly.

The most energetic efforts to establish nuclear-free zones, and those taken most seriously by the West (especially the West German Social Democrats), were those made in the late 1950s and early 1960s by Poland, whose concern about nuclear weapons was twofold. First, nuclear weapons stationed on NATO and WTO territory increased the risk that Poland, wedged between East Germany and the Soviet Union, would be subject to nuclear strikes on the assumption that West Germany would urge NATO planners to avoid German targets and the United States would not want to threaten Soviet territory directly and invite retaliation on the American homeland. Second, while paying lip service to the value of "coalition warfare," Polish military leaders did not share Khrushchev's enthusiasm for nuclear weapons and, in particular, resented having to train Polish troops for a WTO nuclear offensive against NATO rather than developing a national military posture capable of defending Poland.[36]

From the mid-1950s to the mid-1960s, the Polish Foreign Ministry energetically pursued a series of arms-control initiatives designed to create a nuclear-free zone in central Europe. These proposals were clearly designed to counter plans for NATO's nuclear deployments but would equally have precluded Khrushchev's plans to deploy Soviet nuclear-capable systems in Eastern Europe. As such they were not embraced with overwhelming enthusiasm in Moscow. Even though the comprehensive disarmament proposals which the Soviet Union offered in the United Nations in the mid-1950s often included nuclear-free zones, there was considerable apprehension in Moscow about the Polish initiative and especially the Polish concept of "constructive coexistence" and Foreign Minister Rapacki's desire to act as a bridge between East and West in solving the German problem.[37]

Apprehension about the reliability of the Soviet umbrella increased throughout Eastern Europe during the early 1960s. The Soviet humiliation as a result of the Cuban missile crisis suggested that, far from the strategic superiority of which Khrushchev had boasted, the Soviet arsenal could not protect its own interests let alone those of the WTO allies. In addition, the doubling of NATO's stockpile of American battlefield nuclear weapons during President John F. Kennedy's tenure in office exacerbated East European fears that central Europe would quickly become a nuclear battlefield in any conflict between NATO and the WTO.

These concerns combined with the onset of East-West detente and the fading of the West German threat tended to shift the locus of East European fears away from German revanchism on which the initial cohesion of the Pact had rested to two other more likely threats: intervention from the East and the risks of becoming embroiled in a superpower nuclear conflict. Thus not only in Poland but also in Czechoslovakia, Romania, and to a lesser extent Hungary, the military sought ways to establish national defense postures and dissociate their national security policies from Soviet nuclear doctrine.[38]

When the Warsaw Pact was first established in the mid-1950s, the Czechoslovak arms industry received a welcome boost as the Soviets began a post-Stalin facelift of the East European armies. Once Khrushchev had launched a nuclear doctrine for the Pact in the early 1960s, however, conventional forces—and thereby the importance of the Czechoslovak contribution—were downgraded. Nuclear war-fighting missions for an offensive into Western Europe were assigned to Polish and East German national forces, together with stationed Soviet troops, whereas the Czechoslovak People's Army (CPA) was to hold down NATO forces in southern Germany. A later shift in Soviet doctrine suggested that initial conventional fighting would precede the nuclear phase of any East-West conflict. But by this time, the Czechoslovak military leaders were thoroughly disenchanted with Soviet domination of WTO doctrine and especially with Soviet concepts of nuclear war-fighting and the prospects of enormous destruction and high casualties on Czechoslovak territory in such a war.

These differences simmered below the surface through the early 1960s as the Czechoslovaks resisted pressure from Khrushchev to station Soviet troops and nuclear-capable missiles in Czechoslovakia.[39] Multicapable Frog and Scud missiles were deployed with Czech troops in 1965 but without nuclear warheads, and Czechoslovakia remained free of Soviet troops for another three years. In the mid-1960s, the military increasingly made public its differences with the Soviets and together with the Romanians began to demand a greater voice for the East Europeans in the formulation of WTO doctrine. A memorandum issued from the Klement Gottwald Military and Political Academy in Prague in July 1968 outlined these concerns and also called for Czech initiatives in the disarmament and security field, specifically proposing a nuclear-free zone and the removal of all foreign troops from central Europe.[40] In March 1968 Prague Radio suggested that Czechoslovakia follow the example of General Charles de Gaulle, who in 1966 had withdrawn France from the integrated military command of NATO because he disagreed with American nuclear policies. The Czechoslovaks' hopes for military reform were ultimately crushed when the Soviets invaded Czechoslovakia in August 1968, and since then CPA leaders have been passively orthodox.

In Romania, by contrast, President Ceausescu continued to articulate his opposition to Soviet domination of nuclear decision making in Pact force planning and arms control through the 1970s and early 1980s. In the 1960s Ceausescu was particularly incensed by the discriminatory aspects of the Non-Proliferation Treaty. His arguments were analogous to those articulated in West Germany, objecting to the balance of rights and obligations between the nuclear and non-nuclear weapons states that were parties to the treaty, with all the rights accruing to the weapons states and all the obligations to those that renounced an independent nuclear weapons capability. More recently Romanian spokesmen have been at pains to attribute equal blame for the nuclear weapons buildup in Europe to both the Soviet

Union and the United States and have called for the dismantling of Soviet missiles.

WTO RESPONSES TO EUROPEAN NUCLEAR FORCE MODERNIZATION

Two developments in NATO's nuclear force planning were particularly disturbing to the Warsaw Pact countries in the 1970s: the effort to produce and deploy battlefield nuclear weapons that purported to be "cleaner" and therefore more usable and the decision in December 1979 to deploy new longer range American missiles in Western Europe which could directly strike Soviet targets. The new generation of battlefield weapons threatened to lower the threshold between conventional and nuclear conflict, while the new long-range missiles drastically reduced the Soviets' warning time of an American strategic attack and threatened to destroy command and control centers in the western military districts of the Soviet Union.

In NATO, there were conflicting pressures in the early 1970s about whether to withdraw or upgrade the short-range battlefield nuclear weapons. Many defense analysts argued that these systems should be withdrawn and dismantled because there was no rational way they could be used and they were no longer credible deterrents in view of Soviet retaliatory capability.[41] Others believed that battlefield weapons were useful both as munitions and as bargaining chips at MBFR and should be upgraded.[42] The decision to upgrade the Lance missile and the 203mm nuclear artillery shells with a reduced blast-enhanced radiation warhead (the so-called neutron bomb) was eventually taken by the Ford administration in 1976.

Touted as ideal antitank munitions and designated only for the shorter range systems, neutron weapons seemed most likely to be used against second-echelon Warsaw Pact armored forces as they advanced through Eastern Europe and thus appeared to pose a greater risk of early use than existing NATO arsenals. Discriminating battlefield weapons of any kind are thus regarded by most Europeans as destabilizing. These were not the arguments raised by the East Europeans, however. Rather, they focused on the emotional and moral aspects of the "capitalist bomb that kills people but preserves property" and stressed that deployment would undermine detente in general and ongoing arms-control negotiations in particular. In a press conference in Vienna on 31 July 1978, for example, the Polish delegate to MBFR, Tadeusz Strulak, deplored the fact that NATO's December 1975 offer to limit battlefield weapons at MBFR had been overtaken by plans to deploy the neutron bomb, which endangered detente and greatly complicated the Vienna talks.[43]

In late 1977 and early 1978 President Jimmy Carter and Chancellor Helmut Schmidt both raised the possibility of using the neutron bomb as a bargaining chip, but it was far from clear whether restraints on American neutron weapons were to be offset by limits on Soviet tanks at MBFR or on SS-20 missiles in what were then expected to be the SALT III negotiations. Either option might have been welcomed in Eastern Europe, but the Soviets threatened to match any neutron weapons deployed by NATO and, in effect, rejected both bargaining offers by announcing that American restraints on neutron weapons would be met only by reciprocal guarantees not to produce and deploy Soviet neutron bombs. After President Carter's announcement in April 1978 that he was deferring a decision on neutron bomb production the Soviets' propaganda campaign subsided.[44]

Meanwhile, both the Soviet Union and the United States were upgrading their medium-range nuclear systems. Soviet spokesmen claim that the persistent refusal of the United States to accept limits on her forward-based nuclear systems, either in SALT I or in the Vladivostok understanding reached by Presidents Gerald Ford and Brezhnev in late 1974, made replacement of the vulnerable and obsolescent SS-4 and SS-5 in the late 1970s inevitable.[45] After SALT I would certainly have been an ideal time to freeze medium-range missiles and nuclear-capable bombers, as proposed by the London-based International Institute for Strategic Studies in its annual *Strategic Survey* for both 1972 and 1973, but neither side was willing to show restraint. Instead, parallel to the SALT II negotiations, the United States upgraded its forward-based aircraft in Europe, accelerated development of cruise missiles, and initiated the "Longbow" project to develop a new medium-range ballistic missile for deployment in Western Europe.[46] Meanwhile, the Soviet Union developed the medium-range Backfire bomber to replace the missions of the Badgers and the Blinders and the SS-20 missiles to replace the aging SS-4 and SS-5s.[47]

Reports from Eastern Europe suggest some opposition within the WTO in the mid-1970s to plans to deploy SS-20 missiles in the western military districts of the Soviet Union. Apparently both Romanian and Hungarian leaders argued that increasing the nuclear threat to Western Europe could undermine the progress in East-West detente just codified in the 1975 Helsinki Final Act. By contrast, a small group of Western defense analysts was developing an appetite for new long-range missiles in Western Europe because of resentment that

SALT II had failed to impose limits on the SS-20 and the Backfire bomber, while applying restrictions, albeit modest and temporary, on cruise missiles, which might be useful in the defense of Western Europe. The result was a decision to replace 108 Pershing IA missiles deployed with American forces in West Germany with 108 longer range Pershing II missiles and to distribute 464 long-range cruise missiles to the NATO allies. All 572 new missiles would be able to strike Soviet targets, thereby reversing NATO policy of the previous decade and a half.

The intra-NATO debate about the need for new long-range missiles in Western Europe generated considerable alarm throughout the Eastern bloc. In an effort to avert deployment of ground-launched cruise and Pershing II missiles, on 6 October 1979, President Brezhnev announced the unilateral withdrawal of twenty thousand Soviet troops and one thousand Soviet tanks from East Germany and offered to reduce Soviet medium-range missile deployments and begin negotiations immediately to limit this category of weapons if NATO would cancel its missile modernization plans.[48] Brezhnev's offer—presumably the result of intense debate within the Politburo and pressure from the WTO leadership—was summarily dismissed by NATO. In response to pressure from Western Europe, however, NATO ministers coupled the decision to deploy new long-range missiles with the withdrawal of one thousand obsolete nuclear warheads—previously assigned to atomic demolition mines, short-range missiles, and air defense systems—and with an offer to negotiate limits on land-based intermediate-range forces. Brezhnev, however, asserted that the deployment part of NATO's "double decision" removed the basis for negotiations, and though some preliminary INF talks were started in October 1980, serious negotiations did not get under way until late November 1981.

Meanwhile, the Soviet campaign against the new NATO missiles intensified. The Soviets based their opposition on five main arguments, not all of which were endorsed with equal enthusiasm by the East Europeans. First, the Soviets claimed that because the new missiles could strike Soviet targets they were strategic systems and would undermine the SALT II treaty signed in June 1979; second, as qualitatively new systems the Tomahawk ground-launched cruise missiles and Pershing II extended-range ballistic missiles posed a new, more serious threat to the security of the Soviet homeland and upset Soviet-American strategic parity; third, the new missiles would also undermine a longstanding nuclear equilibrium in Europe, which would have to be reestablished; fourth, the new systems suggested that the United States was preparing to engage in limited nuclear strikes in an effort to confine future nuclear exchanges to the European continent; and finally, by assigning a prominent role to West Germany as host nation for the new missiles, NATO was undermining the gains of *Ostpolitik* and East-West detente in Europe.[49]

For East Europeans who had been within range of NATO nuclear weapons since the early 1950s and who knew that they would be the likely first victims in any NATO–Warsaw Pact nuclear exchange, the prospect of longer range missiles in Western Europe posed no new dangers. Indeed, the intense concern in Moscow about the new threat to Soviet territory tended to underscore Soviet indifference to East European security over the past two decades, a criticism which East European human rights activists also directed against the antinuclear movements in Western Europe.

Nevertheless, although the proposed new NATO missiles posed no immediate threat to their physical security, East European leaders were concerned about the planned deployments for three other reasons: that a further deterioration in East-West relations, through a breakdown in the INF talks for example, would reduce Soviet tolerance for economic and political liberalization in the bloc; that NATO cruise missiles in particular would generate demands for higher East European contributions to upgrade the Pact's integrated air defense system;[50] and that Soviet countermeasures to the new missiles could undermine East European security.

In late 1981 and early 1982, East German and Czechoslovak officials emphasized that one important difference between Soviet and American nuclear doctrine was that the Soviets did not use allied territory as a launching pad for their nuclear missiles.[51] On one level such statements can be viewed with cynicism as those of loyal allies supporting the Soviet line in opposing NATO's modernization plans. Given the geographical asymmetries between NATO and the WTO, the Soviets do not need East European territory as forward bases for their SS-4s, SS-5s, and SS-20s. The western military districts of the Soviet Union are both adequate and preferable in providing secure command and control.

It seems likely, however, that East Germany and Czechoslovakia stressed that Soviet INFs were not deployed in Eastern Europe because they wanted to preserve the nuclear status quo and discourage the Soviets from countering the new NATO missiles with systems that required forward basing. Until the early 1980s no new land-based, nuclear-capable missiles had been deployed in Eastern Europe since the multicapable Frogs and Scuds were distributed to non-Soviet Pact forces in the mid-1960s, and it was widely assumed that all nuclear warheads assigned to these systems were stored in the Soviet Union as were all Soviet nuclear artillery pieces that are not dual-capable.[52] Soviet missile tests monitored by the West in the early 1980s suggested, however, that new systems were being developed to replace the Frogs and Scuds in Eastern Europe and the Scaleboards in the western military districts. NATO designated these new systems SS-21, SS-23, and SS-22.

On several occasions through 1983, WTO leaders were summoned to meetings to discuss appropriate countermeasures to the new NATO missiles. Kremlin spokesmen insisted that Pershing and cruise must be countered in kind with both new Soviet missiles in Eastern Europe to reassert the European nuclear equilibrium and new systems that would directly threaten United States territory to restore the Soviet-American strategic balance. Party leaders in Eastern Europe, particularly in East Germany, Czechoslovakia, and Hungary, were thus caught between pressure from Moscow to welcome the necessary countermeasures and increasingly vocal opposition to any new Soviet missiles from the fledgling antinuclear groups that emerged in these countries in the early 1980s. Not surprisingly, there were no ringing endorsements from WTO leaders for new nuclear-capable systems in Eastern Europe.[53]

As in the 1950s and 1960s, East European military and political leaders were apprehensive that hosting new Soviet nuclear systems would make their territory a more likely target for NATO missiles, particularly if the Soviets should begin to stockpile nuclear warheads with shorter range delivery systems.[54] These concerns are analogous to those articulated in Western Europe whenever new nuclear systems are proposed for NATO because the nonnuclear powers in both alliances share the same anxiety that the two superpowers will deploy forces so as to leave their own territories nuclear-free sanctuaries in the event of an East-West nuclear exchange.

NUCLEAR-FREE ZONES REVISITED

In the early 1980s, with no direct input to the bilateral INF talks, East European concerns about the proposed new NATO missiles and possible Soviet countermeasures were channeled into various revived proposals to establish European nuclear-free zones. In contrast to the late 1950s, Poland was not actively engaged in this effort, being preoccupied with domestic unrest, but several other East European governments took up the cause, some with Soviet blessing and some without. As usual, the most independent action was in Romania. Unlike the other WTO allies, who focused their public criticism on NATO plans to deploy Pershing and cruise, Romanian spokesmen used language that specifically opposed, and called for the removal of, already deployed Soviet systems.[55] Similarly, in calling for the abolition of foreign military bases Romanians specify seventy bases in eighteen European countries to include Soviet installations in Eastern Europe.[56] In December 1981, three hundred thousand people marched in a government-sponsored demonstration in Bucharest against both the SS-20 and the new NATO missiles and in support of President Ceausescu's call for a Balkan nuclear-free zone. The latter was also endorsed by President Zhivkov of Bulgaria, the post-Tito leadership in Yugoslavia, and President Andreas Papendreou of Greece.[57] Meanwhile, to the north the Finnish government revived proposals for a Nordic nuclear-free zone, which initially appeared more attractive to Norway and Sweden than similar proposals in the 1960s because in June 1981 the Soviets suggested a willingness to include the Kola peninsula.[58] These offers looked less convincing, however, when Soviet submarines began to probe Scandinavian territorial waters in 1982 and 1983. In the early 1980s proposals by several international groups for a variety of nuclear-free zones increased the prestige and credibility of the concept. One of these groups, chaired by Swedish Prime Minister Olof Palme, proposed a narrow 300km nuclear-free strip in central Europe, an idea which Palme then launched as an official Swedish proposal.[59] The WTO governments welcomed the Palme initiative, seeing in it an opportunity to reintroduce NATO nuclear weapons into the MBFR negotiations. Soviet and East European leaders proposed a doubling of the Palme zone to 300 km each side of the NATO-WTO border, thereby including most of NATO's short-range nuclear hardware, and suggested that the details could be negotiated at the Vienna talks.[60]

CONCLUSION

There are obvious political advantages for the Soviet Union in using the WTO as the base from which to launch its arms-control initiatives in East-West negotiations, but it is less clear what benefits membership in the WTO brings to East European countries in pursuit of their security needs. As Peter Bender wrote in the early 1970s, the Soviet Union seeks maximum security in as much bloc unity as possible and as little collaboration with the West as necessary, whereas most East Europeans see their interests best served by as much collaboration with the West as possible and as little bloc unity as necessary.[61]

Willy Brandt's *Ostpolitik* and the East-West detente, which flourished in the early to mid-1970s, provided tangible political and economic benefits to East European populations, thereby posing a threat to WTO cohesion. Western influence increased in Eastern Europe, but Moscow could no longer invoke the German threat to bind the Eastern bloc together. Consequently, despite continuing to proclaim the inevitable momentum of the correlation of forces in the direction of world communism, Soviet objectives in East-West arms-control negotiations through the 1970s and early 1980s were actually more damage-limiting than dynamic, defined in terms that did little more than codify the territorial gains of World War II and the existing military balances. Assessments of how well WTO arms-control diplomacy has met East European security needs therefore depend largely on the extent to which different national Communist parties were satisfied with the status quo in this period and how successful East European leaders were in nudging the Soviets toward more ambitious arms-control positions.

Tighter integration of the WTO has precluded the energetic pursuit of independent East European arms-control initiatives, which characterized Poland's persistent effort with different versions of its Rapacki Plan through the late 1950s and early 1960s. Nevertheless, the East Europeans now have many more opportunities to press their own arms-control objectives on the Soviet leadership during the policy formulation stage. How effective this input has been remains an open question, but some analysts see East European influence at work in the Soviets' greater willingness to open up Soviet territory to on-site inspections, to accept more militarily significant confidence-building measures both at the CSCE and MBFR, and to reduce the number of SS-20 missiles targeted on Western Europe.

Despite progress in intraalliance consultations, however, East European governments, in common with the smaller NATO allies, still find their security and arms-control interests better served in multilateral negotiating forums, in which they participate directly, than in bilateral Soviet-American agreements, which often seem to be concluded at the expense of European needs. Similarly, states in the Southern Tier of the WTO, like the northern and southern flanks of NATO, preferred the Conference on Security and Cooperation in Europe, in which all Europeans participated on an equal footing, to the Mutual and Balanced Force Reduction talks in Vienna, at which those with no forces deployed in central Europe were assigned second-class status.

Beyond the general issue of status, East European attitudes toward CSCE and MBFR vary according to the orthodoxy of their regimes. East Germany and Czechoslovakia, which are closest to the Soviet line in both foreign and domestic policy, found their interests better served at the interalliance talks in Vienna than at the multilateral CSCE. This may seem paradoxical since MBFR stemmed from a NATO initiative whereas the CSCE was designed to codify the Soviet Union's political and territorial gains of World War II. MBFR, however, was the forum most unambiguously geared to maintaining the status quo in Europe, whereas the CSCE opened up the prospect, however distant, of a pan-European security system based on new norms of international restraint, which could eventually impose limits on Soviet control over its East European buffer zone. Many East Europeans believe, for example, that the Helsinki Final Act and subsequent review process were important factors restraining the Soviets from direct military intervention in Poland in the early 1980s.

The less orthodox, more independently oriented East European governments used the CSCE to press their own interests. Romania in particular used this forum to pursue ambitious military confidence-building measures that would impose stricter limits on Soviet military activity in the vicinity of the Balkans. But Hungary and Poland also used CSCE to put distance, albeit more discreetly, between their own views and those of Moscow, an effort encouraged by Western and neutral delegates at the Madrid review conference, who noted the relatively benign Hungarian and Polish records on human rights compared with the rest of the bloc.

Although more bloc discipline was in evidence at MBFR than at CSCE, the three East European participants with "direct" status in Vienna did not behave in a uniform manner. The East Germans and the Czechoslovaks tended to react even more nervously than the Soviets to NATO's insistence on more transparency in the WTO force posture, while Polish delegates on numerous occasions tried to bridge the data discrepancy and to persuade both superpowers to adopt more imaginative and ambitious arms-control positions.

In both NATO and the WTO, the smaller nonnuclear states found their interests not well served by the bilateral superpower effort to manage the nuclear balance in Europe. From late 1981 through late 1983 both sides in the bilateral INF negotiations in Geneva seemed more interested in scoring propaganda points than in pursuing what Europeans viewed as the two critically important objectives of the talks: a lessening of the nuclear confrontation and an improvement in East-West relations. On the contrary, both the United States and the Soviet Union invoked the intransigence of the other at the negotiating table to rationalize the deployment of redundant nuclear hardware which manifestly undermines the security of the smaller European powers, East and West. Thus for the WTO countries, as for many West Europeans, the INF talks became part and parcel of the latest round in the nuclear spiral, serving primarily to exacerbate an already uncomfortable European dependency on the nuclear strategies of the superpowers.

Nevertheless, to the extent that the Soviets sought to portray their INF diplomacy as coordinated WTO policy, the East Europeans had opportunities to exert some influence on Moscow in the early 1980s. The available evidence suggests that whenever the Soviets called the East European leaders together to endorse the latest INF initiative, be it a variant of the basic negotiating position or a statement on appropriate Soviet countermeasures to the new NATO missiles, the East Europeans modified Soviet rhetoric if not operational policy. Communiqués from the WTO as a whole were always more conciliatory than unilateral Soviet statements, and there were no ringing endorsements of plans to base new Soviet nuclear-capable missiles on East European soil. On the contrary, even the most orthodox allies, Erich Honecker and Gustav Husak, expressed misgivings about proposed Soviet countermeasures to cruise and Pershing and deplored the breakdown of the INF talks in November 1983.

One reason why even the orthodox regimes in East Germany and Czechoslovakia were reluctant to host new Soviet missiles was the new antinuclear sentiment in the East, which permeated through from Western Europe in the early 1980s. WTO leaders were clearly confused by this new phenomenon because it meant reversing their initial enthusiasm for the Western peace movement as it developed in the wake of the December 1979 NATO missile decision. At that time Soviet propagandists praised the antinuclear protestors in Western Europe as enlightened anti-imperialists, while East European dissidents chastised the same activists as naive dupes.[62]

Through the early 1980s, however, western antinuclear activists visited the Soviet Union and Eastern Europe and wrote and spoke out more on human rights. At the same time civil rights activists in the Eastern bloc began to embrace the peace issue, denouncing the nuclear forces of both sides, in stark contrast to the official state-run peace committees in the Warsaw Pact countries who only condemn Western arsenals. Independent groups in East and West grew increasingly impatient with traditional arms-control diplomacy and saw one another as natural allies in the search for peaceful change.

In Moscow in June 1982, the Group to Establish Trust between the USSR and the USA launched itself with a press conference for Western journalists, claiming it wanted to harness the enormous creative potential of ordinary people in the USSR in the quest for peace.[63] In Czechoslovakia in August 1982, Charter 77 called on the government to open bilateral negotiations with Moscow on the withdrawal of Soviet troops, claiming their "temporary stationing" in Czechoslovakia in 1968 had changed the balance of forces between the two blocs and was now obstructing the Vienna talks. The group claimed that withdrawal of Soviet forces would further detente, unlock the MBFR talks, "assert our republic's full sovereignty," and "could lead to the renewal of the naturally healthy friendly ties between the peoples of the Czechoslovak Peoples Republic and the people of the USSR."[64]

In Budapest, the Peace Group for Dialogue offered a detailed proposal for a nuclear-free zone modeled on the Rapacki Plan, in the third stage of which all foreign troops would leave the country.[65] An East German group initially petitioned for alternatives to military service but took up the nuclear disarmament issue in 1981 encouraged in part by the Evangelical church, which endorsed an antinuclear position similar to that of the Lutheran churches in West Germany and the Netherlands.

WTO governments were obviously unsure how to deal with the new pockets of protest, sometimes punishing the more prominent members of each group, sometimes trying to co-opt the antinuclear issue by official state-run peace committees. Predictably, the Soviet and East German authorities were the most harsh and the Hungarian the most lenient in coping with the problem. Soviet propagandists reversed their judgment of the Western peace movement in a pamphlet published in April 1983, which criticized those in the West "bringing the cold war spirit into the peace movement and sowing the seeds of hostility towards the socialist countries and their sociopolitical system" and "organizations which declare that they dedicate themselves to nuclear disarmament and become cats paws and meddle in the internal affairs of socialist states."[66]

Thus, much as West Germany's *Ostpolitik* was too threatening to Moscow when attempted as a series of bilateral maneuvers between Bonn and East European capitals in the 1960s, so were new pan-European disarmament links being forged at too unsettling a pace for the Andropov leadership in the early 1980s. East European leaders who saw no alternative to membership in the WTO for the foreseeable future were thus caught once again between the need to demonstrate allegiance to the Soviet Union and the need to meet the demands of their increasingly anti-Soviet polities. This difficult task will require extraordinary skill and pragmatism and not a little understanding from the West.

PART IV

FUTURE PROSPECTS

[8]

The Future of Political Relations within the Warsaw Pact

J. F. BROWN

Neither of the two Great Power blocs is immune to change. NATO and the Warsaw Pact are subject to both internal and external pressures, and, if the recent disarray in NATO brought gloomy prognostications of an early demise, it should not be forgotten that in the Pact, based on domination rather than sovereignty, evolution does occur and change remains a possibility.

Predictions, therefore, are legitimate. But with an alliance such as the Warsaw Pact, whose workings proceed behind a veil of secrecy, the greatest caution, even humility, is necessary. The future can be considered only as far as the myopic eye can see, say, to the end of the 1980s, and even this short span of time invites the most egregious errors of prognostication. But the risks must be run.

THE SOVIET FACTOR

Political relations within the Warsaw Pact in the future, as in the past, will depend on a number of interacting factors, of which the most important are the Soviet Union, Eastern Europe, and the West. Each of these can, in turn, be broken down into parts.

The Soviet factor is obviously the most important. The Soviet Union founded the Warsaw Pact in 1955 and has dominated it, militarily and politically. The Pact's future depends, primarily on that of the Soviet Union. The Soviet factor involves both purely domestic considerations and Soviet perceptions of their allies. It includes, for example, the internal stability of the Soviet Union and the future strength and unity of its leadership. The most immediate question concerns the ability to survive the forthcoming leadership succession without crisis.[1] A basic longer-term question, although not directly relevant during the present decade, is the ability of Soviet leaders to handle the growing problem of nationalities, which they claim was solved by establishment of the Soviet Union. Soviet economic strength is also of crucial importance, affecting not only the power and even survival of the Soviet Union itself but also its relations with its allies. Economic control can be used as a coercive or a bargaining instrument—or both. Lack of it could result in the alliance crumbling.

The military dimension is crucial in Soviet assessments of their East European allies.[2] Are the allies considered primarily as providing a strategic defense zone to strengthen Soviet security in a conventional conflict? Are they primarily to serve as a forward base for offensive military operations? Are they bases for, and instruments of, political subversion against Western Europe, particularly against the Federal Republic of Germany? Conversely, are they defenses for the Soviet Union against political subversion from the West? Is the ideological importance some may have attached to them as the vanguard of a world revolution still considered viable? After nearly forty years of dominance—achieved after massive suffering—is control over the area a crucial psychological underpinning of Soviet self-confidence? Obviously, the process of separating these possible perceptions is an artificiality. All by now are so intertwined in the Soviet psyche as to defy unraveling. There may be others, too. A historical perception, for example, dating back at least 250 years, sees the East European region as Russia's natural and rightful sphere of influence. Rational and intuitive perceptions such as these constitute the hard core of Soviet foreign policy and view of the world.

They must also tend to color the Soviet perception of the condition of the East European countries, collectively or severally, at any particular time: stable or unstable, economically viable or unviable, confident or lacking confidence in the different national leaderships. These are questions vital to the health of the alliance, and the Soviets clearly attach great importance to them. They are extremely well informed about what goes on in Eastern Europe. But their appraisal could well be clouded by their multiple preconception about what should be going on. Sometimes the Soviets are without illusion; sometimes they are victims of their own.[3]

THE EAST EUROPEAN FACTOR

Any discussion of the East European factor in Warsaw Pact relations must begin with the standard admonition about the individuality and distinctiveness of each of the countries. Almost as many factors are involved as countries. But at the risk of serious over-simplification, the East European factor can be broken down into a number of parts many of which are, again, interconnecting.

One factor, obviously, is regime stability. Another is the economic viability of the individual countries and its interaction with the level of expectations of society. This interaction is crucial: what is important is never the economic situation itself but what people think about it. And it is this truism that very often dictates the nature of the relations between regime and society—the degree to which society accepts or tolerates an authority the form and composition of which it has never been consulted on. The relations between the various East European regimes and the Soviet leadership—in some cases the relations between factions of one and the other—are also basic, and in this connection the developed skills of some East European leaders—Kadar and Ceausescu, each in his own way and in his own interest, for example—should be noted. Less important up to now have been the relations of the different countries of the region with each other. Traditional antagonisms, coupled with a Soviet jealousy of groupings from which it is excluded, have prevented this factor from assuming real importance.[4] Indeed, a depressing feature of contemporary East European history has been a tendency to perpetuate old antagonisms, with Moscow sometimes undemonstratively stirring the pot. Many of the younger generation, however, appear free of the prejudices of their elders.[5] If so, a constructive new dimension could eventually be introduced into Eastern Europe's intraregional relations and its relations with both East and West.

THE WESTERN FACTOR

Finally, there is the Western factor. In the early years of Soviet domination in Eastern Europe, this was of minimal importance. The Hungarian revolution of 1956 and the Soviet invasion of Czechoslovakia in 1968 seemed to confirm Eastern Europe as a zone of exclusive Soviet influence. But in the 1970s the Western factor began to play a more important role, both in Eastern Europe and in Soviet relations with the region. The two most important aspects were detente diplomacy and its momentous offshoot, the massive Western financial involvement in Eastern Europe.

The detente diplomacy of the 1970s was made up of several factors and processes, dominated perhaps by the Soviet-American relationship but neither totally initiated nor dependent on it. Very briefly, it involved Henry Kissinger's concept of relations with the Soviet Union and the policy emanating from it, the West German *Ostpolitik*, the Helsinki CSCE process, French policy toward Eastern Europe, and, finally, the Vatican's relations with Eastern Europe including the phenomenon of the Polish pope (the latter, of course, hardly fitting within the framework of the superpower relationship).

Western economic and financial involvement had, by the end of the 1970s, resulted in such massive debts owed by all East European countries—except Czechoslovakia and almost totally isolated Albania—that it was the overriding issue in relations with the West. The great economic, political, and psychological significance these debts assumed will be referred to later.

BACKGROUND TO THE 1980S

Before making predictions for the 1980s, some background on the 1970s is necessary. It would appear that the nature of relations among Warsaw Pact countries underwent some important changes during the second half of that decade. Some—or, at least, the full extent of their importance—were not evident at the time. But in retrospect, the course of events after 1975 seems to have taken a turn.

The first half of the 1970s could be characterized by a determined and successful Soviet effort to reestablish authority in Eastern Europe after the Prague Spring and the danger of its contaminating influence. The Soviets were determined that the situation that prompted them to invade Czechoslovakia should never be allowed to happen again. They rallied and subsequently consolidated "safe," orthodox, and conservative forces in the East European leaderships. The exception was Hungary, where the Kadar regime skillfully used its bargaining power with Moscow to press on with its economic reform. This bargaining power probably derived from Hungary's record as a dependable ally; Kadar's agreement to join the invasion of Czechoslovakia despite his obvious reluctance; his protestations that, politically, his regime remained satisfactorily orthodox; and Brezhnev's understandable reluctance to interfere openly in another allied country so soon after invading Czechoslovakia and on top of the rift with Romania, which had openly opposed the invasion.

The post-1968 consolidation was accompanied by an unprecedented economic prosperity. The Western prosperity of the 1960s came to Eastern Europe in the wake of the great expansion of commercial relations—ironically, just about the time the West's prosperity was threatened by the oil price explosion. In addition, the massive Western credits began to be felt. Some of the prosperity, notably in Czechoslovakia and in Poland after the upheaval of 1970, was politically engineered rather than economically induced. The Soviet Union extended hard currency loans to the new Husak and Gierek regimes to boost living standards. The resulting consumerism helped facilitate a general passivity of society in Eastern Europe basically caused by the Czechoslovak disaster of August 1968 and the Polish catharsis of December 1970. Reformists and dissident elements became disheartened and retired within themselves.

The Soviet Union, therefore, had reason to be satisfied. The dangers of the late 1960s had been averted. The alliance seemed stable, and in the early 1970s institutional steps were taken both to strengthen it and to make it more palatable to its lesser members. (Here, Brezhnev after 1968 was acting like Khrushchev after 1956.) There are several examples; the Warsaw Pact reforms of 1969 and the CMEA comprehensive program of 1971 are good ones. Ostensibly, the lesser members of the Pact were given more say. A "directed consensus" became standard operational procedure, and it seemed to work from the Soviet point of view. True, the self-assertiveness of Romania continued; but this could be contained, and even in the early 1970s Moscow may have foreseen that Romania, and not the alliance, would suffer most from Ceausescu's policies.[6]

The change that came about in the middle of the decade was caused by a combination of factors, the common denominator of which was a Soviet complacency about the alliance and its members. Among the most important of these factors was the deceptive stability and apparent viability of the region, leading the Soviets to believe they could relax their concentration on it. Eastern Europe was quiet and improving economically. Its leaders seemed effectively in control. Three new leaders had emerged since 1968: Gustav Husak, Erich Honecker, and Edward Gierek. All appeared from Moscow to be performing well (Gierek, in particular, had the extraordinary knack of being able to convince everybody—East and West—of his leadership qualities). Zhivkov had always been considered safe. As for Kadar, whatever the skepticism about the New Economic Mechanism and its possible consequences, the party seemed firm, and Hungary was a loyal ally.[7] Romania was containable. True, the situation was not one of unbroken calm. The Polish price riots of 1976[8] and the emergence of Charter 77 in Czechoslovakia, a small dissenting group determined to keep alive the spirit and principles of the Prague Spring, were not negligible. Charter 77 is a brave movement that persists and has taken on new life by embracing the antinuclear issue.[9] Neither movement, however, was a basic challenge on the regional level.

This seeming quiet made it easier for the Soviet leaders to make far-reaching shifts in their perception of the importance of Eastern Europe in a broader setting. In the military-strategic context, for example, Eastern Europe's role as a defensive *glacis* was no longer so crucial as it had been thirty years before in light of spectacular developments in nuclear weaponry. In a conventional war, however, Eastern Europe would remain of paramount importance.[10]

Moreover, the global political and expansionist ambitions of the Soviet Union, perfectly clear by the mid-1970s, inevitably tended to reduce the importance of Eastern Europe. As the "seven seas" psychosis assumed a larger role in motivating Soviet behavior, Eastern Europe assumed a smaller one. Again, this shift was facilitated by the assumption that Eastern Europe was safe.

Finally, there was a shift in the Soviet ideological attitude toward Eastern Europe. This shift is difficult to identify, let alone measure. First, it needs defining. Opinions may differ on how far Soviet leaders ever saw Eastern Europe as a physical extension, potential vanguard, or springboard of the Marxist-Leninist revolution. Khrushchev at times may have done so. Brezhnev appears to have had fewer illusions (and Andropov probably even fewer) about the messianic or therapeutic properties of the communist ideology, despite all the ritualistic lip service paid to it. After the trauma of the Prague Spring, there was, inevitably, another of the ideological offensives that have punctuated the history of Soviet domination in Eastern Europe. But by the mid-1970s little trace of it was left. The ideology in which Soviet state interests had been so demonstratively clothed was getting threadbare, leading to a certain laxity, even permissiveness, toward Eastern Europe. If, for example, Gierek assured the Kremlin that Poland was under control, if Kadar protested Hungary's loyalty—and could show economic viability to boot—there was little disposition to submit the evidence to closer examination. Eastern Europe began to be taken for granted.

By the mid-1970s, however, the cement binding the surface stability was beginning to crack. Economic recession crept into Eastern Europe, heralded by the drastic increases in the price of Soviet raw material exports, particularly oil, to its clients beginning in 1975[11] and the delayed impact of Western "stagflation," itself a symptom of growing East-West economic relations. The second half of the 1970s was characterized by a steadily sharpening economic deterioration in all the countries of the alliance, including the Soviet Union. The scattered strikes in Poland in 1976 protesting price increases on basic foodstuffs were an early warning. But most economies were shielded from the worst impact of the deterioration by that new phenomenon of East-West relations: massive Western loans.

Western loans achieved several results, not all of them unconstructive; but one of their most unfortunate effects was to delay for several years the moment of truth for the extensive, command structure, socialist economies of Eastern Europe.[12] The Soviet Union, by its invasion of Czechoslovakia in 1968, had killed two hopes or illusions: first, that a Communist party could ever be allowed to reform itself enough to command the loyalty of society; and second—and more relevant here—that the overpowering, modernizing need to switch from an extensive to an intensive ecomony could be achieved through unimpeded reform.[13] By the late 1960s not only the Czechoslovak economy but all others in Eastern Europe including, to some extent, the Romanian and Bulgarian, needed this basic transformation. But the events of August 1968 condemned them to continued unviability in the old structure.

For a time, though, it did not seem to matter. Trade with the West and Soviet subsidies,[14] often politically motivated, helped. But it would certainly have begun to matter by the mid-1970s, when Soviet subsidies had apparently decreased and when the new raw material prices and Western stagflation began to bite. Just then, however, Western credits, state and private, stepped in and bailed out the ideologically inviolable, economically suicidal old methods for another few years.

Hungary, of course, is an exception. The New Economic Mechanism was an imaginative reform program, conceived and carried out by skillful officials. The Western loans were, on the whole, well spent, although the problems of repayment are just as painful for Hungary now as for any other debtor country.[15] Why and how Hungary became a case apart is a study in itself, characterized by the long shadow of 1956 and the unwritten social contract resulting from the revolution; the phenomenon of Kadar; the maximum use of bargaining leverage with Moscow; an economic policy both bold and sound allowing, among other things, for a flourishing secondary economy; and an astute *Westpolitik*. These are some of the explanations that make Hungary a salutary warning against sweeping generalizations. But Hungary's experience does not disqualify the generalizations made above. It rather serves as a counterpoint by which the rest of Eastern Europe (excluding nonaligned Yugoslavia) can be seen in better focus.

[203]

The beginning of the 1980s was dominated by two events, the importance of which still remains to be assessed: the rise and fall of Solidarity in Poland and the deaths of both Brezhnev and his successor Andropov, with the ensuing uncertainty in the Soviet Union.

The rise of Solidarity in Poland meant the near collapse of the Polish regime.[16] It was a direct product of the late 1970s and was typically and uniquely Polish. Nothing similar in its majesty and tragedy may happen again for many years in Eastern Europe. But what happened in Gdansk and after should be seen as a symptom, albeit a spectacular one, of the growing malaise in Eastern Europe as a whole. Much speculation has recently been legitimately expended on the effect the Polish revolution might have on the rest of Eastern Europe. There may be eventual, delayed effects, but it would be missing the point about the last and the next ten years in Eastern Europe to view the Polish events solely as a future cause and not also as a symptom of a continuing situation.

Taking the three major determining factors mentioned at the beginning of this chapter—the Soviet, the East European, and the Western—a veritable profusion of scenarios could be depicted for the few years ahead. What follows are not scenarios but a discussion of possibilities based on the interaction of these three factors.

As for the Soviet factor, the choice of Chernenko to replace Andropov—the last stand of the old guard?—makes a continuing lack of decisiveness a real possibility. It can be assumed, though, that, for any new leadership, the upheavals in Poland would be proof that neglect does not pay. Eastern Europe, in general, and Poland, in particular, should then become an area of priority concern once again. But what is to be done? What immediate and longer term steps should be taken to see that disaster does not recur? The dilemma is exactly the same as after 1956 and 1968.

But on both those occasions, the response was energetic, decisive, and, in some measure, successful. Now it promises to be less so. True, the first surgical measure—that of 13 December 1981—was decisive and successful, with the added attraction of not involving direct Soviet participation. But the constraints on a comprehensive response such as followed 1956 and 1968 now seem most formidable. Personally and economically, the Soviet leadership is now appreciably weaker. Militarily, of course, it is far stronger; but Eastern Europe is a problem that cannot be solved by military means alone. Such means are the ultimate guarantee of control, but resort to them is the most abject confession of failure. Something else is needed from the Soviet leadership. Will it come from Chernenko—or his successor?

The thousands of pages and millions of words written about Andropov on his succession told us more about journalists and political scientists than they did about Andropov.[17] There is considerably less curiosity about Chernenko, mainly because he appears a less interesting personality than his short-lived predecessor, very much the machine-politician in the Brezhev mold. Unless, therefore, Chernenko turns innovator at the summit of his career, few basic changes in policy toward Eastern Europe need be expected. Indeed, his inclinations, plus the system inertia his election reflects, could ensure that the Soviet holding, rather than movement, pattern will continue.

Andropov was considered, on the basis of scanty evidence, to be sympathetic toward the reform in Hungary. He certainly knew Hungary, and many Hungarians seemed convinced of his good-will. Chernenko may instinctively be less sympathetic but probably not to the point of actively interfering. On the other hand, any spread of Hungarian principles, particularly to the strategically vital "Northern Tier" of satellites, would almost certainly be discouraged.

There remains, therefore, the question of the three basic approaches seemingly open to the new Soviet leadership (this and the next) and which they might opt for.

The first could loosely be termed the decolonizing approach. Putatively advocated by technocratic leadership elements, among whom Chernenko can hardly be counted, this approach would countenance a looser association of states within the Warsaw Pact. Each member would have more domestic and external leeway, provided that the sacred canons of party rule and alliance membership were not violated, although even the former might be stretched to allow for a more viable pluralism. Those advocating this course would presumably argue that the resulting risks and losses would be less than those from a more restrictive, traditional approach. Whether this approach has much support, or will have in the foreseeable future, is doubtful.

The second would be a directly repressive approach, representing a primitive attitude based on a totally defensive view of Eastern Europe. After more than thirty years in power, the only effective method of rule perceived would be a neo-Stalinist one, involving the rigorous use of both military and economic instruments to retain control. Little attempt would be made to disguise Soviet domination of both the Warsaw Pact and the CMEA. A closer watch would be kept on the domestic and foreign policies of all the states concerned; flexibility and diversity would be viewed with great suspicion. Such diversity as might develop would be subjected to the *Gleichschaltung* process. An effort to recreate total Soviet control over the East European security apparatus, reminiscent of the Stalin era, might also be involved here.[18]

The third could be called the conservative "muddle-through" approach, best personified by the latter-day Brezhnev. The difference between the second and third is basically one of method and style rather than principle, with the third approach more ready—though considerably less so than several years ago—to tolerate flexibility and diversity. The more blatant forms of domination and repression would be avoided wherever possible, and various tactics including *divide et impera* might be used.[19] But this approach could also involve Soviet efforts to strengthen their secret police network and contacts in Eastern Europe—a milder version of the second approach. Basically, though, this approach would lack decisiveness and would often be characterized by the saving grace of procrastination.

Of these three possibilities it would perhaps be naive to expect the decolonizing approach to have much chance during this decade, if ever. It is doubtful whether the real change in Soviet leadership, after Chernenko, will make a basic difference in the Soviet approach to Eastern Europe, which seems to be one of the least reformable aspects of a very conservative system.

What is most likely to happen, then, is a continuation of the conservative muddle-through approach, particularly if Chernenko shows some durability. The dilemma for any new leader is not so much the priorities facing him but how to order them. The societal revolt in Poland obviously raised Eastern Europe higher in the priority table. But it would have been higher for Brezhnev than it presumably is now for Chernenko, who, like Andropov, faces the same kind and urgency of priorities as existed for Brezhnev in 1964 after he had ousted Khrushchev. The top priority is, of course, stabilizing one's own power. Andropov attempted this; so must Chernenko. Then there is the economy. Chernenko is believed to be more cautious here than his predecessor. But, still, the situation demands some changes. And if, as seems likely after the anticlimax of Solidarity's demise, there is a period of stagnation rather than turbulence in Eastern Europe, the chances are that there will be no major changes in Moscow's relationship with it. The muddling through may be a bit more systematic and watchful, but basically it will remain. The Soviet Union and, of course, the relationship with the West, in general, and the United States, in particular, will dominate.

Briefly, then, Soviet policy toward its East European allies in the 1980s is likely to be based on makeshift decisions. It could also depend in part on whether any Soviet factional struggles are reflected in Eastern Europe and on the interaction between factions in Eastern Europe and their counterparts in Moscow. But that is a wholly unpredictable variable. It is likely to be defensive in that it will respond to situations rather than seeking any basic change or promoting any concept. The traditional goal of Soviet policy in the region—to balance cohesion and viability[20]—would go by default for lack of decisiveness and a conceptual overview. The obvious need, dramatized by the events in Poland, to "do something about" Eastern Europe would at least be met only partly.

THE EAST EUROPEAN FACTOR

Assuming a temporary stagnation after the success of reaction in Poland, what situation might eventually develop in Eastern Europe to which the Soviet Union would need to respond and which could seriously affect the Warsaw Pact alliance?

One can assume the economic deterioriation will continue. It will be most immediately acute in Poland and Romania but will seriously affect all other countries, Hungary not excepted.[21] Societal tensions will, therefore, increase as standards of living stagnate or decline and material expectations appear further out of reach. The pattern of societal response, almost impossible to predict, will vary from country to country. But there need be no direct correlation between the degree of economic decline and the level of social tension in any particular country. Other factors are involved, such as the degree of economic advancement, national temperament, and perceived strength and likely response of the authorities.

Generalization here can lead to oversimplification, and a more detailed look is necessary. The economic difficulties of some countries are not and will not be as serious as in others, and the deterioration will not be uniformly swift or deep. The case of Hungary is obvious, but neither Bulgaria nor the GDR is yet in a serious crisis.[22] By the standards of its Balkan communist neighbors—Romania and the Yugoslav republics of Serbia and Macedonia—Bulgaria is flourishing in many respects. But this prosperity is not entirely the result of its own efforts. As a Warsaw Pact outpost facing two uncertain NATO allies—and a most loyal and quiet one at that—Bulgaria receives Soviet help and special dispensations not available to others.[23] But these may not be eternal. Above all, in spite of the progress it has made, it is still in the relatively extensive, undeveloped stage of industrial development. Progress, therefore, has been relatively easy, and Bulgaria has a little time yet to contract the ills of its Northern Tier allies. The GDR and Czechoslovakia, the two most economically advanced East European states, can, in this context, be viewed together. Both are encountering recession; the regimes of both are very worried and make no secret of it although the GDR economy has recently shown some signs of revival. But their distress cannot be remotely compared with that of either Poland or Romania. Czechoslovakia, with its already obsolescent industrial plan and infrastructure, could face catastrophe by the end of this decade.[24] It draws present comfort from its not laboring, as its allies are, under huge debts to the West. But it will need massive credits for the economic modernization it knows is essential. And where will they come from? If the direct and indirect financial help the GDR receives from West Germany, altogether amounting to a massive annual subvention,[25] is taken away, its future would be precarious. Little is left of the "economic miracle" of the 1960s. Less would be left without these West German injections—injections that would become transfusions if the economy continues to sicken.

The most effective response to such deterioration would be far-reaching measures of economic reform such as those applied in Hungary over a number of years. But there are few signs that other countries are prepared to follow suit. In Poland regime spokesmen promise much—particularly to Western journalists, visiting politicians, and economic representatives. A program based on "three S's" is promised: self-financing, self-sufficiency, and self-government. But it has been difficult to ascertain how much progress has been made in any of these spheres.[26] In Bulgaria an economic reform program with some superficial similarities to the Hungarian was begun in 1982.[27] The Bulgarian government is also making determined efforts to reduce its considerable Western debt.[28] There are murmurings from Prague about the need for economic rationalization, but here the paranoia over the consequences of economic reform dating back to the Prague Spring—the Sik psychosis—is likely to preclude any basic changes.[29] All in all, therefore, the outlook for economic reform is bleak. And there is yet no lead from the Soviet Union—no Liberman article in *Pravda* that was the starting gun for reform twenty years ago.[30] Without such an impetus one can expect little.

Economic dissatisfaction is, therefore, unlikely to be easily assuaged and, in the presumed absence of any bent for reform, it is likely to lead to more conservatism—more repressiveness when necessary—at all levels of the political leadership. And this trend might well be strengthened by uncertainty over the course of events in the Soviet Union.

DECLINE OF THE PARTY?

A possible trend, in light of recent developments in Poland, is worth examining more closely. There the party collapsed; so did the state apparatus except for the military and the security forces, which carried out the coup of 13 December 1981. Through them the party has been creeping back toward the center of the stage, where Soviet-style "real socialism" has fixed its position. But has a precedent been established here, one that could be invoked elsewhere? Other parties in Eastern Europe might crumble under less pressure than beset the Polish and have to be bailed out by army and police. Is it possible, therefore, that the Polish events may have begun a gradual shift in power relationships within the communist system? For Poland has dramatically demonstrated that, in the last analysis, the system's salvation rests, not with the party, but with the forces of coercion and repression. The militarist potential arising from the December coup has been referred to many times: the coup itself; General Jaruzelski's simultaneously holding the posts of first party secretary, prime minister, and minister of defense; senior officers filling other key posts; the militarization of key industries and, at the beginning, the media.[31] This pattern could be repeated elsewhere.

But the key role of the security apparatus should also be noted. It brings to mind the struggles of the post-Stalin party leaderships in the Soviet Union and several East European states to gain mastery over the police power. In Eastern Europe it was reflected at the highest level in spectacular duels between the party leader and the interior minister: Antonin Novotny against Rudolf Barak in Czechoslovakia;[32] Zhivkov against George Tsankov in Bulgaria,[33] Ceausescu against Alexandru Draghici in Romania.[34] first Gomulka and then Gierek against Mieczyslaw Moczar in Poland;[35] not to forget Tito (untouchable though he was) against Alexander Ranković in Yugoslavia.[36] (In Hungary the revolution broke the security apparatus. It was revived later but under Kadar's party control.) These struggles at the top were replicated at every level down the scale of authority until finally the party won. It was the biggest step away from Stalinism so far: everybody benefited. But was the victory final? As the system that has prevailed in Eastern Europe for more than thirty years becomes manifestly unviable, is the party now in the twilight of its power, propped up by the army, which never challenged it, and by the police, which it once mastered? Every effort, of course, is being made to revive the Polish party. It may become much smaller, leaner, and "fitter" (partly because nobody wants to join it and droves have left it). The trend toward mass parties in the entire region might be reversed. Attempts might be made to revive the elite or vanguard concept of the party. But how can this be done when communist idealism and motivation now scarcely exist? Only when it did exist—even if only fitfully— could party supremacy, strength, and resilience mean anything. The possibility, therefore, of this crucial shift in power relationships taking place should not be dismissed, particularly if the societal challenge to authority in Eastern Europe proves strong. The party, to be sure, would still remain formally and ritualistically in charge of everything as before. But the reality of power would be elsewhere—and would be seen to be so.

A Brighter Possibility?

Developments in Poland, however, could possibly point to a brighter future in Eastern Europe—at least in the short term—than any sketched out previously. The prospects at present seem almost totally dim, but some thoughtful Poles are not completely pessimistic—unlike the majority of their countrymen, who most definitely are. A confluence of forces and a constellation of circumstances could, say, in the next two to three years, come about in Poland leading to that genuine compromise or accord which all sides—the Jaruzelski government, the church, and underground Solidarity, which still holds the sympathy of most Poles—profess to desire. The ingredients needed would be Jaruzelski's sincerity; his ability to control those powerful reactionaries in and supporting his regime who want no compromise; firmness and skillful leadership from the church in both Warsaw and Rome; continued resistance tempered with moderation and flexibility on the part of underground Solidarity; continuation of mass sympathy for Solidarity yet mass readiness for a dignified compromise, especially on the future of the trade union movement, perhaps involving Solidarity's replacement by something less inspiring but still representative of many aspirations; and a continuation of the desperate economic situation, forcing all sides to come together to avert collapse.

Such a confluence of events is a tall order.[37] It calls for luck, strength, skill, moderation, and restraint—blessings that seldom coalesce even in the best of situations, let alone in the hate-charged atmosphere that characterizes Poland today. Its success would also obviously depend on acceptance by the Soviet Union under Chernenko. But this might not be as difficult to secure as it seems. The Soviets would have invaded Poland if they had considered it the only course left, but they desperately wanted to avoid doing so. The Polish army and security apparatus did their work for them—brilliantly, as it turned out. They have every reason to be satisfied with Jaruzelski and might accept a blueprint recommended by him containing all the necessary safeguards. They would do so reluctantly, as they did in the case of the Kadarite evolution. Jaruzelski has great bargaining leverage vis-à-vis Moscow if he wants to use it—as much as Kadar ever had with Khrushchev and later with Brezhnev. Does he realize it? Would he use it? This is probably the most crucial condition of all for the necessary compromise, and the enigma of Jaruzelski makes it impossible to answer. Time for him is running out. The reluctant and grudging hopes once placed in him need fulfillment. Otherwise his place in Polish history will be unenviable.

The odds against such a compromise, therefore, look depressingly long, but they could narrow as time—perhaps the most basic condition of all—tempers passion and obstinacy. If it were to succeed, the effect on the rest of Eastern Europe could be profound. Whereas many Poles would still view the compromise in terms of what they had lost, many other East Europeans would view it in terms of what they might gain—in the case of the Hungarians, of what they might maintain. The fears many expressed over the rise of Solidarity—that it would lead to a severe Soviet response engulfing them all and the relief, even *Schadenfreude*, after the December coup—would dissolve into a cautious optimism about their own future. Reform would be permissible; reformers could come out from hiding.

Again it is a picture closer to the ideal than the real, but it is not to be discounted entirely. And pessimists could rightly point out that, even if it did materialize, it could bring only short-term relief to the inexorable trend toward the decay of the system in Eastern Europe. Only basic changes of principle, policies, and methods can reverse that trend—and obviously no remedy presented by Jaruzelski and approved by the Kremlin is going to involve these. But such a compromise could be all that was attainable at present and, most important, it would buy time: time that staves off disaster; time that could give the unexpected a chance to appear, to transform, to transmute.

THE WESTERN FACTOR IN THE FUTURE

The Western economic factor, negligible until the late 1960s, began playing a major role in Eastern Europe in the 1970s. When efficiently used, as in Hungary, Western credits contributed to economic progress. When squandered, as in Poland and Romania, they added to the nightmare. They also had profound effects other than economic. Before the bubble burst in the summer of 1980, they had resulted in a dramatic shift of Polish trade toward the West and had enabled Hungary to chart new paths in trade with the West which were not without political and diplomatic significance. Barred from pursuing an independent foreign policy, Hungary sought compensation in seeking an independent foreign trade policy.[38] Western credits also buttressed, for a time, the ramshackle Romanian regime's determination to keep the Soviet Union at arm's length.

The role of Western credits in postponing the necessity of initiating economic reform had indirect political results. The forces of conservatism that feared the political consequences of economic change were strengthened. Now, the adverse effects of Western credits are evident in every country except Hungary, which used the credits well, and Czechoslovakia, which took hardly any. They have simply added hugely to the accumulating economic difficulties. Paying them back seems almost impossible. Moreover, after first seeming to foster more independent attitudes, they are now tending to force the East European debtors back toward the Soviet Union and CMEA.[39] Internationally, the prospect of defaults has led to widespread nervousness and fierce debate about consequences.

What, then, should Western policy toward Eastern Europe be now? The East European members of the Warsaw Pact cannot help themselves, nor can the Soviet Union for any length of time. The fate of Eastern Europe, its future domestic and foreign policies, therefore, could lie in the hands of the West.

What are the immediate alternatives for the West, making, of course, the immodest assumption that at least a modicum of coordination among the major Western powers, public and private, could be reached? They would seem to be the following: (1) Declare debtor countries in difficulties with repayment—Poland and Romania—to be in default and break all economic relations with the East European states generally. This option now seems unlikely but could be revived. (2) Show patience over rescheduling but offer no more economic help. (3) Put together a package of economic and financial aid, without preconditions, for East European economies in difficulties. (4) Use the "carrot and stick" approach. This would involve offering generous rescheduling terms, further credits, and economic aid, provided that meaningful economic reforms are undertaken, their political consequences accepted, and elementary human rights guaranteed.

At the risk of being prescriptive rather than analytical, it is worth speculating on the possible effects of these different options. Both the first and second would almost certainly produce serious breakdowns in many branches of organized life, sending the standards of living plummeting further. They might hasten discontent and possibly violence, repression, and Soviet intervention.

The third option, hardly a likely one, would simply reward inefficiency, coerciveness, conservatism, and cynicism. Much more obviously, and less excusable than in the 1970s, it would give a moribund system yet another new lease on life.

It is the fourth option, already much touted in the Western media, that captures the imagination without necessarily blunting a sense of realism. It would be denounced, of course, by the Soviet and East European leaderships as the most blatant interference; but in the face of what could be approaching disaster, how long would they be able to preach—or practice—pride and principle? The great mass of the East European populations would support it strongly.

East Europeans, however, would not support a Western policy that seemed to be using them as a pawn in larger struggles involving East and West or in diplomatic tangles that have no bearing on them. A Soviet invasion of Poland, for example, might have strengthened the NATO alliance but would not have done much for the average Pole. Nor does Poland's involvement in the second half of 1982 in the huge Atlantic row over the Soviet gas pipeline project seem relevant to Poles. If Western involvement in Eastern Europe is to mean anything to East Europeans it must be, and be perceived as, primarily in their interests. They have been used by others too often in history to like it—and to be unaware of it.

The risks of involvement would, of course, be enormous. If not adopted consistently, patiently, and with some unison by the Western powers, it could result in a grotesque disproportion between small reforms and large volumes of aid. The fourth option would then turn out to be no different from the third. On the other hand, if the effects were too swiftly and demonstrably successful, the ensuing change could alarm even an indecisive Soviet Union, with the same result as in August 1968. Also, where would the new reform leaders come from? Because the present political elites are corrupt, they would obviously have to come from deeper down in the political and especially the economic and intellectual hierarchies and from outside the power structure. There they could presumably be found. Capable, dedicated people, party and nonparty, still exist who would react positively to the prospects presented, as was demonstrated in Poland between August 1980 and December 1981.

Whatever happens, the West, whether through commission or omission, will play a major role. The paradox is obvious: at a time when detente is being buried by some participants, when many aspects of East-West relations have slowed or are at a standstill, the West through a fortuitous combination of circumstances is entering its most important—perhaps its most constructive—period of relations with Eastern Europe in forty years. In the early 1960s the notion of peaceful engagement by the West in Eastern Europe was touted.[40] Perhaps it was too early then. In a year or two from now it might be too late.

[9]

Intrabloc Economic Relations and Prospects

PAUL MARER

This chapter examines three sets of issues that describe the economic context in which the Warsaw Pact functions. First, the evolution of Soviet–East European economic relations from the late 1940s until the early 1980s is discussed. These relations in the more recent period are then examined in a cost-benefit framework, contrasting the different views on whether Eastern Europe is an economic asset or a liability for the USSR. This middle section concludes with observations on the relationship between economic subsidies and dependence and the use of political-military leverage by the USSR. The final section looks ahead to the rest of the 1980s. The economic forecast shows that even though there are very important differences in the environments, economic systems, and policies of the Warsaw Pact countries, at the beginning of the decade the region as a whole entered a new and fundamentally more difficult economic era with implications for political stability, alliance cohesion, and military burden-sharing. The section concludes with a discussion of the future prospects for trade and economic reforms in the region.

POSTWAR EVOLUTION OF SOVIET–EAST EUROPEAN ECONOMIC RELATIONS

During the first postwar decade, the Soviet concept of regional economic integration was for each East European country to carry out Soviet instructions. Eastern Europe is defined here as the six Warsaw Pact members: Bulgaria, Czechoslovakia, the German Democratic Republic, Hungary, Poland, and Romania. The orders given by the

USSR under Stalin were demonstrably exploitive. Rough calculations show that the Soviets used methods ranging from war reparations to joint stock companies to unfair prices in trade to obtain unrequited resources roughly estimated to have totaled about $14 billion, with East Germany bearing the brunt of this burden. This was approximately the same amount as was spent by the United States in Western Europe under the Marshall Plan.[1]

Soviet economic policy toward Eastern Europe changed markedly after 1956, when the high political cost of economic extraction and pervasive direct interference was brought home to the Russian leaders by the uprisings, revolts, and revolutions in East Germany, Hungary, and Poland. The discrediting of certain aspects of Stalin's dictatorial methods also influenced policy. Furthermore, as the Western embargo was relaxed and as the more developed East European countries fell behind Western technological standards, the USSR probably began, gradually, to attach less strategic importance to imports from Eastern Europe.

The essence of the post-1956 policy was an effort to move trade with Eastern Europe toward a more equitable, commercial basis. The Soviet Union has continued to view its trade with Eastern Europe as yielding important economic, military, security, ideological, and political benefits.

This background provided the basis for the Soviet decision to activate the Council for Mutual Economic Assistance in the late 1950s. Economic integration among a group of centrally planned economies is fundamentally different from that among market economies, such as in the European Economic Community. In the West, much of international commerce is conducted by private enterprise seeking profit opportunities so that a reduction of barriers to the movement of goods, factors of production, and money across national borders is integrative. By contrast, for a country under central planning, all movement of goods and factors across national borders requires explicit government action. Agreement about specialization is difficult to reach, as is finding a workable mechanism to implement agreed-upon policies. Suggestions for CMEA integration have ranged from Khrushchev's proposal in the early 1960s for a supranational authority that would extend the traditional institutions of central planning to the regional level to Hungarian and Polish proposals favoring greater reliance on market mechanisms. Khrushchev's proposal brought to the surface the fear of the East European countries that bloc integration under a supranational authority would mean even more domination by the USSR. The most uncompromising stand against supranationalism was taken by Romania. Perhaps recalling that earlier pressures on Yugoslavia and Albania had contributed to those countries' defection from the bloc, the USSR decided not to press its proposals.

During the 1960s, economic integration among the Warsaw Pact countries proceeded on two bases. One was technical decisions involving large, blocwide infrastructure projects such as electricity grids and oil pipelines, for which engineering considerations provided the economic rationale. The other was Soviet willingness to export increased quantities of energy and raw materials in exchange for East European manufactured products.

Joint CMEA investment projects represented the major new form of regionwide activity during the 1970s. The Soviet Union pressed the East European countries to participate in joint investment projects, pointing out that it had the natural resources which such projects would exploit.

The total value of joint investment projects agreed upon for the 1976–1980 period was approximately $12 billion. The largest undertaking was the Orenburg project, consisting of a natural gas complex at Orenburg in Siberia and a 2,667km natural gas pipeline connecting it with the Soviet Union's western border. The low and high estimated costs of the project were from $5 to 6 billion, so that it alone accounted for about 50 percent of the value of all CMEA joint investment projects during the period. Approximately half of the total cost—about $2.5 billion—was spent on materials (mainly pipe) and equipment (mainly compressor stations), 80 percent or more purchased from Western countries on credit. The second largest joint undertaking was a giant pulp mill at Ust Ilim in Central Siberia—the largest forest-based industrial complex in the USSR.

The two features that distinguish the Orenburg and Ust Ilim projects from all other joint CMEA investment projects are the participation of the investing countries in the construction on the territory of the host country (the earlier CMEA projects were jointly planned but not jointly built, each country being responsible for construction on its territory) and the extensive contribution of Western technology, machinery, equipment, and financing. The ownership benefits, however, accrue to the USSR. It is repaying the East European countries' investment with resulting products at a 2 percent simple interest rate. The East European countries do gain, however, certain quantities of assured supplies and enjoy price concessions as long as CMEA prices are set on the basis of historical world market prices and as long as world market prices of energy and raw materials continue upward.

The joint investment formula used for the Orenburg project apparently is not being continued during the 1980s, certainly not on the scale implemented during 1976–1980. The reasons for this pullback are a growing perception in Eastern Europe, and possibly in the USSR, of the excessive costs of such projects; the immense logistical problems of employing large East European work crews in a faraway region with a hostile climate; the difficulty of finding mutually acceptable cost and profitability calculations in the absence of meaningful prices, exchange rates, and convertibility; and the exhaustion of pipeline projects, which lend themselves more readily to joint construction and financing than projects in the manufacturing sector. Instead of the Orenburg formula, there appears to be a new emphasis on bilaterally determined investment specialization in the East European economies to provide machinery and other inputs for multilateral resource developments projects in the USSR.

COST-BENEFIT ANALYSIS OF SOVIET–EAST EUROPEAN ECONOMIC RELATIONS

CMEA countries employ different pricing mechanisms in East-West and in intra-CMEA trade. With partners outside the bloc they try to trade at current world market prices, generally succeeding in imports but obtaining lower prices on exports; in intrabloc trade, prices are linked to Western world market prices of an earlier period, according to formulas periodically agreed upon. Western prices are used because each CMEA country sets its domestic prices differently and essentially arbitrarily, so that no country is willing to accept the prices of the others for valuing exports and imports.

One consequence of this price-setting mechanism is that it prompts bargaining because it is difficult to establish the precise world market price, especially for manufactured products. A very important aspect of bargaining is that power may be exerted through prices (obtaining high prices for exports and paying low prices for imports) or through quantities (supplying small or zero quantities of goods and forcing the trade partner to sell certain goods in specified quantities). Thus the price of a commodity may be high or low relative to current world prices because the price that is out of line may be compensated by offsetting deviations in the prices or quantities of other export and import items; one country exploits or subsidizes the other; or current world market prices have moved higher or lower than the historical Western prices on which the CMEA price is based.

[218]

CMEA prices can be determined relatively easily for energy, raw materials, and other primary products because these are mostly standardized commodities traded on the world markets at published prices. Between 1973 and 1982 world prices of energy and many raw materials rose sharply; CMEA prices, because of the price rule, more slowly. Thus as net exporter of energy and raw materials, the USSR has obtained for those goods prices lower than current world prices, which one may call implicit Soviet subsidy to Eastern Europe. For most manufactured goods, there is a world market price range for similar but in most cases not identical products. There is very little accurate information on intra-CMEA prices of manufactured goods; what there is suggests that prices may be relatively high, though much of the evidence is for the 1960s.

A significant recent development complicating any cost-benefit analysis is that a growing share of intrabloc trade is valued at current world market prices and settled in convertible currency. This trade involves goods in strong demand in the bloc exported to a CMEA partner over and above the quantities agreed upon in the five-year trade agreements. Thus a certain portion of Soviet oil and raw materials is sold to the East European countries at current world prices and paid in dollars, and a portion of Soviet imports from Eastern Europe is also priced and settled in the same way. No systematic information is available on the size and balance of this trade except for Hungary, for which it represents 8 to 10 percent of its trade with the socialist countries.

In addition to this direct trade there is also indirect convertible currency trade. The latter refers to the import content of East European exports to the USSR and other CMEA countries that have to be purchased from the West for convertible currencies, which, according to the calculations reported by Hungarian economists, have increased rapidly in recent years.[2]

Credits are among the most important and complex issues in Soviet–East European economic relations. The size of credits, the type of goods or currency in which the loans are given, settlement provisions, and the grant equivalent of credits jointly determine the distribution of costs and benefits in a loan transaction. In recent years credit transactions between the USSR and the East European countries have become significant, but no comprehensive, balance-of-payments accounting is available on them. During 1971–1973, the East European countries combined had a positive trade balance with the USSR of about $2 billion. During 1974–1981, however, East Europe had a negative trade balance in every year, the cumulative total reaching about $10 billion, a portion of which represents ten-year Soviet terms of trade credits, publicly announced.

A great deal of uncertainty, however, surrounds the interpretation of the observed trade balances because they typically reflect some combination of delays in planned deliveries by one partner, settlement of balances on invisible transactions, extensions of new credits, and repayment of earlier loans. Matters are further complicated by the involvement of the CMEA's International Bank for Economic Cooperation (IBEC) and the International Investment Bank (IIB) in convertible currency credit transactions. Only one side of such a transaction appears in intra-CMEA trade statistics. In recent years the IBEC and IIB have borrowed, in behalf jointly of the USSR and the East European countries, billions of Eurodollars, primarily to finance Western imports for CMEA projects located in the USSR such as the Orenburg gas pipeline. The East European countries are responsible for servicing their share of these loans. The USSR repays with additional gas shipments that may show up as a Soviet trade surplus with Eastern Europe while the hard currency portion of the credits the East European countries have given to the USSR remain invisible. A further important aspect of such credits is that although the East European countries pay the Euromarket rate of interest, which in recent years fluctuated between 8 and 20 percent per annum, they receive from the USSR between 2 and 5 percent interest per annum. These transfers may be considered partial offsets to the implicit or explicit subsidies the USSR may grant to Eastern Europe on its commodity exports and imports.

This background discussion has indicated some of the conceptual and practical problems of carrying out an accurate cost-benefit analysis of Soviet–East European economic relations; quantification is also hampered by insufficient data. Therefore, the conclusion one reaches will be influenced by how the problem is conceptualized, what assumptions are made, whether the time horizon is the short run or the long run, and whether the perspective is that of the USSR or that of one or another East European country.

Two American economists, Michael Marrese and Jan Vanous, have recently published dramatically high and controversial estimates of Soviet subsidies to Eastern Europe.[3] According to their calculations, from 1960 to 1980 Soviet subsidies to the six East European countries totaled $65 billion. These estimates have been prominently reported in influential publications, such as the *Wall Street Journal* (15 January 1982), *Time* (18 January 1982), and *Fortune* (13 July 1982).

Marrese and Vanous conceptualize the problem by posing the following question: would the Soviet Union have been better off if it could have substituted trade with the industrial West, settled in dollars, for the transactions it entered into with the six East European countries, settled (mainly) in transferable rubles? The prices paid to or received from the West represent the Soviets' opportunity cost, hence trade should be repriced and revalued at those hypothetical dollar prices.

Estimating the true dollar value of Soviet–East European trade in energy, raw materials, and semimanufactured products is possible with modest error margins because most of these commodities can be repriced meaningfully in dollars. Not so, however, for intrabloc trade in manufactured products. To price these goods, Marrese and Vanous were forced to make two crucial assumptions: (1) that intra-CMEA prices of manufactures are 25 percent higher than world market (that is, West selling to West) prices, and (2) that the Soviet Union and the East European countries could sell to the West the manufactured goods they trade with each other only at a 50 percent discount from the world market (West to West) price because of the poor quality of these products. Although there is strong evidence that the East can sell its manufactured products only at a substantial discount, the size of the assumed discount is arbitrary. The larger the assumed East-to-West discount and the larger the assumed difference between CMEA and West-West price levels, the lower will be the estimated dollar value of the machinery and industrial manufactures traded. Since the East European countries are large net exporters of these commodities to the USSR, the estimated dollar value of their exports will be small and the amount of computed Soviet subsidy very large.

It is my view that even if one accepts the Marrese-Vanous conceptualization of the problem, their estimated subsidy on trade in manufactures is biased upward for several reasons. One is that even if intra-CMEA prices were higher than West-West prices in the 1960s, they probably increased less than world market prices during the 1970s, so that the gap has narrowed. Regarding the second assumption, even if Marrese and Vanous guessed correctly that the East could export its manufactures to the West only at a 50 percent discount, it is important to note that such a large discount arises for three sets of reasons. One is the poor quality of the East's products. Another is the systemic shortcomings of Eastern export pricing, including exporting on the basis of plan directives, which impedes the flexibility required to obtain the best price. The East frequently enters into barter and compensation deals inconvenient for the Western partner, who therefore discounts substantially the price of such products. Persistent hard-currency balance-of-payments pressures may also force Eastern countries to make drastic price concessions to acquire hard currency. The third set of reasons for the Eastern export price discount is Western discrimination in the form of high tariff and nontariff impediments to CMEA exports. For example, the CMEA states are just about the only countries in Europe without preferential access to the EEC, their main export market, because nonmember European (and many Third World) countries receive tariff and nontariff preferences under various agreements.

Since Marrese and Vanous argue that a portion of Soviet subsidy arises because the Soviet Union pays more for imports from Eastern Europe than it would have to pay if the same goods were purchased from the industrial West, the correct dollar opportunity cost is not East to West export prices, which is what they use, but East from West import prices. The point is that if the Soviet Union imported the same manufactured goods from the West it now purchases from Eastern Europe, it would not be able to obtain as large discounts as when the East exports those products to the West because the second and third sets of discount factors would be absent. This point is missed by Marrese and Vanous, who assume that they can substitute East European export prices for Soviet import prices to value Soviet purchases from Eastern Europe. This assumption introduces a very strong bias.

Marrese and Vanous are probably correct that, as net importer of manufactures, the USSR provides some subsidy to the exporters, but not enough statistically meaningful information is available to put a dollar price tag on the amounts that might be involved. Until further, more reliable computations can be carried out, a preliminary resolution of the debate requires that the subsidy estimates be decomposed into amounts that arise because the Soviet Union sells to Eastern Europe its net exports of primary products below world market prices (which are acceptable estimates) and the Soviet Union pays for its net imports of manufactures higher than world market prices (which are unacceptable). Net Soviet subsidies and taxes on 1960–1980 trade with Eastern Europe by five commodity groups are presented in Table 9.1, including annual figures for 1971–1980. Of the total cumulative subsidy of $65 billion, $39 billion, or 60 percent is accounted for by net Soviet imports of manufactures and 40 percent by Soviet exports of primary products. Net fuel exports dominate the latter category, accounting for 43 percent of all subsidies. More than half of the cumulative 1960–1980 total fuel subsidy of about $28 billion arose in 1980 and was the result of the explosion of the world market price of crude oil in 1979 and 1980, which the CMEA price formula and other

Table 9.1. Net Soviet subsidies (+) and taxes (−) on trade with six East European countries combined by major commodity groups, 1960–80 (millions of current dollars)

Year	Total (1)	Fuel (2)	Nonfood raw materials and semimanufacturing (3)	Agriculture (4)	Primary products (2) + (3) + (4) (5)	Machinery (6)	Industrial consumer goods (7)	Manufactures (6) + (7) (8)
1960–70	3,862	−2,099	−3,502	−594	−6,195 (−160%)	4,953	5,104	10,057 (260%)
1971	900	−31	−311	−38	−380 (−42%)	472	808	1,280 (142%)
1972	1,134	−114	−411	22	−503 (−44%)	736	901	1,637 (144%)
1973	2,001	293	−132	2	163 (8%)	934	904	1,838 (92%)
1974	6,227	3,525	1,450	215	5,190 (83%)	449	588	1,037 (17%)
1975	5,030	2,028	31	496	2,555 (51%)	1,304	1,171	2,475 (49%)
1976	5,144	2,547	43	298	2,888 (56%)	1,155	1,101	2,256 (44%)
1977	5,209	2,333	106	288	2,727 (52%)	1,165	1,317	2,482 (48%)
1978	5,637	959	−145	345	1,159 (21%)	2,856	1,622	4,478 (79%)
1979	9,653	4,041	−376	481	4,146 (43%)	3,527	1,981	5,508 (47%)
1980	20,482	14,294	−341	477	14,430 (70%)	3,933	2,120	6,053 (30%)
Totals								
1960–80	65,279	27,776	−3,588	1,992	26,180 (40%)	21,484	17,617	39,101 (60%)
As percent of total								
1960–80	100%	43%	−5%	3%	(40%)	33%	27%	(60%)
1960–79	100%	30%	−7%	3%	(26%)	39%	35%	(46%)

SOURCE: Michael Marrese and Jan Vanous, *Soviet Subsidization of Trade with Eastern Europe: A Soviet Perspective* (Berkeley: Institute of International Studies of the University of California, 1983), Table 5 (1960–78 data) and Table 13 (1979–80 data, using the method shown on p. 39/a to decompose subsidies and taxes by commodity groups).

considerations did not allow the Soviet Union to pass on to Eastern Europe.

During the 1973–1980 period, the USSR is shown to have been subsidizing the East European countries to the tune of $60 billion, of which $34 billion (56 percent) arose from USSR net sales of primary products, mainly fuel ($30 billion), and $26 billion (44 percent) from USSR net purchases of manufactures.

The distribution of the subsidies by countries and commodity groups is determined by the CMEA price system and the commodity composition of trade, the latter a function of an East European country's level of development and resource endowment, as well as Soviet willingness to supply energy and other "hard goods" to its trade partners. Thus both the GDR and Czechoslovakia, being relatively poor in energy and raw materials, import large quantities of these commodities from the USSR, which, along with the CMEA price formula, yielded $4.8 and $2.6 billion in subsidies to them, respectively, during 1971–1978, an amount that would be significantly higher if the 1979–1980 subsidy breakdown were available by commodities and countries. For both countries, however, even larger subsidies were granted by the Soviet Union on manufactures, $5.4 (53 percent of total) and $3.6 (59 percent of total) billion, respectively, amounts which of course are not acceptable, for the reasons indicated.

Poland and Hungary, being better endowed with primary products (Poland with energy, Hungary with agricultural goods), received not only smaller subsidies on primary products than the GDR and Czechoslovakia but also a smaller share of their total subsidy (37 and 25 percent, respectively) derived from primary products (Table 9.2).

Bulgaria is the most poorly endowed East European country in energy and imports a large part of its total energy consumption from the USSR with which the predominant share of its global trade is conducted. It is for this reason primarily that 71 percent ($3.5 billion) of its 1971–1978 subsidy of $5 billion is on trade in primary products. The remaining almost $1.5 billion subsidy is on manufactures, of which Bulgaria became a large net exporter to the USSR in the 1970s. Thus Bulgaria's heavy dependence on the USSR and poor resource endowment explains much of the relatively large subsidy it receives, although preferential treatment by the USSR (which is the main explanation of Marrese and Vanous) may also be an important factor.

Romania has received only small subsidies because until recently it was self-sufficient in energy, because a much smaller share of its trade has been with the USSR than for the other countries of Eastern Europe (until recently, partly or mainly its own choice), and because it is the only East European country to which the USSR is still a large net exporter of machinery. During the last few years, when suddenly Romania needed large energy imports, it was unable to obtain these from the USSR except in small amounts and for convertible currency, whereas Bulgaria and the other East European countries, long dependent on Soviet energy, have had continued access to Soviet supplies.

In sum, since 1974, when the price of energy and some raw materials skyrocketed, Eastern Europe has benefited from the inertia built into the CMEA price mechanism. Although it was not so intended, the price system has become a vehicle for implicit subsidies in trade. Soviet policy makers have not intended to transfer these grants, but political considerations have led them to accept them.[4] For example, in 1975 the CMEA price of crude oil was only about half of the world price. Between 1976 and 1980, when the world price rose only moderately, the price of Soviet oil exports continued to increase so that by early 1979 the Soviet and world prices were almost equal. When the world price shot upward again during 1979–1980, the price of oil exports to Eastern Europe again became only about 50 percent of the world price. Since 1982, however, the gap—and thus the implicit subsidy—has declined rapidly as world energy prices softened while intra-CMEA prices continued to rise; in a few years Eastern Europe may be subsidizing the USSR by paying above world prices.

The conclusion reached by Marrese and Vanous is that the USSR would be much better off economically if it reoriented trade away from Eastern Europe. By implication, the East European countries would be very much worse off if that were to happen.

The East European perspective on this issue is quite different. East European economists would point out that the benefit of Soviet price subsidies is offset, at least in part, because the Soviet Union imposes on them very different composition and quantities of imports and exports than they would choose freely at the prices prevailing. To be sure, these costs would be even more difficult to quantify than the Soviet disadvantage conceptualized by Marrese and Vanous. This is not to deny that all the East European countries would face tremendous economic problems if they were forced, on very short notice, to reorient all of trade from the CMEA to the world market. The reason essentially is that many of their producers are not equipped to stand their ground in world market export competition. But the East Europeans would also note that this cost was imposed on them largely by the USSR, which forced them to adopt a Soviet-style economic system and development model. Moreover, being pulled into a political-military alliance with the USSR has forced them to espouse an adversary

Table 9.2. Net Soviet subsidies (+) and taxes (−) on trade with East European countries by major commodity groups, 1960–80, by subperiods (millions of current dollars)

Year	Total (1)	Fuel (2)	Nonfood raw materials and semimanufacturing (3)	Agriculture (4)	Primary products (2) + (3) + (4) (5)	Machinery (6)	Industrial consumer goods (7)	Manufactures (6) + (7) (8)
GDR								
1960–70	2,297	−597	−886	−373	−1,856	2,843	1,310	4,153 (181%)
1971–78	10,196	3,523	1,160	156	4,839	3,911	1,446	5,357 (53%)
1978–79	3,400							
1979–80	7,200				(47%)			
Czechoslovakia								
1960–70	1,303	−708	−548	−248	−1,504	1,931	876	2,807 (215%)
1971–78	6,166	3,110	−638	81	2,553	2,387	1,226	3,613 (59%)
1978–79	2,000				(−115%)			
1979–80	4,100				(41%)			
Poland								
1960–70	730	−281	−519	−107	−907	792	845	1,637 (224%)
1971–78	5,573	1,992	−5	75	2,062	1,476	2,035	3,511 (63%)
1978–79	1,700				(−124%)			
1979–80	3,500				(37%)			

Hungary

Period										
1960–79	659	−422	−395	−11	−828	(126%)	683	804	1,487	(226%)
1971–78	3,910	609	51	305	965	(25%)	1,453	1,492	2,945	(75)
1978–79	1,200									
1979–80	2,600									

Bulgaria

Period										
1960–70	−863	−318	−628	110	−836	(−97%)	−760	733	−27	(−3%)
1971–78	4,906	2,190	464	826	3,480	(71%)	542	884	1,426	(29)
1978–79	2,000									
1979–80	4,100									

Romania

Period										
1960–70	−271	223	−526	33	−270	(−100%)	−536	535	−1	(0%)
1971–78	537	119	−401	187	−95	(−18%)	−698	1,330	632	(118%)
1978–79	100									
1979–80	200									

NOTE: The 1979–1980 totals are slightly higher than those shown in Table 9.3 because of differences in the treatment of transferable ruble trade balances.

SOURCE: Marrese and Vanous, *Soviet Subsidization of Trade*, Appendix Tables 32–37.

relationship with the West, which denied them technology and other trade benefits, although more so in the 1950s than in the 1970s.[5] Many East European economists would note also that the Soviet market's willingness to absorb poor quality goods and obsolete equipment appears to be an advantage only in the short term and will impose a large cost in the long run because it reduces the pressure and incentive to innovate and produce for the market, causing their firms to fall more and more behind competitors on the world market. This cost appears to fall mainly on the more advanced CMEA countries—the GDR, Czechoslovakia, Hungary, and Poland. The "bill" is presented when they must expand their manufactures exports on the world market to pay for goods and services unavailable on the protected CMEA market.

One might note also that public opinion in most of the East European countries—in Poland most emphatically—believes that the Soviet Union continues to exploit them economically. Unscientific as this opinion may be, it reflects some combination of the public's distrust in its country's leadership, which it sees as being subservient to Russia in many ways, skepticism that the Russians would discontinue economic exploitation (well documented for the Stalin era), desire for a scapegoat to blame for their country's economic problems, and a fundamental belief that the Russians ultimately are responsible for maintaining an inefficient economic system in their country.

By contrast, the official Soviet view appears to be that in recent years the USSR has provided significant subsidies to Eastern Europe, the amount being a function of the volume of energy and raw materials sold (net) at below current world market prices.

I would be surprised, however, if Soviet economists and policy makers would consider trade in manufactured products as embodying significant subsidies. Public opinion in the USSR, however, appears to be closer to the Marrese-Vanous view in that it considers much of trade as fraternal assistance to cement the alliance. For the average Russian, evidence to support this view is the significantly higher living standards in most of the East European countries than in the USSR.

Whatever the differences in the cost-benefit perceptions on Soviet–East European economic relations, it still appears paradoxical that the CMEA's strongest economic and political power would agree to prices and to a division of labor that in some ways are disadvantageous for the USSR. There are probably several explanations: economic, historical, and political. In the 1950s the exchange of primary products for East European manufactured goods was advantageous for the USSR because its partners were able to supply machinery and other manufactures denied to the Soviets by the Western embargo and because there was no world shortage of energy and raw materials and therefore no strong demand for Russia's supplies. By the 1960s the pattern of Soviet trade with Eastern Europe became to some extent ossified, and planners on both sides had gotten used to the routinized bilateral trading relationship. Moreover, during this period there was not great economic pressure on the USSR to alter the trade pattern because it was able to expand energy and raw material production rapidly and at a reasonable cost.

During the 1970s circumstances changed. The Soviet Union's rapid expansion of trade with the West increased the opportunity cost of being a large net supplier of "hard goods" to Eastern Europe, as did the rising domestic cost of extracting and transporting these commodities from the increasingly remote Siberian oil and gas fields and mining regions. The Soviet Union began to complain that some of its trade with Eastern Europe was disadvantageous. But a very important mitigating circumstance was the large windfall gain the USSR enjoyed arising from its improved terms of trade with the West, the rising price of gold, and its ability to tap into the Organization of Petroleum Exporting Countries (OPEC) surplus by selling military hardware to these countries. During 1973–1980 these windfall gains may have yielded the USSR in the neighborhood of $50 billion, enabling it to increase its hard currency export revenues almost as rapidly as it expanded its hard currency imports, that is, without having to incur an excessively large foreign debt. Thus the opportunity cost of supplying increased amounts of energy and raw materials to Eastern Europe, even at subsidized prices, did not appear to be a crushing burden. Moreover, the USSR managed to obtain at least partial compensation, in the form of East European investment contributions, partly in hard currency; agreements to settle a portion of intra-CMEA trade in convertible currency; and East European subsidies to the non-European members of the CMEA—Mongolia, Cuba, and Vietnam—which, along with proxy interventions in Third World countries (especially by East Germany) have supported the Soviet Union's global political and military objectives.

Furthermore, during the 1970s the rate of growth of the volume of Soviet hard goods exports to Eastern Europe declined steeply, prompting the East European countries to step up purchases from the world market, forcing them to assume considerable additional burdens trying to earn or borrow the requisite hard currency.

Toward the end of the 1970s another factor became increasingly important in Soviet calculations: the growing economic weakness of the East European countries and the related political instability, actual or potential. This factor has prompted the Soviet leaders to proceed cautiously about raising export prices too steeply or curtailing energy and raw material shipments too precipitously.

Has the USSR used economic leverage to achieve its military or political objectives in Eastern Europe because the countries are un-questionably dependent on the USSR (as they are on the West also), both in their obvious need for Soviet supplies and markets and in the more subtle sense of countries receiving a "subsidy" being depen-dent on the country that bestows it? The usual inference is that the USSR, having a much smaller stake in bilateral economic relations than the East European countries, is able to bend these customers to its will by threats that the economic benefits might otherwise be withdrawn.

Economic dependence does not, however, translate automatically into leverage that can be exercised freely.[6] First, a superpower like the USSR is normally preoccupied with its more vital other interests around the globe. As long as Eastern Europe was calm, the Soviet Union's global political ambitions tended to reduce their relative im-portance. Disparity of economic size and political importance gener-ates disparity of attention, or at least high-level attention, that is especially important in Soviet decision making and mitigates against the blatant use of economic leverage by lower-level officials.

Second, the use of leverage is more likely if the desired quid pro quo is very important and if the dependent country has unified lead-ership which begins to oppose the USSR (if the leadership is not united, the Soviets are more likely to find other avenues to exert pressure). But it is precisely in such a situation that the use of lever-age is the most risky. In the past, the Soviet Union has attempted to use economic leverage to try to maintain foreign policy conformity in the region. But as its experience with Yugoslavia and Albania shows, the ability to inflict economic deprivation is more apparent than the willingness of the dependent country to accept it or to switch to new economic and political patrons.

A third consideration limiting the use of economic leverage, es-pecially today, is the growing economic weakness of the East Euro-pean countries. To the extent that the explosion in Poland was trig-gered at least partly by the country's deteriorating economy, the Soviet Union must be doubly cautious in threatening or using eco-nomic disruption.

[230]

This enumeration of the limitations on the use of economic leverage is not intended to suggest that Soviet–East European trade is guided only by commercial considerations. It is bilateral bargaining between governments in which economic, political, and perhaps military issues are intertwined, though exactly how and to what degree is not known. On issues the Soviets consider important, such as to have an East European country contribute more resources to build up the Warsaw Pact militarily or to provide more economic help to Poland, there is no need to use blatant economic leverage to get approximately what the Soviets want. For instance, if they believe that an East European country can and should contribute more to Poland and the country is unwilling, the Soviets can divert some hard goods deliveries from the country to Poland or insist that a larger portion be settled in convertible currency. In recent years, Soviet energy and raw material shipments to the East European countries have stagnated and in some cases declined. It is difficult to ascertain to what extent this trend might reflect slowed demand by an East European country as its growth rate declines and it conserves scarce resources, across-the-board cuts in deliveries to the region triggered by the Soviets' own economic problems, or the application of subtle economic leverage to achieve desired ends. All one can say is that neither logic nor the admittedly incomplete evidence that is available suggests that in recent years the Soviets have relied in a major way on economic leverage to have the East European countries comply with this or that Soviet political or military objective.

ECONOMIC PROSPECTS AND IMPLICATIONS

All the East European countries are small or medium-sized economies, which means that they are heavily dependent on foreign trade, including trade with the West, since they cannot satisfy fully from domestic and CMEA sources all the energy, raw materials, intermediate products, and modern technology their economies need to function smoothly. Eastern Europe's Western imports must increasingly be paid for by exporting manufactured products.

During the last three decades the East European countries appear to have performed well, some exceptionally well, by international comparisons. Western experts consider the exceptionally high growth rates reported by some East European countries to be exaggerated because of unconventional statistical methods of index number construction. More important is the fact that the growth rate of output should not be the only performance indicator; that would be like judging the performance of an automobile on the basis of speed only, disregarding economy of operations and passenger comfort. The performance of an economy, too, should be evaluated by multiple indicators, including efficiency, consumer satisfaction, and the external trade and financial balance. If these factors are taken into account, their economic achievements are less spectacular, even though during the past thirty years the countries were able to make good economic progress. The least developed countries grew faster than the more developed ones, so that the development gap has narrowed. One reason for the relatively good growth performance is that a traditional, Soviet-style centrally planned economy is able to mobilize unemployed and underemployed resources which, for a time, can generate impressive increments to output. But in the case of Eastern Europe, a further reason was that until the beginning of this decade, the countries were able to rely on three consecutive sets of temporary support mechanisms.

During the early 1950s, the regimes used extreme methods to mobilize unemployed or underemployed resources and to squeeze agriculture and the consumer to finance a rapid growth in investments. These strong-arm methods, however, proved to be economically and politically counterproductive. Political excesses and the absence of material incentives undermined political stability and the economic efficiency of resource use.

During the 1960s, the East European economies were boosted by increased trade with the USSR, exchanging Soviet energy and raw materials for machinery and other manufactured products. Energy and raw materials were obtained cheaply, reflecting the favorable prices of these products on the world market. By the early 1970s, however, the Soviet Union concluded that large increases in energy and raw materials exports in exchange for manufactured products were no longer in its economic interest. During the 1970s the annual increments of Soviet exports to Eastern Europe slowed; by the early 1980s their absolute level began to stagnate (in volume, not in value), exerting further economic pressure on Eastern Europe. Furthermore, since the mid-1970s, the cost of Eastern Europe's energy and raw material imports from the USSR has been rising much more rapidly than the price of Eastern Europe's exports to the USSR (reflecting world market price trends). This has put further, more permanent economic pressures on Eastern Europe because having to increase the volume of exports to the USSR to pay for a given quantity of imports means a lower rate of domestic investment and consumption as well

as more Western imports to substitute for Soviet imports and to produce the incremental exports required by the deteriorating terms of
Soviet trade.

During the 1970s, the growth rates of the East European countries
were helped by Western government and private bank credits. Lending to Eastern Europe was considered safe because central planning
was viewed as synonymous with effective control over the balance of
payments since planners, supposedly, could always cut imports and
expand exports. A Soviet umbrella was said to exist also: for economic
and political reasons the USSR would not allow these countries to
default. But the most important reasons for extending credit were to
finance exports, to reduce unemployment, and to increase business
profits. By the end of the 1970s debts reached dangerously high levels
in all the countries except Czechoslovakia as exports to the West
lagged behind imports because of problems in the economic system,
mistakes in policy, and unfavorable economic and financial conditions on world markets. In 1981 Poland was forced to reschedule; in
1982 Romania did the same. Net lending to the East European countries stopped, largely because of reduced credit-worthiness but in
part also because of political considerations.

By the late 1970s and early 1980s, all the East European countries,
in varying degrees, began experiencing greatly increased economic
pressures—from their own consumers, who expected that living standards would continue to improve or at least not deteriorate; from
their trade situation with the USSR, whose energy and raw materials
became less readily available and much more expensive; and from
Western creditors, who stopped making new loans.

The most immediately observable outcome of the new situation
was a substantial decline in the growth rates and in some countries
absolute—in the case of Poland, drastic—declines in production levels. The already modest initial growth targets of the 1981–1985 five-
year plans have repeatedly been revised downward, as were the
plans for the growth of investments and improved living standards.
Eastern Europe has entered a new economic era. The pressures are
not cyclical or temporary but fundamental, and there are no easy or
obvious ways to overcome them. Improved economic conditions in
the West would ease the pressures a bit but would not be sufficient to
make them disappear.

There are important similarities but also significant differences between the economic conditions and prospects of the East European
countries and the USSR. One similarity is that the USSR, too, has a
bureaucratic, centrally planned economic system, which, though not

[233]

highly efficient, has until recently been able to achieve comparatively good growth rates. But the USSR is different because of its size and resource endowment: its huge economy (GNP roughly 50 to 60 percent that of the United States) is well endowed with energy and other natural resources, though the Soviets need Western technology to maintain or increase production of some of the energy and raw materials in which they are well endowed. Up until now the Soviet Union has been able to finance its Western imports largely with energy and raw material exports, so that its level of debt is more manageable than those of East European countries. Thus the Soviet Union is in a more comfortable foreign trade situation than are the other Warsaw Pact countries that must compete on the world market with manufactured products.

The Soviet economy grew rapidly until about 1960. GNP growth rates averaged 6 percent in the 1950s, 5 percent in the 1960s, and 3 percent in the 1970s. They are unlikely to surpass 1 to 2 percent in the 1980s. The major problems are low and declining growth rates in the labor force, with small new additions coming from the non-Russian (mostly Moslem) peoples, who prefer to remain in agriculture and not migrate from the regions where they were born; a fall in productivity growth rates, typical of mature, centrally planned economies, which are better at resource mobilization than at their efficient use; increasing costs of extracting and transporting raw materials and energy; and sluggish agriculture, which does not respond to central planning methods. Short of fundamental economic reforms, which in the short to medium run are unlikely in the USSR, there is probably little that even the new Chernenko leadership can do to speed up substantially the 1 to 2 percent growth rate projected for the 1980s.

What are the broader implications of the economic situation and prospects of the Warsaw Pact countries? As a broad generalization (which is therefore an oversimplification), the findings suggest increased instability in the domestic economies of the countries and in Soviet–East European relations. To be sure, there are important environmental, systemic, and policy differences among the East European countries and in their relations with the USSR, which require qualifying statements by country. Country-specific issues are discussed in Chapter 8, and I will focus on a few general conclusions and implications.

The economic prospects for the rest of the 1980s are not conducive to the Warsaw Pact moving toward greater alliance cohesion. The Soviet Union does not appear to be in a position to increase trade with the East European countries in ways that will promote cohesion:

providing increased quantities of energy and raw materials in exchange for manufactured products. Although sudden and drastic cuts in Soviet exports, credits, and subsidies are unlikely, the USSR appears to have decided to give reduced priority to meeting Eastern Europe's economic needs in the 1980s. In 1982 Soviet oil exports to Eastern Europe were cut (compensated only partly by increased exports of natural gas), and the trade surplus also declined. For some time, the Soviet Union has been encouraging the East European countries to set moderate growth targets and to turn to the world market to purchase items in short supply in the CMEA.

Another possible avenue to increase alliance cohesion would be to improve CMEA integration through inter- and intraindustrial specialization in manufactured products. This integration is unlikely to happen owing to the many systemic impediments, including the absence of meaningful cost and price calculations on which to base specialization decisions and the incompatibility of traditional central planning with direct entrepreneurial contacts between manufacturing firms in the member countries. The complementary relationship between CMEA integration and East-West trade is also a factor. Given the inability of the CMEA countries to satisfy fully from CMEA sources their needs for many goods, ranging from basic materials to state-of-the-art technology, a precondition for increasing manufactures exports to a CMEA partner is obtaining additional imports from the West. Because imports from the West must be paid for with exports to the West, CMEA integration in manufactures cannot be considered an alternative to East-West economic relations.

The contemporary state of economic affairs thus would appear to reduce the Soviet Union's degree of freedom to enforce alliance cohesion. Earlier, J. F. Brown identified succinctly the Soviet Union's policy dilemma in Eastern Europe: conflict between its desire for alliance cohesion and political viability in the region.[7] Cohesion requires conformity of ideology, domestic and foreign policies, and implementing institutions. Viability demands credible and efficient economic performance that would help legitimize communist rule. The two objectives are not fully compatible because a uniform set of institutions and policies is at odds with the need for flexible responses to country-specific problems. Stalin opted for cohesion; the post-Stalin leadership has been emphasizing viability so long as East European policies have remained within limits that are uncertain and changing.

The post-Brezhnev leadership's basic policy options, examined by Brown in Chapter 8, are still essentially those of viability versus cohesion. Emphasis on the former would mean that the Soviets would allow greater economic liberalization, provided that the party's rule and the country's membership in the Warsaw Pact alliance were not threatened. Emphasis on cohesion would mean increased use of military, political, and economic instruments to control the institutions and policies in Eastern Europe.

Focusing principally on the economic aspects of Soviet policy, I am somewhat more optimistic than Brown that the first option, stressing viability, has a chance of prevailing. Given the economic pressures in Eastern Europe, perhaps the single most important issue for the second half of the 1980s is whether the countries will move toward fundamental, market-oriented economic reforms and whether the Soviet Union will oppose such reforms being expanded in Hungary and introduced in other countries. To be sure, the implementation of market-oriented reforms faces formidable domestic opposition in each country. Reform pressures typically become stronger when economic performance worsens and shortages intensify. At the same time, reforms are more difficult to introduce and sustain in a worsened economic situation because some slack in the economy would be needed to help bridge the difficulties bound to arise during the transition period. Domestic political opposition to reforms is based on the fear of the party bureaucracy that economic reform must be accompanied by political reform, for example, in the nomenclature system. There is no firm basis to predict the outcome a priori; the strength of the forces supporting and opposing major reforms is country-specific and partly a function of the precise reforms and implementation strategies.

The attitude of the USSR toward economic reforms is obviously very important. Whether the issue will become a source of conflict in the future is a key question in the policy choice between viability and cohesion. No outsider can give a categorical answer. Detailed study of the Hungarian reform experience places me in agreement with Wlodzimierz Brus, who states that whatever conflict there was on this issue in the past

between "reformist" countries and the USSR (plus other "conservatives") [was] not basically because of the economic content of the reform, but mainly because (and to the extent which) the economic reform was conceived as part of a broader political blueprint aiming at some sort of democratic pluralism connected with national aspirations and the denunciation of the Soviet-type [system]. . . . Consequently, it would seem that the (generally) unsuccessful reform attempts so far can scarcely be regarded as a result of Soviet pressure, or the single case of

[236]

relative success (Hungary) as a hard-won and exceptional concession. This is not to say that there were (or are) no political obstacles to economic reform; [only] that these political (and other) obstacles are in the main not of the "Soviet–East European conflict" category.[8]

[10]

The Warsaw Pact in the International System

JONATHAN DEAN

Thirty years ago, the Soviet Union was consolidating its hold over Eastern Europe in the aftermath of World War II. In Western Europe and the United States, political leaders were concerned that the expansion of the Soviet system into Eastern Europe and the victory of the communists in China marked, as the Soviets claimed, the beginning of a new era in world history. Western leaders feared the evolution of communist governments in Europe, Asia, and the developing world, knit together by a common ideology, monolithic in their unity, and controlled from a single center in Moscow. Soviet success in installing communist regimes in the widely different countries of Eastern Europe, with uniform institutions of totalitarian control— Communist parties, secret police, controlled public media, mass organizations and educational systems—was impressive. Many feared that this success would lead to the emergence in Eastern Europe of self-sustaining political systems, which would serve as a base for a similar advance into Western Europe and propel the Soviet Union toward world domination.

These apprehensions led to the establishment of NATO and of the Federal Republic of Germany. Today, their mere recital appears outdated and exaggerated.

The enormous human costs of the Soviet state; the serious weaknesses evident in the Soviet economy and social system, the military interventions of the Soviet Union against its allies; the defection from alignment with Moscow of China, Yugoslavia, and Albania; and the ensuing strains and fissures in relations of non-Soviet Communist parties with Moscow all have reduced the attractions of Soviet Marxism-Leninism and the ideological influence of the Soviet Union. Although the Soviet Union is militarily powerful, its power today is little more than that of an imperialist state.

It has also become evident that the Warsaw Pact system is far from a political success. With the limited exception of Hungary, communist governments in the East European member countries of the Pact have failed to gain the voluntary support of even a sizable minority of their populations. Each of them still must spend great sums on repressive police institutions and on controlled public media and propaganda and, with few exceptions, on fencing in their citizens with barbed wire, guard towers, and minefields. The East German and Czechoslovak riots in 1953, the Hungarian uprising of 1956, the political turmoil in Czechoslovakia in 1967–1968, the Polish workers' riots in 1956, 1970, 1976, and 1980, and the rise of Solidarity in 1980, followed by de facto replacement of the Polish Communist party by military rule, demonstrated that the communist systems in these countries, and concomitantly, the Warsaw Pact, are not politically self-sustaining. Pact governments remain in power only by virtue of Soviet military power.

Nor has the Pact produced a viable economic system. Lagging productivity and foreign trade deficits exist in nearly every country of Eastern Europe. Continued operation of unprofitable plants, production of low-quality goods, and consequent inability to produce for sale in competitive market economies are nearly universal. The failure to elicit enduring motivation to work and to produce is widespread. Each of the countries of the Pact has large-scale concealed unemployment and is plagued by widespread corruption, graft, "fixing," and nepotism. With the limited exception of Hungary, central Communist parties retain their rigid grip over economic decision making, and it has not been possible to maintain a continuing flow of consumer goods to reward higher productivity from workers.

The economic and political deficiencies of the Pact system in Eastern Europe have had to be compensated for by the Soviet Union in the form of large economic subsidies and massive political-military interventions: direct Soviet intervention in East Germany in 1953, in Hungary in 1956, and in Czechoslovakia in 1968, and local military intervention backed by the threat of Soviet intervention in Poland in 1981. Soviet economic subsidies to Eastern Europe in recent years are variously estimated but substantial, a reversal of earlier Soviet exploitation of the Eastern European economies. Likewise, the incurable political instability of Eastern Europe represents a nearly complete reversal of earlier Western expectations that these states would serve as a springboard for political penetration of Western Europe and beyond.

In affecting East European public attitudes, the actions of the Western coalition in the period of detente have compounded the problems of sustaining the Pact system. Federal German acceptance of postwar eastern borders has made it difficult for Pact leaders to exploit the image of aggressive German irredentism to maintain cohesion within the Pact. Western credits have financed levels of consumer consumption which will not recur in Eastern Europe for a long time to come, but their memory will intensify dissatisfaction.

To assess the importance of detente for future developments in Eastern Europe, its effects should be examined. The roots of the Solidarity movement and of other dissident stirrings in Eastern Europe have been said to lie in the detente policy pursued by Western governments during the late 1960s and 1970s, especially those of the Nixon and Carter administrations in the United States and the Brandt and Schmidt governments in Federal Germany.

In one sense, this conclusion is correct; in another it is not. Detente between the NATO countries and the Soviet Union began in the late 1950s and early 1960s. It found specific form in early arms-control agreements—the "Hot Line" Agreement, Limited Test Ban Treaty, and Outer Space Treaty. The period was also marked by the cessation of radio jamming (except for Radio Liberty and Radio Free Europe) by the Soviet Union and the countries of Eastern Europe. Detente was accelerated in the late 1960s and early 1970s. The willingness of the Nixon administration to enter the SALT I agreement, of the Brandt government to enter treaties with the Soviet and Polish governments pledging not to change postwar borders by force, and of the Western governments to endorse these frontiers in the Helsinki Final Act, to conclude the Four-Power Agreement on Berlin, and to accept entry of the GDR into the United Nations, and Willy Brandt's dramatic act of kneeling atonement at Auschwitz, all were historic evidence that the countries of the Western alliance accepted the postwar situation in Eastern Europe.

These actions made it difficult convincingly to present the United States, Federal Germany, and the other countries of the NATO alliance as aggressive. The active participation of Western governments in arms control and the development of highly visible antinuclear movements in Western Europe in the early 1980s reinforced these earlier positive impressions. The leading Soviet role in all these negotiations legitimized Eastern Europe's closer relations with the West. Their direct participation in the Vienna MBFR talks and the negotiations leading to the Helsinki Final Act as well as the ensuing review conferences in Belgrade and Madrid formally sanctioned continuing relations with NATO countries even in matters relating to security. Huge Western credits to Poland and other East European countries, accompanied by greatly increased trade and expanded tourism and cultural exchanges all had considerable impact on the governments and populations of Eastern Europe.

In Czechoslovakia in the late 1960s and in Poland in the late 1970s, these developments affected the public's perception of what changes were acceptable to domestic and Soviet leaderships. At any given time, this perception acts as an inner regulator to restrain or release public demonstrations of dissatisfaction and other pressures on Eastern European governments. Yet, as Edwina Moreton and Stephen Larrabee have noted elsewhere in this volume, all the major outbreaks of protest or manifestations of desire for change in Eastern Europe, notably those in East Germany, Hungary, Czechoslovakia, and Poland, were motivated mainly by reaction to internal conditions. The concepts and formulations used in statements of Solidarity members and supporters show preoccupation with the Polish society and domestic economy and seldom use Western actions as justification. The exception is comparison of domestic performance with Western economic practices and living standards, a ubiquitous cause of public unrest in Eastern Europe. But the focus was on Polish national issues and reforms, and the intellectual impetus came from within. This conclusion has considerable relevance for East European developments in the next decades.

FUTURE OF THE PACT SYSTEM

Few would dispute that the present situation of the Warsaw Pact is bleak, whether seen from the West or from Moscow. Is there a chance that the Warsaw Pact system may become self-sustaining as it enters the twenty-first century? As matters now stand, the East European states are likely to continue to exhibit continued dissatisfaction, periodic political unrest, and stagnant economies, deeply in debt to Western banks and to the Soviet Union. Far from becoming self-sustaining, the Pact system in Eastern Europe would, if left on its own, collapse under the weight of its shortcomings and failures. The Pact system is sustainable only as long as it is backed by the willingness of the Soviet leadership to make up for economic and political deficiencies with subsidies and, ultimately, with the use of force. The possibility of broad adherence to official beliefs by the general population and elites and of widespread voluntary support for the political systems of the individual Pact member states is gone—if it ever existed. But the class of newly privileged officials, which replaced the elites of the precommunist system, will keep day-to-day operation of the Pact states going. The economies of the Pact nations are not efficient in maximizing productivity or producing high-quality goods, but they are capable of maintaining distribution of basic necessities at low, subsidized prices. Living standards are stagnating but are well above those of twenty years ago. The Soviet Union will continue to serve as a vast market for low-quality East European products. During the next decade, popular discontent is likely to flare up again in one or more Pact countries. But if national authorities cannot maintain control, Soviet forces will intervene.

In short, the possibility of Soviet intervention will in all probability continue to maintain the Warsaw Pact system in Eastern Europe over the next decade and beyond, albeit at a relatively low level of economic productivity and individual satisfaction.

POSSIBLE CHANGES IN THE EXTERNAL ENVIRONMENT

These depressing prospects could, however, be affected by major changes in the external environment of Eastern Europe—in the political, economic, and military strength of the Soviet Union or of the Western coalition or marked improvement in East-West relations. The coming decades could, for example, bring acute economic and political difficulties inside the Soviet Union as well as acute unrest in Eastern Europe. Under increasing external and internal pressure, the Soviet leadership might decide to cut its losses in Eastern Europe and relax its hold over the area. Some Western leaders theorized early in the Cold War period that inner contradictions of the Pact system would cause its progressive deterioration and that the countries of the Western coalition would, through the accumulation of economic and social strength and their superior social systems, exercise a "magnetic" effect on the countries of Eastern Europe, causing them to gravitate toward a more successful, free Western Europe.

Or the reverse development might take place: Soviet fortunes might rise under more decisive leadership from Chernenko's successors, the Soviet economy might begin to improve, and Soviet military capabilities might increase still further. Encouraged by the growth of neutralist sentiment in the Federal Republic of Germany, a more confident Soviet leadership might decide to relax its hold over East Germany and other parts of Eastern Europe in order to gain greater influence over the Federal Republic of Germany, seeking to dissolve the NATO alliance through Federal German withdrawal and neutrality. The potential gains would be enormous: if such an approach were successful, the Soviet Union could achieve decisive influence over the human and material resources of Western Europe and tip the world balance of power decisively in its favor. In one form or another, this possibility has been the nightmare of Western political leaders since the Cold War and the postwar division of Germany. Today, with controversy over NATO nuclear strategy a divisive issue, it appears to some observers closer than ever to realization.

But each of these possible lines of development of the Soviet system—its sharp decline or its outstanding success—is extreme and highly unlikely. It is improbable that the Soviet Union can gain enduring, decisive military superiority over the NATO countries in the coming decade. A rough balance in conventional forces between NATO and Pact forces will continue, particularly in view of the questionable loyalty, inferior equipment, and limited military value of the bulk of the armed forces of the East European countries. Achievement of enduring Soviet superiority in the strategic nuclear field is highly unlikely because of U.S. resources and technical capacity. Decisive Soviet inferiority is also unlikely. The Soviet Union has shown its capacity to keep abreast of the United States by catching up in nuclear armaments from far behind. Consequently, the present rough Soviet-American parity in strategic nuclear armaments will also probably continue in the coming decades and will be a main factor in the U.S.–Soviet and the general East-West relationship. Both sides may make innovations, but neither can outstrip the other.

As a result, the Soviet Union will maintain its military hold over Eastern Europe, and the Western coalition will continue to abstain from contesting that hold by military means, even in the event of widespread unrest and repression in Pact countries, because of the high risk that the Soviet Union would resort to all-out war if NATO forces should enter the area.

The Soviet economic and political system will surely change over the next decade, but it is likely to be gradual and incremental, with only modest increases in economic strength. On the other hand, even if the post-Brezhnev Soviet leadership does not solve the many problems of the Soviet society and economy, deterioration of the Soviet system is likely to be slow and undramatic. Neither the brilliant success of the Soviet system nor its total collapse is likely within the next decade.

One factor will almost certainly remain constant: whatever the direction of internal change in the Soviet Union, maintenance of the Warsaw Pact in Eastern Europe will continue to hold top priority for the Soviet leadership. The continued existence of communist governments in Eastern Europe is an important confirmation of the correctness of Soviet institutions and values, assuring that the sacrifices of World War II were not made in vain and will not be repeated. Change would have to go very far indeed inside the Soviet Union before Soviet leaders would dare to gainsay these deeply held values. In sum, it is most improbable that the Soviet hold over the Pact states will be relinquished in coming decades.

Nor are developments over the next decade likely to lead to an increase in Western economic power, military strength, or political unity of sufficient dimensions to place the NATO countries in a position to bring about major change in Eastern Europe either against the will of the Soviet Union or through inducement. As already pointed out, the prospect is remote that the United States and other members of the Western coalition could gain decisive and enduring military superiority over the Soviet Union. Western economies are unlikely to have at their disposal enough private or government money to lend to Eastern Europe or to the Soviet Union to induce far-reaching internal change.

Marked decline over the next decade of West European or American military power relative to that of the Soviet Union is also improbable. The West will keep up militarily. Nor is decline of the Western economies to such an extent as to give the Soviet or East European systems a marked superiority likely. Instead, the cultural and personal freedoms of the Western countries and their advanced consumer products will continue to exercise strong attraction for the populations of Eastern Europe, contributing to a continuing ferment of discontent in the Pact countries.

Further decline in the unity and cohesion of the NATO alliance in coming years does seem possible, however, particularly if no East-West arms-control agreements are concluded. The benefits for the European NATO allies from the American contribution to their defense have declined with the Soviet Union's achievement of strategic parity with the United States. A program to modernize American nuclear weapons based in Western Europe, intended to restore public confidence in that contribution, has miscarried, particularly in West Germany, Britain, and the Netherlands, resulting in mounting skepticism and doubt about the soundness of NATO's reliance on nuclear deterrence. This skepticism is based on the realization that the American nuclear umbrella can no longer provide the protection it did during the period when the United States had superiority over the Soviet Union in both strategic and tactical nuclear weapons and on the perception that the risk of outright Soviet attack on Western Europe is limited. These doubts are likely to continue, leading to further discontent with American leadership, skepticism as to the utility of the alliance relationship with the United States, and increase in neutralist and nationalist sentiment and anti-American, "Gaullist" attitudes in the northern tier of Western Europe, especially Federal Germany. Under these conditions, some observers see the possibility of the Soviet Union disengaging Federal Germany from the NATO alliance.

But this picture, too, is unrealistic. Soviet efforts to manipulate the German desire to be left in peace and German interest in some form of reunification of the two German states will continue. These efforts will influence German public opinion. But they will remain in the realm of diplomatic maneuver, with limited impact, unless the Soviet Union moves from gestures to actions. The population of the Federal Republic is apprehensive, cautious, and suspicious of the Soviet Union, highly unlikely to relinquish even a devalued security connection with the United States for insubstantial Soviet offers on German unity. To have real effect on Federal German opinion, the Soviet Union would have to undertake far more than conciliatory rhetoric. It would have to make a series of actual, important moves in relinquishing control over East Germany and to back these moves by convincing arms-control and force reductions.

But East Germany is the keystone of the Pact system in Eastern Europe. Therefore, relinquishment of Soviet control over the German Democratic Republic would mean renunciation of Soviet control over the entire Warsaw Pact system in Eastern Europe. Given the security and ideological importance to the Soviet leadership of maintaining its position in Eastern Europe, such actions are unimaginable unless the Soviet system has changed beyond recognition, and there are no such prospects for the next decades. Consequently, Soviet actions are not likely adversely to influence the West's problems of coping with changing attitudes of the Federal German public.

The East-West friction following the 1979 Soviet invasion of Afghanistan illustrates in a negative sense the importance of overall East-West relations for the degree of latitude permitted East European governments to engage in modest experiments both in domestic and in foreign policy. It also illustrates the interaction of external and domestic developments in Eastern Europe. The Polish Solidarity movement was a child of the detente period. Its repression has contributed to an increase in East-West frictions.

Although far-reaching change in the East-West power balance is improbable in the next few decades, a marked improvement in East-West relations could provide a more favorable international framework for developments in Eastern Europe. Conclusion of a series of arms-control agreements, particularly a U.S.-Soviet START agreement and increasing Soviet-American and Soviet–West European political and economic cooperation, could improve the outlook for significant political and economic change in Eastern Europe. Yet, however desirable, positive developments on a major scale appear improbable during the next decade.

Soviet-American relations since their formal beginning in 1933 appear to show a cyclical pattern in which periods of strain and friction alternate with shorter periods of better relations. This pattern will probably continue in the future, influenced by domestic political developments in both countries as well as their actions toward each other. But the swings of the cycle are long term—from the Soviet revolution to formal relations took sixteen years; slowly improving relations and wartime cooperation to Cold War, thirteen years; Cold War to beginning of detente, another decade or more.

Some individual East-West arms-control agreements may be concluded in the coming period. But it took the West more than a decade to generate the concepts and the changed public attitudes during the period of improvement of East-West relations which extended from the 1960s to result in signature of the SALT II agreement in mid-1979. Western, especially American, disappointment with that detente, and the accompanying reversion to disillusioned suspicion of the Soviet Union, are firmly rooted. Under the best circumstances some time would be needed for these attitudes to diminish sufficiently to permit any lasting rapprochement. Public concerns over nuclear war and the high costs of defense are now considerable inside the Western coalition. But the blows to Western hopes of enduring U.S.-Soviet and East-West cooperation caused by the continued Soviet arms buildup, Soviet interventions abroad, and the repression of the Solidarity movement in Poland have resulted in skepticism among even the most optimistic Western leaders. The capacity of the Western economies to offer important economic inducements, credits, or concessions, whether governmental or private, is likely to remain low both because of the state of the Western economies and the disarray among Western views on this subject. The most likely course of development in U.S.-Soviet relations in the next decade or longer is toward isolated individual agreements in a larger continuum of suspicion and friction, while cyclical pressures for improvement gradually gather strength for a period of more decisive change. And the quality of the U.S.-Soviet relationship is likely to be decisive for overall East-West relations.

The new Soviet leadership under Chernenko has not yet consolidated its internal position. Given Chernenko's age and apparent poor health, it appears a further transitional leadership, unlikely to break the pattern of incremental change. Shaken in its expectation of greater U.S.-Soviet collaboration by what it considers erratic and hostile American behavior, the new leadership is also likely to adhere to a cautious and restrained approach, eschewing far-reaching moves and gestures toward the West. Moreover, repression of efforts at greater freedom and independence in Eastern Europe by Pact police and military forces, and large-scale Soviet political and economic intervention in Third World areas—and even military involvement—are all possible. Such developments will continue to elicit reactions of frustrated outrage from Western governments and publics, causing the climate of East-West relations to deteriorate.

The next decade may well see the replacement of the present Albanian leadership by a new leadership willing to improve relations with the Soviet Union. A result could be the reopening of important Soviet naval facilities on the Albanian coast. This development would cause sharp concern in the West, especially to Italy and other Mediterranean NATO countries, and to Yugoslavia. It would probably confirm the Soviet military hold over the Pact countries. All in all, there does not seem much prospect, at least in the coming decades, of improvement in East-West relations of a scope and duration which could affect internal developments in the Eastern European Pact countries.

EVOLUTION OF THE PACT SYSTEM

This brief review suggests that fundamental changes in the external environment of Eastern Europe resulting in major change in the Pact system are unlikely.

Yet the Soviet–Eastern European relationship will inevitably evolve in coming decades. Direct intervention will become even more costly and difficult for Soviet leaders both politically and economically—costs in the country which is the object of intervention, costs in Western opinion and relations and in relationships with the allies and well-wishers of the Soviet Union, and questions within the Soviet Union itself. The inhibitions against military intervention increase each time it is practiced, as shown by the long decision period before intervention in Czechoslovakia and by the decision not to intervene directly in Poland.

Moreover, it is questionable whether the Soviet Union any longer possesses the instruments for intervention available to it in the 1950s, when Soviet officials held positions inside key agencies of the East European governments or exercised surrogate government functions from accredited Soviet embassies, as Iuryi Andropov did in Hungary. The police controls of the 1950s, including their Soviet components, have been cut back by most East European governments and probably could no longer be reinstituted in their previous scope. As Christopher Jones has noted, Soviet influence on the military forces and economies of the Pact countries remains very great. But Soviet control mechanisms are no longer capable of the comprehensive effectiveness of the past.

The leaders of the Warsaw Pact countries know that the Soviet Union may someday replace them and that, ultimately, their failure and poor performance may bring bloodshed and Soviet occupation to their countries. But as several chapters in this study have shown, all the East Europeans—not only the Romanians—have learned to bargain more toughly with the Soviet Union. And there has been some evolution in Soviet attitudes over the years. There is evidence from the more than ten years of negotiation in the CSCE and MBFR that Soviet officials may be slowly learning to treat their East European counterparts as colleagues rather than inferiors.

Soviet interaction with Eastern Europe will, of course, continue to be intense, but understanding on the part of Soviet leaders that change and reform are necessary will conflict with concerns about the possible results of reform to produce caution, immobilism, and avoidance of difficult decisions—something like the caution and restraint of a bomb-disposal squad. Thus the main changes in Eastern Europe, as in past decades, will probably be generated inside the area. If so, against this background of a relatively unchanged external environment, what main trends can be expected in the Pact system in coming years?

The Warsaw Treaty will lapse in 1985, having been prolonged for ten years beyond its original twenty-year span. It lacks provision for further automatic renewal, probably because of the Pact's commitment to the political objective of dissolution both of itself and of the

NATO alliance. Backed up by its network of bilateral treaties with Pact countries, the Soviet Union could dispense with the Pact structure and might conceivably dissolve it in order to influence Western public opinion.

It is far more likely, however, that the trend will be toward increased reliance on the Pact mechanism. Policy statements by Andropov in June 1983 spoke of a "further perfection of political interaction, of which the Warsaw Treaty organization is the major instrument," as well as "a new level of economic integration."[1] It is doubtful that Pact membership will be expanded to include countries outside the East European–Soviet Union area. The NATO-oriented mission of the Pact, its geographic focus on Eastern Europe and the western Soviet Union, as well as probable strong resistance from the East European members all argue against expansion except possibly for the restoration of Albanian membership. The next decades are likely to bring gradual continued development of the Warsaw Pact structure to make it an increasingly important mechanism of international coordination as well as Soviet control. Uncertain which way to go in delicate, complex bilateral relations with the East European states, the Soviet Union may increasingly seek the reassurance of expanded multilateral machinery, while the East European governments may see benefits in insulating their bilateral relationships with the Soviet Union through the Pact mechanism.

The Warsaw Treaty Organization began as a propaganda echo to the inclusion of Federal Germany in NATO, but organizationally, it has developed into an increasingly important and complex international mechanism. After the Pact intervention in Czechoslovakia in 1968, a Committee of National Defense Ministers, a Military Council, a committee for coordination of arms technology, and a joint armed forces staff were established. In 1976, a permanent Commission of Foreign Ministers and a Joint Secretariat were added.

The Pact mechanism has also grown in importance as a forum for political relations among member states. For example, after Ceausescu's refusal to participate in the 1968 invasion of Czechoslovakia, his willingness to attend the Pact meeting on Poland in December 1980 was a signal that the meeting would not decide on military intervention in Poland. It is probable that Brezhnev deliberately called the meeting to exploit Romania's opposition to intervention so as to counter pro-intervention forces inside the Soviet Union and in the governments of the GDR and Czechoslovakia, whose diplomats abroad were openly talking of the inevitability and desirability of military intervention in Poland. Romania's demonstrative Soviettweaking could not be so overt without the reluctance of other Pact governments to join in repeated Soviet efforts to organize corporate disapproval of such behavior. The meetings of Pact leaders have provided some mutual support against recurrent Soviet efforts to increase the military contribution of the East European member states, the Pact version of familiar NATO frictions over burden-sharing in defense. Pact meetings have served as a forum for members, usually with the exception of the more politically exposed GDR, to lobby corporately with the Soviet Union in favor of more arms-control gestures and as an increasingly important vehicle for coordinating Pact positions in arms-control negotiations such as CSCE and MBFR, even though this is done by bilateral consultation as well. During the mounting Soviet campaign against new American intermediate-range nuclear missiles in 1983, corporate statements from the Pact were markedly more conciliatory and negotiation-oriented and less threatening than unilateral Soviet statements. The Pact mechanism will continue to be a device for transmission of Soviet impulses and for ratification of Soviet initiatives but perhaps also for group reluctance and resistance to Soviet suggestions from the East European members.

One possible future expansion of Warsaw Treaty Organization functions would be in the coordination of military assistance to developing countries: arms sales, providing military instructors in the recipient countries, and training their military personnel in Eastern Europe. As Condoleezza Rice and Edwina Moreton have noted, the level of activity in this field has steadily increased over the past decade. For example, the value of military deliveries by East European countries has doubled in the past five years and the number of East European military personnel in Africa and the Near East has increased three times in the last few years to about three thousand. These trends are likely to continue. Over the past five years, the most active sellers in order of activity have been Romania, Czechoslovakia, and Poland. The main recipients have been the radical Moslem states of North Africa and the Near East: Libya, Syria, Iraq, and Iran, all capable of paying in hard currency, which is a major consideration for the East European states. Czechoslovakia and Bulgaria have also been major suppliers of arms to the PLO.

Institutionally, however, there does not seem much prospect that arms sales will be actively pursued in the mechanisms of the Warsaw Treaty Organization. Coordination of military programs has been almost entirely bilateral between the source country and the Soviet Union. Continuation of the present specialization between the East

European states and the Soviet Union is probable, with the Soviet Union supplying more technically advanced weapons and the East Europeans selling tanks, armored personnel carriers, trainer aircraft, small arms, uniforms, communications equipment, and medical units. That there is close political coordination of these sales is clear: East European countries sold military supplies to both Iraq and Iran in the early stages of the Iraq-Iran war, while the Soviet Union deliberately held back in an ostensibly evenhanded approach toward both countries. But subsequently, the Soviet Union entered a $3 billion arms delivery program to Iraq, and the East Europeans appear to have cut back. Obtaining hard currency and promoting sale of domestic products, rather than political aims, appear to be the main East European motive in arms sales, and it is difficult to see these activities expanding very rapidly in other developing countries in the future.

THE CMEA MECHANISM AND ITS FUTURE

All East European Warsaw Pact members are also members of the Council for Mutual Economic Assistance, whose mechanisms were expanded in the 1970s with a major statute revision and increases in standing commissions and the Secretariat. In the future, the Soviet Union will continue to seek to expand the Secretariat in the face of resistance from East European members. Consequently, the importance of this mechanism will probably increase in the next decade, but only gradually.

A possible area of expansion of the CMEA mechanism would be in coordination of aid to developing countries. But despite Soviet pressures, actual prospects for such expansion appear limited owing to the discrepancy between the interests of the Soviet Union and those of the East European states. On the one hand, the Soviet Union is interested in further integration of CMEA members and in using the CMEA mechanism to elicit greater efforts from the East European countries in the development and support of Soviet foreign policy objectives. On the other hand, the manifest desire of the East European countries is to use their economic aid and expanding technical assistance in direct support of their own export sales. Most economic aid from East European states takes the form of selective short-term credits tied to purchase of specific products of the donor country.

There is some coordination within CMEA of economic support activities to "fraternal" developing countries, including Ethiopia, Mozambique, and South Yemen. But this activity has been unpopular, as is indicated by East European resistance to Soviet efforts to gain Mozambique, now an observer, full membership status in the CMEA. There has been some loose discussion of general guidelines for aid to developing countries within CMEA and some exchange of information on actual programs once decided but no apparent coordination in CMEA of specific projects. Soviet efforts to encourage joint projects of two or more CMEA members in developing countries are unlikely to be successful. In short, there seems little prospect in the next decades of a major shift in foreign aid motivation of East European CMEA members away from national economic considerations to bloc or ideological motives.

To date, economic credits and grants, mainly from Romania, East Germany, and Czechoslovakia, have gone mainly to developing countries in the Near East, who pay in hard cash or oil, or to countries that are a source of minerals and raw materials or are willing to enter into barter deals. East European technical assistance personnel in developing countries—a source of hard currency for the sending countries—increased to more than seventy-five thousand in 1982 (more than forty thousand in Libya alone). But because of East European economic problems over the past two years, the total amount of credits and grants extended to developing countries has fallen sharply from highs in the late 1970s and early 1980s of well over $1 billion to the more normal average for the 1970s of about $700 million per year, of which only about half is actually drawn on by recipient governments.[2]

There may be prospects for increased technical assistance and services sold for hard currency by the Eastern Europeans in the future, but the chances seem remote within the next few decades either for major increases in East European economic aid to developing areas or the major increases in the trade which this aid is intended to further. East European countries have been intensifying their efforts to increase their sales to developing countries in the current period of economic recession, political frictions with the West and slowdown of Soviet economic growth. But the developing countries in the Group of 77 have categorized the countries of the Warsaw Pact as developed industrial countries from which a higher level of aid is expected and are becoming more selective and demanding about the conditions of economic aid and terms of trade they will accept from Eastern Europe. Their interest in barter deals has diminished. More important, they are themselves increasingly producing goods, such as shoes of quality comparable to those made in Romania and Czechoslavkia, which compete with East European products both in developing countries and in the markets of industrialized countries. The outlook in coming decades is for slow growth of relations between individual Eastern European states and developing countries, without an expanded role for CMEA as such.

EAST-WEST PULLS ON EAST EUROPEAN ECONOMIES

The countries of Eastern Europe are small and, with limited exceptions, poor in natural resources and heavily dependent on foreign trade. These disadvantages can be overcome only by favorable terms of trade and by high-quality production backed by adequate technology. These two requirements will continue to result in some tension between the economic links of the East European states with the Soviet Union and their links with Western industrialized countries. Except for Romania, Eastern Europe still obtains about 90 percent of its energy supplies and many raw materials from the Soviet Union, which has a decreasing surplus of energy sources and a decreasing desire to subsidize East European purchases of energy and other raw materials at concessional prices but a continuing desire to foster economic integration among CMEA members. The slow progress in the early 1980s toward a CMEA summit meeting, originally proposed by Romania, reflects the difficulty in coming to a revised basic understanding between the Soviet Union and the East European members of CMEA on pricing policy of energy and raw materials and terms of trade with the Soviet Union. Tension will continue between the Soviet Union's desire for more integration among CMEA members and the desire of the East European states to preserve their remaining national economic sovereignty. East European governments are divided between advocates of increased CMEA integration and retrenchment of economic links with the West, at present the Czechoslovak and Polish governments, and those favoring expansion of links with the West, currently Romania and Hungary. The difficult and drawn-out nature of the negotiating process and the recalcitrance of some East European states in acceding to Soviet desires, as indicated in such matters as the rejection of CMEA association for the "fraternal" development countries, suggest that their economic bargaining with the Soviet Union is fairly tenacious. It is likely to become even more so in coming years.

Today, about two-thirds of East European trade is with the Soviet Union or with one another and about one-third with developed and developing countries. Over the years, trade with non-CMEA countries has increased. At the outset of the 1980s, Romania and Hungary conducted over half their trade with noncommunist countries, and Poland was not far behind. The $60 billion debt of the East European states, the economic recession of the Western countries, and the cessation of Western credits have slowed this trend. Nevertheless, despite their current failure to produce goods of sufficient quality to be competitive in Western markets, the East European states may well increase the proportion of their trade with noncommunist countries up to the 50 percent level over the next decades.

One reason for this conclusion is that the Western industrialized countries are the main source of the new technology which the East European states will need to increase their productivity. Even the Soviet Union has acknowledged the need for continuing East European trade with the West. In the early 1980s, Brezhnev, Prime Minister Nikolai Tikhonov, and other Soviet leaders urged the East European states to maintain and expand their Western trade but to avoid dependency relationships.[3] (Despite Soviet warnings, the East Europeans are already dependent on Western suppliers for spare parts and replacements for many industrial plants.) An underlying desire to bolster national independence and reduce dependence on the Soviet Union will also promote trade with the West.

Detente has educated East Europeans in the ways of the Western economies and, by comparison, the weaknesses of the Soviet bloc economy, as it has educated the West about the Soviet Union and Eastern Europe. Thus a combination of Western motives—geographic contiguity, pan-European solidarity, the promotion of peaceful evolution in Eastern Europe, and the desire to maintain existing credit investments in a logical market area—will probably bring renewed West European credits for Eastern Europe within a decade, even though these will be on a smaller scale than during the 1970s and always vulnerable to political developments such as the repression of uprisings by force.

If East European trade becomes as heavily oriented toward the West as forecast, there will ultimately be political consequences. Even with the present degree of trade contact and the associated two-way travel, ideologically motivated control over the flow and content of information about Western countries becomes difficult. The operation and performance of Eastern economies will be even more subject to continued comparison with that of the West. Expanding trade links with the West will strengthen the already existing inclination of East European governments to resist actions that would have harmful effects on their economic relations with Western countries.

FORCES FOR CHANGE WITHIN THE PACT:
ECONOMIC ASPECTS

It would be wrong to assume that the coming decades in Eastern
Europe will be uniform and drably uninteresting because of probable
lack of major change in the external environment and the continued
predominance of the Soviet Union. To the contrary, there will probably be considerable experiment, ferment, and turbulence, both political and economic. There are several built-in reasons why pressures
for economic and political change will remain strong and why worried Pact governments will continually experiment with the economy
and, ultimately, even the political structure.

East European leaders are well aware of the deficiencies of the
built-in Soviet command economy model and have strong motivation
to succeed and survive as governments and as individuals. In the
coming period, they will be under unremitting pressure from their
own populations to do better and from the Soviet Union to become
more efficient and self-sustaining and less dependent on Soviet support. Economic experiments are a less risky way to satisfy political
discontent than changes in political institutions. The educational systems of the individual Pact countries will turn out increasing numbers
of trained professionals who operate on rational rather than ideological grounds, and these people will join those arguing for economic
reform. Nearly all East European leaders, even the East German computer technocrats, are aware of the attractions of decentralizing economic decision making and looser control of microeconomic processes, including the versions proclaimed by the Hungarians since
1968 in their New Economic Mechanism and those they have actually
put into effect.

In the coming decade, most Pact governments will attempt to deal
with the problems of low public support and poor economic performance through experiments aimed at decentralizing economic decision making and eliciting improved leadership skills and worker motivation. These experiments will be continual. But they are also likely
to be modest in scope and slow in application because of important
obstacles to far-reaching economic change. In the past, an alliance,
sometimes tacit, sometimes explicit, between workers interested in
continuation of full employment and subsidized prices for food and
housing and party officials anxious not to have their authority decreased has repeatedly frustrated reform efforts. Even stronger than
the conservatism of entrenched interests is the caution of Pact governments about the adverse political effects of economic experiments,

which has stifled numerous experiments at birth and has been rein-forced by the Solidarity experience. The Soviet Union, whose influence can be decisive, is likely to be permissive in the long run but stultifying, cautious, and slow in reaching decisions.

The net result of these conflicting motives is likely to be timid but nonetheless continual experimentation with the institutions and processes of the domestic economy. Many East European governments will follow the course already taken by Hungary, particularly its efforts to elicit more individual initiative within state-owned enterprises, its more flexible prices, and its market-oriented agricultural reforms. These innovations have already been tolerated by the Soviet Union, and some have even been mentioned by Soviet leaders for use in the USSR. It is probable that, over time, experiments and innovations will result in some cumulative increase of the role of the free enterprise sector of the East European economies—privately owned or operated enterprises and services. In Poland, for example, up to 25 percent of the work force is already employed in the private sector. In time, East European governments will realize the value of closing inefficient plants and of retraining and reassigning workers. It is also probable that greater scope will be allowed to price mechanisms and to market forces, with prices open within controlled limits to the effects of supply and demand.

It is doubtful that these slow, limited changes will have decisive effects in unlocking reserves of ingenuity and motivation or that the productivity of the East European economies will greatly increase over coming decades. The adjustments will be too cautious, and there are too many obstacles to success, particularly in a period when most investment will have to come from inside the area. But although the overall performance of East European economies may remain weak, this does not mean that there will not be gradual change in the pattern both of external trade and of the institutions and policies of the individual economies. These will increasingly become those of a mixed economy, combining state ownership with market economy elements.

POLITICAL CHANGE

Political change is another matter. It is unlikely that any more nationwide trade unions or groupings similar to Solidarity will be permitted in Eastern Europe in coming decades. But we should avoid the pitfall of permitting justified pessimism about the present sorry state of Poland and its short-term prospects to dominate long-range perspectives. In the longer run, there will be political change in Eastern Europe, even in Poland.

In the coming decades, domestic politics in the East European countries are likely to be turbulent. As with their economic systems, both populations and political leaderships know the shortcomings of the Soviet political model and know that its institutions cannot be made to work without real change. The populations of the East European countries have two characteristic attitudes on political matters: first, considerable self-imposed discipline and awareness of the limits to which their governments and that of the Soviet Union can be pushed (the inner regulator mentioned earlier), and second, a continuing desire for more personal scope, more accountability of government authorities, and more unbiased information and factual content in the public media. This desire will generate unremitting pressures for change.

In coming decades, Communist party leaders will continue to emphasize national cultural and historical traditions in the hope of increasing popular support. To the same end, they will probably follow the example of Romania and engage in limited but documented disagreement with the Soviet Union on individual issues, hoping to make a record of defending the national interests of their countries. Managers of major plants will become still more important in a combined role of directors of industrial production and local controllers of incipient unrest. Their turnover will be heavy.

There will be periodic unrest, especially among dissatisfied workers and students, sometimes leading to shuffles of personnel in the Communist party leadership. Dissatisfaction could again lead to one or more outbreaks of widespread unrest followed by repression. Large-scale unrest is unlikely in Hungary after the searing experience of 1956 despite signs of growing economic troubles. It is unlikely in Czechoslovakia, whose population continues subdued, or in pro-Russian Bulgaria. Soviet forces are numerous in East Germany and would probably be used ruthlessly and immediately to repress any unrest the East German armed forces could not quell. Here in particular, a nervous Soviet leadership would be highly apprehensive about action from the Federal Republic in support of dissidents, even though organized Federal German intervention would be improbable. The strategic nuclear forces of both sides would probably be on alert, and the possibility that a huge East-West military confrontation in Germany or a U.S.–Soviet nuclear confrontation would ignite by mischance would increase.

[257]

Romania and after it, Poland, are the most likely areas of widespread unrest in the next decade. In Romania, where repeated strikes have been repressed by force, replacement of the Ceausescu government by a military coup motivated by the desire to preclude or to deal with public dissatisfaction is possible. Romania is also the most likely site for public unrest of such proportions as to bring intervention by the Romanian armed forces and, if this proves ineffective, military intervention by the Soviet Union.

Even though Soviet capacity to prevail in the long run does not seem in doubt, it is possible that, at some point during the next decade, unrest in one of the other East European countries may become so extensive that its duration and the difficulty of repressing it, whether by indigenous or Soviet forces, may be considerable. Each such occasion will incur high political and economic costs to all Pact governments, whether or not they intervene directly.

The political lessons of the Prague Spring and of the Solidarity development in Poland are twofold. First, the Soviet leadership can be brought to accept major departures from socialist orthodoxy which are intrinsically repugnant to it, for example, the existence of independent trade unions organized on a countrywide basis or of freer public media. But, second, such changes can be enduring only if, however initiated, they are carried out by disciplined national Communist party leaderships which demonstrably are in a position to maintain control over their own populations, to assure the continuing primacy of the Communist party, and to avoid any appearance of leaving the Pact security system.

Accordingly, it is possible that, at some point in the next decade, a cohesive national Communist party leadership in an East European Warsaw Pact country could carry out enduring major political reforms under evident public pressure, if that leadership is able to control the public and conservative pro-Soviet elements in its own ranks. Chances for the combination of visible, strong public pressures for change with a tough, change-minded party leadership prepared to carry out the necessary reforms are not great. Evident public pressures are more likely to lead to changes of regime or to repression than to be translated into enduring reform. And a tough national Communist party leadership is more likely to choose repression of its own population over confrontation with the Soviet leadership for the sake of innovation. Riding the tiger of public discontent toward political reforms in Eastern Europe without being thrown off has not yet been successfully accomplished. Thus the chances of tougher, more cohesive versions of the Dubcek or Kania leaderships appearing at some time in the next decade and surviving the combined pressures of expectant public opinion and Soviet efforts to unseat them are slim. Failures are likely to be more sensational and more visible than successes.

Yet despite repression, public pressures for political reform and change in Eastern Europe will be strong and recurrent in the next decades. A slow, gradual movement toward institutions and conditions of greater personal freedom can be expected among the East European member states of the Warsaw Pact. This advance will be uneven and punctuated by repression, but in the long term it will be cumulative. Among the political institutions in which this trend may become evident are parliaments, which in Eastern Europe may gradually gain in authority and importance, including exercise of oversight and control over economic decisions and performance, the public media, which will probably become more informative, and even the judiciary, which in individual instances has shown up well in resisting illegal actions of the martial law administration in Poland. As the Warsaw Pact enters the next century, most East European countries will have moved perceptibly closer to West European models both in decentralization of the economy and in political life. And some of these changes will spread, slowly and hesitantly, to the Soviet Union.

WESTERN POLICY TOWARD EASTERN EUROPE

Given the political realities, Western policies aimed at supporting movements toward pluralism in Eastern Europe can have only limited effect. The cooperation or acquiescence of East European governments, however grudging, will be necessary. Yet even marginal inputs can have long-term effects. Even where political relationships are sharply restricted, diplomats can have useful effects on a small scale, and their impact can be increased if Western countries agree on the policies to be pursued.

Broad, enduring improvement of Western relations with the Soviet Union is improbable in the next decade for reasons that already have been reviewed, not least, the chilling effects of continuing repression in Eastern Europe. Yet certain developments in the next decades could improve Western relations with the Soviet Union to a partial and limited extent. A U.S.-Soviet agreement on reduction of strategic nuclear arms may be concluded or an understanding reached on control of intermediate-range weapons in Europe. The NATO countries may develop effective coordination of their economic policies toward the USSR and the Pact countries. Such coordination could in time place the Western countries in a position to use their economic resources, considerable even in periods of economic slump, in a positive way by offering credits and investments on condition of general loosening up, or of specific economic reforms in the recipient East European countries, or of more positive positions about arms control. Some resumption of Western, especially West European, credits to the countries of Eastern Europe appears possible in the coming decade, whether or not in coordinated form.

It may be also possible to achieve limited accords on reduction of NATO and Pact forces in Europe similar to those now under discussion in the MBFR negotiations in Vienna. The crushing weight of defense establishments, which on both sides consume more than half of the world's annual expenditures on armed forces of over $600 billion, as well as the intrinsic risks of a military confrontation, will provide continuing motivation to seek agreement. A NATO–Warsaw Pact arms reduction agreement like MBFR could create a rudimentary East-West security structure in Europe. It could reduce and limit the armed forces of both sides and provide a system of inspection and other measures of warning against surprise attack. It could also provide assurance to the Soviet leadership that NATO countries would not seek to convert economic and social change in East European countries to their military advantage, whether by increasing their own forces, deploying them in a more aggressive posture, or seeking to detach individual countries from the Pact.

Under such agreements, Soviet forces would probably remain in Eastern Europe to ensure against a shift of alliance, but their size and deployment would be checked by Western observers on a reciprocal basis. The armed forces of the East European countries would be smaller and less of an economic burden. The agreements would insulate these countries to some degree from recurrent deterioration in the continuing competitive U.S.-Soviet relationship and from related Soviet pressure to increase their defense efforts. The Soviet Union would have confidence, which it could check through its own observers in Western Europe, that NATO forces were not in a position to attack it. These assurances could induce Soviet leadership to accept greater social and economic diversity in Eastern Europe and thus to create conditions for a less turbulent and repressive, more orderly evolution in the area.

The chance for such a positive development is small. But a coordinated long-term Western policy toward Eastern Europe combining political, economic, and arms-control elements, which is now lacking, would seek to increase this possibility.

Any examination from a Western viewpoint of the future of the East European Warsaw Treaty states is bound to begin with deep pessimism. Yet as this review has shown, when looked at more closely, the gloom lightens somewhat, especially if the perspective looks forward for a considerable period. Even under continuing Soviet control, unremitting pressures for change will continue in Eastern Europe. They will come from national leaderships anxious to improve their economies to meet public demand and to become more competitive with Western trading partners. They will come from populations moved by economic dissatisfaction and by desires for broader personal scope and elbow room. These desires will be continually fueled by comparisons with the societies of the Western coalition. On occasion, however cautiously, pressures for change will come from the Soviet Union itself, concerned for the success of the Warsaw Treaty system. Together, these pressures will be strong. Over the years, they will result in important institutional change in the economic and political fields. East European states will slowly develop mixed economies, with many free market aspects. Although Communist parties will remain dominant, individual aspects of more pluralistic polities will be built into East European political systems. The lives of individuals will become more tolerable, and the seeds of still more far-reaching change will be gestating.

Notes

1. The Warsaw Pact in Transition

1. See, for example, Karen Dawisha and Philip Hanson, eds., *Soviet–East European Dilemmas: Coercion, Competition, and Consent* (London: Holmes and Meier, 1981); Stephan Tiedtke, *Die Warschauer Vertragsorganisation. Zum Verhaltnis von Militär-und Entspannungspolitik in Osteuropa* (Munich, Vienna: R. Oldenbourg Verlag, 1978); Christopher D. Jones, *Soviet Influence in Eastern Europe: Political Autonomy and the Warsaw Pact* (New York: Praeger, 1981); Robert W. Clawson and Laurence Kaplan, eds., *The Warsaw Pact: Political Purpose and Military Means* (Wilmington: Scholarly Resources, 1982); William J. Lewis, *The Warsaw Pact: Arms, Doctrine and Strategy* (New York: McGraw-Hill, 1982).

2. See, for example, Malcolm Mackintosh, *The Evolution of the Warsaw Pact*, Adelphi Papers No. 58 (London: Institute for Strategic Studies, 1969); Robin Alison Remington, *The Warsaw Pact: Case Studies in Communist Crisis Management* (Cambridge, Mass.: MIT Press, 1971); Lawrence T. Caldwell, "The Warsaw Pact: Directions of Change," *Problems of Communism*, 25 (September–October 1975), 2–10.

3. Lewis, *Warsaw Pact*, passim.

4. On the integration of non-Soviet forces into the Soviet command structure in time of war see A. Ross Johnson, Robert W. Dean, and Alexander Alexiev, *East European Military Establishments: The Warsaw Pact Northern Tier* (Santa Monica: Rand, 1980), pp. 27–33, 86; Viktor Suvorov, *Inside the Soviet Army* (London: Hamish Hamilton, 1982), pp. 125–33; on the Polish front see Johnson, Dean, and Alexiev, *East European Military Establishments*, pp. 27–33.

5. Lewis, *Warsaw Pact*, pp. 133, 193, 212.

6. Ibid., pp. 144, 166, 199; on the Czechoslovak People's Army see Johnson, Dean, and Alexiev, *East European Military Establishments*, pp. 159–64.

7. A. Ross Johnson and Barbara Kliszewski, *The Polish Military after Martial Law: Report of a Rand Conference* (Santa Monica: Rand, 1982), pp. 24–27.

8. Johnson, Dean, and Alexiev, *East European Military Establishments*, pp. 175–76; see also Dale R. Herspring and Ivan Volgyes, "Political Reliability and Eastern European Warsaw Pact Armies," *Armed Forces and Society*, 6 (Winter 1980), 27–296.

9. On party-military relations see Dale R. Herspring and Ivan Volgyes, eds., *Civil-Military Relations in Communist Systems* (Boulder, Colo.: Westview Press, 1978); and

Jonathan R. Adelman, ed., *Communist Armies in Politics* (Boulder, Colo.: Westview Press, 1982).

10. Johnson and Kliszewski, *Polish Military*, pp. 14–15.

11. Johnson, Dean, and Alexiev, *East European Military Establishments*, pp. 145–50; Jiri Valenta and Condoleezza Rice, "The Czechoslovak Army," in Adelman, ed., *Communist Armies*, pp. 129–48.

12. These themes have been important, for example, in E. P. Thompson's writings. See Thompson et al., *Exterminism and the Cold War* (London: Verso, 1982).

13. The "Havemann Initiative" is quoted in the excellent study by John Sandford, *The Sword and the Ploughshare: Autonomous Peace Initiatives in East Germany* (London: Merlin Press/European Nuclear Disarmament, 1983), pp. 89–91.

14. Sandford, *Sword and the Ploughshare*, p. 60.

15. Zdenek Mlynar, *Nightfrost in Prague* (New York: Karz, 1980), pp. 239–40; emphasis added.

16. *Pravda*, 24 February 1981.

17. In the autumn of 1982 the chairman of the Soviet Peace Committee, Iuryi Zhukov, wrote an open letter to West European peace activists, accusing the organizers of a major conference of European peace movements, which was to be held in West Berlin in May 1983, of "anti-Sovietism and anti-communism," and of trying to blame both blocs for the crisis in Europe. The Soviet committee boycotted the conference. See *Guardian*, April 8, 1983, p. 6.

18. The West's alliance system has been a major theme in recent Soviet analyses of world politics. See, for example, P. A. Zhilin and R. Bruhl, eds., *Voenno-blokovaia politika imperializma* (Moscow: Voenizdat, 1980); B. M. Khalosha, *Voenno-politicheskie soiuzy imperializma* (Moscow: Nauka, 1982).

19. *Pravda*, 7 January 1983.

20. For the Czechoslovak source see Chapter 3, n. 11. The other figures are derived from *The Military Balance, 1981–82* (London: International Institute for Strategic Studies, 1981), pp. 112, 113; and Stockholm International Peace Research Institute, *World Armaments and Disarmament, SIPRI Yearbook, 1980* (London: Taylor and Francis, 1980), pp. 19, 21.

21. Tiedtke, *Die Warschauer Vertragsorganisation*, p. 125.

2. The Warsaw Treaty Organization: A History

1. The East German forces, whose existence was not officially admitted by the Soviet Union in 1955, were incorporated into the Pact in January 1956.

2. See Marshal Tito's account of the equipment Yugoslavia received from the USSR before the 1948 split in his speech on 28 December 1950, quoted in Royal Institute of International Affairs, *Documents on International Affairs, 1949–1950* (London: Oxford University Press, 1953), p. 506.

3. The struggle with Molotov and his colleagues came to a head two years later with Khrushchev's victory over the Anti-Party Group in 1957 with military support.

4. Statement by the Czechoslovak General Prchlik at a Prague press conference on 15 July 1968, as reported by Prague Radio.

5. TASS interview with Army-General P. I. Batov, the chief of staff of the Warsaw Pact, on 11 May 1965 on the occasion of the Pact's tenth anniversary.

6. *Pravda*, 15 May 1955.

7. The treaty with Poland was signed on 17 December 1956, that with Romania on 15

April 1957, with Hungary on 17 May 1957, and with East Germany on 12 March 1957. In July 1958 the Soviet Union withdrew its garrison of two divisions from the territory of Romania.

8. Marshal V. D. Sokolovskii, *Military Strategy* [in Russian] (Moscow: Voenizdat, 1962), p. 429.

9. *Scinteia* (Bucharest) 8 May 1966.

10. *Times* (London) 17–18 May 1966.

11. O. Mahler and Ladislav Kopecky in *Mezinarodni Politika* (Prague), July 1966.

12. Similar tactics, though on a larger scale, were used in the early stages of the Soviet invasion of Afghanistan in December 1979.

13. *Pravda*, 26 September 1968.

3. Defense Burden-Sharing

1. Thad P. Alton et al., "East European Defense Expenditures, 1965–1978," in *East European Economic Assessment* (Part II), submitted to the Joint Economic Committee of the Congress of the United States (Washington, D.C.: U.S. Government Printing Office, 1981), pp. 409–33.

2. Michael Kaser, *COMECON* (London: Oxford University Press, 1967), p. 123.

3. I. I. Iakubovskii, *Boevoe sodruzhestvo bratskikh narodov i armii* (Moscow: Voenizdat, 1975), p. 232.

4. Kaser, *COMECON*, p. 125.

5. According to Alexei Kosygin, *Pravda*, 2 March 1965, cited in Kaser, *COMECON*, p. 123.

6. For example, "Have We an Excessively Expensive Army?" *A-Revue*, May 1968.

7. *Rude Pravo*, 1 December 1966. Novotny was not alone. The chief of the Main Political Administration, Vaclav Prchlik, later one of the leaders of the liberalization in the armed forces, declared that the Czechs seemed suddenly unaware of the dangers of imperialism and the existence of an aggressive NATO buildup (*Zivot Strany*, no. 24, December 1965).

8. Prague Domestic News Service, 7 August 1968, in Foreign Broadcast Information Service, Springfield, Va., 8 August 1968, p. D-5.

9. *Lidova Armada*, 5 January 1979.

10. International Institute for Strategic Studies, *The Military Balance, 1980–1981* (London: IISS, 1980); see "Czechoslovakia," p. 15.

11. Oldrich Běhounek, "RVHP and the Defense Capability of Socialism," *Historie a Vojenstvi*, no. 1 (1980).

12. William Reisinger, "East European Military Expenditures in the 1970s: Collective Goods or Bargaining Offer?" *International Organization*, 37 (Winter 1983), 143–55.

13. John Erickson, "Military Management and Modernization within the Warsaw Pact," in Robert W. Clawson and Lawrence Kaplan, eds., *The Warsaw Pact: Political Purpose and Military Means* (Wilmington: Scholarly Resources, 1982), p. 216.

14. Iakubovskii, *Boevoe sodruzhestvo*, p. 164.

15. The United States government found both Poland's and Czechoslovakia's arms capacity noteworthy, examining both wartime and postwar potential (Prague Embassy to the Department of State, 19 September 1946, airgram, DS 860F, 006/30–810).

16. Roy Medvedev, *Khrushchev* (Oxford: Basil Blackwell, 1982), pp. 243–44.

17. "Poland," *Janes' All the World's Aircraft* (London: Janes Publishing Co., 1981), p. 158.

18. Studiengruppe Militarpolitik, *Die NVA* (Hamburg: Rowohlt Verlag, 1979), p. 13.
19. "Czechoslovakia," *Janes' All the World's Aircraft*, p. 37.
20. "Poland," ibid., p. 159.
21. Friedrich Wiener, *The Warsaw Pact Armies* (Vienna: Carl Ueberrenter, 1977), p. 182.
22. Ibid.
23. Minister of Defense Martin Dzur first suggested the committee in a speech at the All Army Conference of the KSCS, reported in *Obrana Lidu*, 27 July 1968.
24. A. Ross Johnson, Robert W. Dean, and Alexander Alexiev, *East European Military Establishments: The Warsaw Pact Northern Tier* (Santa Monica: Rand, 1980), p. 60.
25. Michael Checinski, *A Comparison of Polish and Soviet Armaments Decision-making Systems* (Santa Monica: Rand, 1981), p. 15.
26. Jozef Wilczynski, *Technology in Comecon* (New York: Praeger, 1977), pp. 304–5.
27. "Poland," *Janes' All the World's Aircraft*. The dominance of Soviet technology is acknowledged in "Economic and Scientific Technical Cooperation of the Socialist Governments," in P. I. Efimov, *Boevoi soiuz bratskikh armii* (Moscow: Voenizdat, 1974), p. 272.
28. *Mlada Fronta*, 2 June 1983.
29. Wiener, *Warsaw Pact Armies*, p. 215.
30. Iakubovskii, *Boevoe sodruzhestvo*, p. 162.
31. *Obrana Lidu*, 13 March 1982.
32. Lawrence L. Whetten and James L. Waddell discuss some of the problems in "Motor Vehicle Standardization in the Warsaw Pact: Problems and Limitations," *RUSI Journal*, 124 (March 1979), 55–60.
33. Wiener, *Warsaw Pact Armies*, p. 272.
34. *Svobodne Slovo*, 7 May 1983.
35. *Aviation Week and Space Technology*, 24 January 1983, p. 48.
36. Ibid., 13 December 1982, p. 53.
37. Ibid.
38. Arms Control and Disarmament Agency, *World Wide Military Expenditures and Arms Transfer, 1969–1978* (Washington, D.C.: U. S. Government Printing Office, 1980), p. 130.
39. See Chapter 10. Though statistics suggest that Czechoslovakia and Poland continue to be the major non-Soviet Warsaw Pact weapons suppliers, Romania may have made an effort since 1980 to export greater numbers to the Third World, including both reexport of French arms and export of indigenously produced arms. Since aircraft are a major Romanian product, its sale could bring a high dollar value.
40. The BTR-60 is much more popular among Third World buyers. See the catalog of arms sales in Stockholm International Peace Research Institute, *World Armaments and Disarmament: SIPRI Yearbook, 1981* (London: Taylor and Francis, 1981), pp. 216–44.
41. Interesting anecdotes are contained in a UPI release, "The Guns of Brno," 5 November 1979.
42. Arms Control and Disarmament Agency, *World Wide Military Expenditures and Arms Transfers* (Washington, D.C.: U.S. Government Printing Office, 1981), p. 130.
43. UPI, "Guns of Brno."
44. Arms Control and Disarmament Agency, *World Wide Military Expenditures and Arms Transfers*, p. 159.
45. "Preparation of Law on Weapons," *SMENA*, (Bratislava) 25 July 1979, in Foreign Broadcast Information Service, Springfield, Va., 30 July 1979.
46. G. L. Dvorak, interviewed in *Obrana Lidu*, 6 March 1969.
47. Johnson, Dean, and Alexiev, *East European Military Establishments*, pp. 19–68.

48. Ibid.

49. See the discussion in my forthcoming book *Uncertain Allegiance: The Soviet Union and the Czechoslovak Army, 1948–1983* (Princeton: Princeton University Press).

50. Long-delayed deliveries of the T-72 tank and a number of advanced aircraft have finally been made (International Institute for Strategic Studies, *The Military Balance, 1980–1981*, p. 14).

51. Ivan Volgyes discusses the buildup of the Southern Tier in his *The Political Reliability of the Warsaw Pact Armies: The Southern Tier* (Durham: Duke University Press, 1983).

52. See reports of the Druzhba exercises in both Czech and Russian sources, especially *Obrana Lidu* and *Rude Pravo*, 5 February 1979, and *Krasnaia Zvezda*, 6 February 1979. The trilateral exercises are discussed in numerous issues of the press. See especially *Obrana Lidu*, 2 February 1982. Another important statement appeared in *Rude Pravo*, 5 October 1978.

53. I am grateful to Christopher Jones, who called this trend to my attention. There is some discussion of this phenomenon in his book *Soviet Influence in Eastern Europe: Political Autonomy and the Warsaw Pact* (New York: Praeger, 1981), pp. 106–11.

54. Louis J. Andolino, "Warsaw Pact Sea Power Assets," in Clawson and Kaplan, eds., *Warsaw Pact*, pp. 195–212. Opinions vary on the effectiveness of the Warsaw Pact's naval contribution. For a full discussion and a less charitable view than Andolino's, see Steve F. Kime, "The Navies of the Warsaw Pact," ibid., pp. 275–86.

55. Lt. Col. Jaroslav Ekart, "The Computer in the Research Institute," *ATOM*, no. 12 (1979), p. 11.

56. UPI release, "Conversations with Romanian Journalists," January 1981.

57. "Meeting of the Main Political Administration Heads on Ideology," *Obrana Lidu*, 4 March 1982. The discussion was on foreign policy issues and coordination. Another meeting held on 15 March 1983 was reported on the CBS Evening News, 16 March 1983.

58. "East Bloc Boosts Its Military Aid to Black Africa," *Christian Science Monitor*, 19 July 1979, p. 5.

59. Stockholm International Peace Research Institute, *The Arms Trade and The Third World* (Stockholm: SIPRI, 1979), p. 546.

60. *Communist Aid to Less Developed Countries of the Third World* (Springfield, Va.: Central Intelligence Agency, 1977), p. 12.

61. *Rude Pravo*, 10 Jaunary 1977.

62. Jiri Valenta and Shannon Butler, "East German Security Policies in Africa," in Michael Radu, ed., *Eastern Europe and the Third World* (New York: Praeger, 1981), p. 147.

63. "OAU Indifference," *Africa Research Bulletin*, 12 July 1979.

64. Valenta and Butler, "East German Security Policies in Africa," p. 157.

65. *New York Times*, 20 December 1982.

66. *Communist Aid to Less Developed Countries of the Third World*.

67. Romania is East Europe's leading contributor of economic aid, but there is no indication that its assistance is coordinated through CMEA. In fact, given the foreign policy independence of Romania, the degree to which this aid supports Soviet bloc efforts is open to question (ibid., p. 12).

4. *National Armies and National Sovereignty*

1. Christopher Jones, "Equality and Equal Security in Europe," *Orbis*, 26 (Fall 1982), 637–64.

2. Christopher Jones, *Soviet Influence in Eastern Europe: Political Autonomy and the Warsaw Pact* (New York: Praeger, 1981), pp. 79–94.

3. Ferenc Vali, *Rift and Revolt in Hungary* (Cambridge, Mass.: Harvard University Press, 1961), pp. 364–67. Paul Zinner, in *Revolution in Hungary* (New York: Columbia University Press, 1962), p. 331, agrees with Vali that Nagy's reason for withdrawing from the Warsaw Pact was to win diplomatic support from the West. Zinner does not, however, explicitly say that the threat of Soviet military intervention prompted Nagy to withdraw from the WTO. Raymond Garthoff, in *Soviet Military Policy* (New York: Praeger, 1966), argues on pages 155–72 that the Soviet decision to intervene militarily in Hungary preceded Nagy's decision to withdraw from the Warsaw Pact.

4. A. Ross Johnson, "The Polish Military," in A. Ross Johnson, Robert W. Dean, and Alexander Alexiev, *East European Military Establishments: The Warsaw Pact Northern Tier* (New York: Crane Russak, 1982), pp. 28–29.

5. See Hansjakob Stehle, *The Independent Satellite* (New York: Praeger, 1965), pp. 220–51.

6. Quoted in Colonel Milan Matous, "The So-Called 'Memorandum'—What It Was and the Purpose It Served," *Zivot Strany*, no. 42 (15 October 1969), in Radio Free Europe, *Czechoslovak Press Survey*, no. 2272 (New York: Radio Free Europe Research: 18 November 1969).

7. "O prebyvanii delegatsii Vooruzhennykh sil Sovetskogo Soiuza v Chekhoslovat-skoi Sotsialisticheskoi Respublike" [On the visit of the delegation of the Soviet armed forces in the Czechoslovak socialist republic], *Krasnaia Zvezda*, 23 May 1968, p. 1.

8. For a list of Romania's participation in WTO exercises, see V. G. Kulikov et al., eds., *Varshavskii dogovor—soiuz vo imia mira i sotsializma* [The Warsaw Pact—An alliance in the name of peace and socialism] (Moscow: Voenizdat, 1980), pp. 275–93.

9. Ibid., pp. 153–54; I. I. Iakubovskii, *Boevoe sodruzhestvo bratskikh armii i narodov* [The combat confederation of the fraternal armed forces and peoples] (Moscow: Voenizdat, 1975), p. 152.

10. Kulikov, *Varshavskii dogovor*, p. 185.

11. Maj. Dobosh (Czechoslovak People's Army), "Gotovnost' k podvigu" [Readiness for a heroic deed], *Krasnaia Zvezda*, 10 October 1970, p. 1.

12. Iakubovskii, *Boevoe sodruzhestvo*, p. 155.

13. N. Taratorin, "V edinom stroiu—k edinoi tseli" [In one battle order—for one goal] in E. F. Ivanovskii, ed., *Na boevom postu: kniga o voinakh Gruppy sovetskikh voisk v Germanii* [At the battle station: A book about the group of Soviet forces in Germany] (Moscow: Voenizdat, 1975), p. 291.

14. Ibid.

15. P. A. Zhilin (USSR) and E. Gefurt (Czechoslovakia), *Na vechnye vremena* [For eternity] (Moscow: Voenizdat, 1975), p. 307.

16. Lt. Col. A. Poliakov, "Boevoe bratstvo" [Combat brotherhood], *Krasnaia Zvezda*, 31 January 1982, p. 2.

17. Kulikov, *Varshavskii dogovor*, p. 167.

18. Jones, *Soviet Influence*, pp. 118–21.

19. Ibid.

20. Ibid., pp. 126–30.

21. For more detailed treatment of these agencies see ibid., pp. 137–43.

22. Ibid., pp. 133–37.

23. Kulikov, *Varshavskii dogovor*, p. 167.

24. Z. Studzinski (Polish deputy chief of the WTO staff), "Nash nerushimyi boevoi soiuz" [Our unbreakable combat alliance], *Krasnaia Zvezda*, 28 March 1975, p. 3.

25. See Iakubovskii, *Boevoe sodruzhestvo*, pp. 148, 161, and appendix; see Kulikov, *Varshavskii dogovor*, pp. 151 and 272–93.

26. Velko Palin (Bulgaria) and A. A. Epishev (USSR), *Naveki vmeste* [Forever together] (Moscow: Voenizdat, 1969), p. 296.

27. For instance, the 1973 "Convention on the Legal Competence, Privileges and Immunities of the Staff and Other Organs of Administration of the United Armed Forces of the Member States of the Warsaw Treaty Organization," in N. N. Rodionov et al., eds., *Organizatsiia Varshavskogo dogovora, 1955–75: Dokumenty i materialy* [The Warsaw Treaty Organization, 1955–75: Documents and materials], pp. 160–64.

28. I. I. Iakubovskii, "Boevoe sodruzhestvo" [The combat confederation] in A. A. Grechko et al., eds., *Sovetskaia voennaia entsiklopediia* [The Soviet military encyclopedia] (Moscow: Voenizdat, 1976), 1: 527; see also Kulikov, *Varshavskii dogovor*, p. 158.

29. V. F. Samoilenko, "Voennoe sodruzhestvo stran sotsializma" [The military confederation of the socialist countries] in S. A. Tiushkevich et al., eds., *Voina i armiia* [War and armed forces] (Moscow: Voenizdat, 1975), p. 373.

30. A. A. Grechko, "Boevoe sodruzhestvo armii sotsialisticheskikh gosudarstv" [The combat confederation of the armed forces of the socialist states"], *Kommunist*, no. 15 (1972), p. 47.

31. A. A. Epishev, *Ideologicheskaia bor'ba po voennym voprosam* [Ideological struggle in military questions] (Moscow: Voenizdat, 1974), p. 91.

32. Kulikov, *Varshavskii dogovor*, p. 148.

33. See Jones, *Soviet Influence in Eastern Europe*, pp. 168–69.

34. Col. V. Semin, "Partiino-politicheskaia rabota v armiiakh stran Varshavskogo dogovora" [Party political work in the armed forces of the Warsaw Pact countries] in S. K. Il'in et al., eds., *Partiino-politicheskaia rabota v sovetskikh vooruzhennykh silakh* [Party-political work in the Soviet armed forces] (Moscow: Voenizdat, 1974), p. 599.

35. Ibid.

36. P. A. Zhilin (USSR) and E. Jadziac (Poland), *Bratstvo po oruzhiiu* [Brotherhood in arms] (Moscow: Voenizdat, 1975), p. 355.

37. Kulikov, *Varshavskii dogovor*, p. 192.

38. Jan Khmelik, "Predannost' delu sotsializma" [Devotion to the cause of socialism], *Pravda*, 6 October 1973, p. 5.

39. Iakubovskii, *Boevoe sodruzhestvo*, p. 163; Kulikov, *Varshavskii dogovor*, p. 159.

40. See Jones, *Soviet Influence in Eastern Europe*, pp. 213–14.

41. Quoted in A. I. Radzievskii et al., eds., *Akademiia imeni M. V. Frunze* [The M. V. Frunze Military Academy] (Moscow: Voenizdat, 1973), p. 240.

42. Zhilin and Gefurt, *Na vechnye vremena*, p. 305.

43. V. G. Kulikov et al., eds., *Akademiia generalnogo shtaba Vooruzhennykh sil SSSR imeni K. E. Voroshilova* [The K. E. Voroshilov General Staff Academy of the armed forces of the USSR] (Moscow: Voenizdat, 1976), pp. 230–32.

44. Ibid., p. 244.

45. Joseph Wisniewski, *Who's Who in Poland* (Toronto: Professional Translators and Publishers, 1981), pp. 59, 60, 118.

46. The Soviet literature occasionally discusses such precedents in Soviet military history and their relevance to the Warsaw Pact. Such texts often condemn socialist states that insist on purely national missions for their national military forces. See Kulikov, *Varshavskii dogovor*, pp. 29–36; 147–49; Rear Admiral F. Chernyshev and Col. V. Koniukhovskii, "The Army of the Friendship of Peoples and of Proletarian Internationalism," *Voennaia Mysl*, no. 11 (1967), in *Selected Translations from Voennaia Mysl*, 18

November 1968, Central Intelligence Agency, Foreign Broadcast Information Service, *Foreign Press Digest* 05117/68.

47. *Kommunistischeskaia partiia Sovetskogo soiuza v rezoliutsiakh i resheniakh s"ezdov, konferentsii i plenumov Ts. K.* [The Communist party of the Soviet Union in resolutions, conferences and CC plenums] (Moscow: Politizdat, 1970), 2: 717, cited in Col. P. Rtishchev, "Leninskaia natsional'naia politika i stroitel'stvo Sovetskikh vooruzhennykh sil" [Leninist nationality policy and the development of the Soviet armed forces], *Kommunist vooruzhennyskh sil*, no. 9 (1974), p. 6.

48. Kh. M. Ibragimbei, "Natsional'nye formirovanie" [National detachments], in N. V. Ogarkov et al., eds., *Sovetskaia voennaia entsiklopediia* (Moscow: Voenizdat, 1978), 5: 552.

49. V. N. Koniukhovskii, *Territorial'naia sistema voennogo stroitel'stva* [The territorial system of the organization of a national defense system] (Moscow: Voenizdat, 1961), pp. 61, 68.

50. Ibragimbei, "Natsional'nye formirovanie," p. 552.

51. Ellen Jones, "Minorities in the Soviet Armed Forces," *Comparative Strategy* 3, (1982), 288.

52. Koniukhovskii, *Territorial'naia sistema*, pp. 56–57.

53. Rtishchev, "Leninskaia natsional'naia politika," p. 6.

54. "Iz resheniia o prakticheskikh meropriatiakh po provedeniiu v zhizn' rezoliutsii XII s"ezda partii po natsional'nomy voprosu" [From the decision on practical measures for the carrying out of the resolutions of the Twelfth Congress on the national question], in K. U. Chernenko, ed., *KPSS o Vooruzhennykh silakh Sovetskogo soiuza* [The CPSU on the armed forces of the Soviet Union] (Moscow: Voenizdat, 1969), p. 206.

55. "Itogi plenuma Revvoensoveta SSSR: Rech' v voennoi akademii RKKA" [Results of the plenum of the revolutionary Military Council of the USSR: Speech to the Military Academy of the RKKA], 20 December 1924, in M. V. Frunze, *Izbrannye proizvedeniia* [Selected works] (Moscow: Voenizdat, 1977), p. 237.

56. "Itogi i perspektivy voennogo stroitel'stva v sviazi s reorganizatsei tekushchego goda" [Results and perspectives of military organization and development in connection with the reorganization of the current year], 17 November 1924, in ibid., p. 191.

57. "Itogi plenuma," in ibid., p. 238.

58. "Budem gotovye" [Let us be prepared], *Armiia i revoliutsiia*, nos. 11–12 (November–December 1923), in ibid., p. 111.

59. Koniukhovskii, *Territorial'naia sistema*, p. 81.

60. "O natsional'nykh chastiakh i formirovaniakh RKKA" [On national units and formations of the RKKA], in Chernenko, ed., *KPSS*, p. 294.

61. A. A. Grechko, ed., *The Armed Forces of the Soviet State* (Washington, D.C.: U.S. Government Printing Office, 1975), p. 117.

62. V. A. Muradian, *Boevoe bratstvo* (Moscow: Voenizdat, 1978), pp. 73–74.

63. K. Taskitishvili, *Na frontakh Velikoi otechestvennoi voiny* [On the fronts of the Great Fatherland war] (Tibilisi: Izdatel'stvo Sabchota Sakartvelo, 1975), p. 283.

64. M. K. Kozybaev, "Narody Kazakhstana i srednoi Azii" [The peoples of Kazakhstan and Central Asia] in A. A. Grechko, et al., eds., *Velikaia pobeda sovetskogo naroda 1941–45* [The great victory of the Soviet people, 1941–1945] (Moscow: Nauka, 1976), p. 463.

65. See Ibragimbei, "Natsional'nye formirovanie," for a general account. For a detailed account, which includes bibliographical references to even more detailed accounts, see A. P. Artem'ev, *Bratskii boevoi soiuz SSSR v Velikoi otechestvennoi voine* [The

fraternal combat union of the peoples of the USSR in the great fatherland] (Moscow: Mysl', 1975), pp. 39–53, 68, 75.

66. See Christopher Jones, "The Political Administrations of the Warsaw Pact," in Daniel Nelson, ed., *Soviet Allies: The Issue of Reliability* (Boulder, Colo: Westview, 1983).

67. Artem'ev, *Bratskii boevoi soiuz*, p. 75.

68. Ibid., pp. 52–57.

69. Ibid., p. 54.

70. Ibid., p. 52.

5. *Soviet Crisis Management in Eastern Europe*

1. For a detailed discussion of the uprising see Arnulf Baring, *Uprising in East Germany: June 17, 1953* (Ithaca: Cornell University Press, 1972).

2. According to East German sources, strikes took place in some 272 towns and involved about 300,000 people, or only about 7 percent of the East German work force. The vast majority of the strikers were industrial workers, though farmers were involved in some isolated instances. See ibid., p. 52.

3. Ibid., p. 76.

4. For instance, Jacob Kaiser, the West German minister for all-German affairs, made a radio broadcast late on the evening of 16 June in which he advised the East Germans not to undertake "rash or dangerous actions" that might endanger the prospects for reunification. Chancellor Adenauer made a cautious statement to the Bundestag, and the West Berlin authorities did their best to prevent West Berliners from joining the demonstrations or influencing their development (ibid., pp. 86–87).

5. Khrushchev later charged that after Stalin's death Beria began to take steps to "liquidate" the GDR and undermine friendly relations with the GDR (*Pravda*, 10 March 1963). For a good discussion of Beria and Malenkov's role in the German question at this time see Victor Bares, "Beria's Fall and Ulbricht's Survival," *Soviet Studies*, 27 (July 1975), 381–95.

6. See Bela Kirali, "Budapest—1956, Prague—1968," *Problems of Communism*, 18 (July–August 1969), 52–60.

7. Khrushchev alluded to these divisions in a speech in Budapest on 2 December 1959, stating that some members of the leadership had opposed giving "new help" to Hungary (*New York Times*, 3 December 1959).

8. Strobe Talbot, ed., *Khruschev Remembers: The Last Testament* (New York: Bantam Books, 1976), p. 381.

9. The text of the declaration appeared in *Pravda*, 31 October 1956. For relevant excerpts in English see Tibor Meray, *Thirteen Days That Shook the Kremlin* (New York: Praeger, 1959), pp. 144–48.

10. Paul Kecskemeti, *The Unexpected Revolution* (Stanford: Stanford University Press, 1961), p. 190.

11. Michel Tatu, "Intervention in Eastern Europe," in Stephen Kaplan, ed., *Diplomacy of Power* (Washington, D.C.: Brookings Institution, 1981), p. 220.

12. Ibid.; Christopher Jones, *Soviet Influence in Eastern Europe: Political Autonomy and the Warsaw Pact* (New York: Praeger, 1981), p. 74.

13. See Talbot, ed., *Khrushchev Remembers*, pp. 381–85. Only the Chinese and the Poles appear to have opposed the invasion. To Khrushchev's surprise, Tito, who was also consulted, backed the invasion, see ibid., p. 384.

14. These assurances were given on three separate occasions in rapid succession: first, in a speech by Eisenhower to the Council on World Affairs in Dallas on 27 October; then by U.S. Ambassador to the United Nations Henry Cabot Lodge at the United Nations on 28 October; and finally by Charles Bohlen, U.S. ambassador to Moscow, to the Russians officially on 29 October. See Janos Radvanyi, *Hungary and the Superpowers* (Stanford: Hoover Institution Press, 1972), p. 12.

15. Talbot, ed., *Khrushchev Remembers*, p. 380.

16. Veljko Micunovic, *Moscow Diary* (New York: Doubleday, 1980), pp. 134–35.

17. Khrushchev told Egyptian journalist Mohamed Heikal that "Molotov thought that it was my policies that had led to the trouble in Hungary . . . that my tolerance of Tito had encouraged the Hungarians." See Heikal, *The Sphynx and the Commissar* (New York: Harper & Row, 1978), p. 92.

18. See Melvin Croan, "Czechoslovakia, Ulbricht and the German Problem," *Problems of Communism*, 18 (January–February 1969), pp. 1–7.

19. The danger was posed particularly by Radio Presov in Slovakia, which began to take the lead in calling for a revival of Ukrainian culture. These broadcasts could be received in the Ukraine, where nationalism has traditionally been a strong force. For a detailed discussion see Grey Hodnett and Peter J. Potichnyi, *The Ukraine and the Czechoslovak Crisis* (Canberra: Australian National University, 1970).

20. For a detailed discussion of the development of the crisis in Czechoslovakia see H. Gordon Skilling, *Czechoslovakia's Interrupted Revolution* (Princeton: Princeton University Press, 1976), and Galia Golan, *Reform Rule in Czechoslovakia: The Dubcek Era, 1968–69* (Cambridge: Cambridge University Press, 1973).

21. See Jiri Valenta, *Soviet Intervention in Czechoslovakia, 1968: Anatomy of a Decision* (Baltimore: Johns Hopkins University Press, 1979), p. 13. This section draws heavily on Valenta's book, which is particularly valuable for the light it sheds on positions taken by various members and factions within the Soviet leadership in the period leading up to the invasion on 21 August. Two other studies which also provide valuable information are Pavel Tigrid, *Why Dubcek Fell* (London: McDonald Press, 1971), and Zdenek Mlynar, *Nightfrost in Prague: The End of Human Socialism* (New York: Karz, 1980). Mlynar, who now lives in the West, was a secretary of the Central Committee.

22. Originally, the exercise was supposed to involve only Czechoslovaks and Soviets, but it was expanded into a Pact exercise without consultation with the Czechs and in violation of the verbal understanding reached between the Soviet and Czechoslovak leadership at the bilateral meeting in Moscow in May (Valenta, *Soviet Intervention*, p. 32).

23. For the text of the Warsaw letter, see Philip Windsor and Adam Roberts, *Czechoslovakia, 1968: Reform and Resistance* (New York: Columbia University Press, 1969), p. 150.

24. See the article by S. Kovalov in *Pravda*, 26 September 1968.

25. Valenta, *Soviet Intervention*, p. 73.

26. TASS, 3 August 1968.

27. Referring to the decision to intervene, for instance, Gomulka notes in his memoirs: "It was necessary to weigh very carefully the pros and the cons of the situation. Even in the Soviet leadership itself there was no unanimity as to the final balance of that account. I will tell you very frankly that the scale was tipping both ways until the last minute" (*Noviny Kurier*, 15 June 1973). See also Valenta, *Soviet Intervention*, pp. 13–39, for an extensive discussion of differences within the Soviet leadership.

28. Valenta, *Soviet Intervention*, pp. 23–27.

29. See the memoirs of Gomulka's interpreter, Erwin Weit, *At the Red Summit: Inter-*

preter behind the Iron Curtain (New York: Macmillan, 1973), pp. 199–202, Valenta, *Soviet Intervention*, pp. 52–53.

30. Valenta, *Soviet Intervention*, p. 133.

31. Ivan Svitak, *The Czechoslovak Experiment, 1968–69* (New York: Columbia University Press, 1971), pp. 180–81.

32. In 1977–1978 several attempts were made by Soviet workers to form independent trade unions. The most prominent of these was the creation of the Free Interprofessional Association of Workers at the end of 1977. Although these efforts were quickly and resolutely suppressed by the Soviet authorities, this association was not entirely wiped out. According to samizdat documents smuggled to the West, some of its members expressed sympathy with the Polish workers. See "Russian Group Issues Proclamation of Support for Polish Workers," *Radio Liberty Research*, 24 July 1981. In 1981 there were also reports of efforts to organize by workers in the Donetsk coalmining basin of the Ukraine (*Washington Post*, 31 January 1981).

33. Romanian Foreign Minister Stefan Andrei flew to Moscow on 2 December for special consultations with the Soviet leadership, and it is likely that he was given assurances at that time that there would be no immediate invasion.

34. TASS, 5 December 1980.

35. Bernard Guetta in *Le Monde*, 10 March 1981.

36. *Pravda*, 5 March 1981.

37. John Darnton, "Brezhnev Phone Call Said to Have Protected Hard Liners in Poland," *New York Times*, 14 April 1981. According to Darnton, Olszowski and Grabski were retained after a letter from the Soviet Central Committee was read, urging that, for the sake of "party unity," no changes be made in either the Politiburo or the Central Committee. The letter, it was reported, was backed up by a phone call from Brezhnev to Kania during a crucial two-hour recess in the Polish Central Committee meeting.

38. *Ibid.*

39. Bruce Porter, "The Kremlin and the PUWP since the Ninth Plenum in Poland," *Radio Liberty Research*, 21 May 1981.

40. For the text of the letter see *New York Times*, 11 June 1981.

41. Polish Press Agency, 18 September 1981.

42. *Washington Post*, 23 September 1981.

43. It is estimated that the party lost, either through expulsion or resignation, as many as 600,000 members from August 1980 until the imposition of martial law on 13 December 1981 and another 250,000 in 1982 (David Buchan, "Group Calls for Release of Solidarity Leader," *Financial Times*, 27 August 1982).

44. The decree was originally passed to prepare the country for a nuclear war. In time of a national emergency the country was to be ruled by a Committee for Territorial Defense, composed of the first secretary of the PUWP, the prime minister, the defense minister, and leading military officers. The decree gave the committee wide-ranging powers, including the power to appoint local and regional administrators. At the time of the imposition of martial law Jaruzelski held all three top civilian posts—first secretary, prime minister, and defense minister. Thus in establishing the Military Council of National Salvation he could legitimately claim he was acting within the legal framework of the Constitution. Moreover, according to the decree, only the first secretary—in this case Jaruzelski—can actually dismiss the committee. See Michael Checinski, "Die Militaerfuehrung und der Machtkampf in Polen," *Osteuropa*, 32 (May 1982), pp. 380–85.

45. In 1956 internal security forces were prepared to resist the troops of Marshal Rokossovskii, the Polish defense minister loyal to Moscow, and major navy and air force units were prepared to fight Soviet forces. According to Khrushchev, during the

crisis in October 1956, he and Marshal I. S. Konev held consultations with Rokossovskii, who assured the Soviet leaders of his readiness to put down the counterrevolution. But "when we began to analyze this situation in detail and calculate which Polish regiments would obey Rokossovskii, the situation began to look somewhat bleak" (Talbot, ed., *Khrushchev Remembers*, p. 231).

46. For a highly speculative argument that Brezhnev did, in fact, oppose intervention based on circumstantial evidence, see Richard D. Anderson, Jr., "Soviet Decision-Making and Poland," *Problems of Communism*, 31 (March–April 1982), pp. 22–36.

47. For a good discussion of the U.S. response, see Valenta, Soviet Intervention in Czechoslovakia, pp. 128–34.

48. Based on the author's personal involvement in the crisis at the time as a member of the National Security Council staff.

49. See in particular Samuel P. Huntington, *Political Order in Changing Societies* (New Haven: Yale University Press, 1968.)

50. A. Ross Johnson, *Poland in Crisis* (Santa Monica: Rand, 1982), pp. 55–56.

51. See Jan Vanous, "East European Slowdown," *Problems of Communism*, 31 (July–August 1982), 1–19.

6. *Foreign Policy Goals*

1. The transition of the East European states from satellites to junior allies was first described in Z. K. Brzezinski, *The Soviet Bloc*, 2d ed. (Cambridge, Mass.: Harvard University Press, 1967); see also V. V. Aspaturian, "The Soviet Union and Eastern Europe," in Aspaturian, *Power and Process in Soviet Foreign Policy* (Boston: Little, Brown, 1971).

2. For a useful summary of the factors for change and potential instability see Archie Brown, "Eastern Europe: 1968, 1978, 1988," *Daedalus*, vol. 180 1 (Winter 1979), pp. 151–74. The issue of regime security is considered at greater length in Edwina Moreton, "Security, Change and Instability in Eastern Europe," in Derek Leebaert, ed., *European Security: Prospects for the 1980s* (Lexington, Mass.: D. C. Heath, 1979).

3. For a discussion of these issues see Kenneth Jowitt, "Inclusion and Mobilization in European Leninist Regimes," in Jan F. Triska and Paul Cocks, eds., *Political Development in Eastern Europe* (New York: Praeger, 1977).

4. This argument is put particularly by J. F. Brown, "Detente and Soviet Policy in Eastern Europe," *Survey*, 20 (Spring/Summer 1974), 46–58.

5. GDR-Soviet relations over the German problem have a long and complex history. See N. Edwina Moreton, *East Germany and the Warsaw Alliance: The Politics of Detente* (Boulder, Colo.: Westview Press, 1978).

6. Some initial evidence of a change in public emphasis away from protestations of impotence on the part of the Polish regime is offered in Jeanne Kirk Laux, "Intra-Alliance Politics and European Detente: The Case of Poland and Romania," *Studies in Comparative Communism*, 8 (Spring/Summer 1975), 98–122. It remains to be seen whether practice matches rhetoric in this case, especially in view of the imposition of martial law.

7. The origins and development of Romania's dispute with the Soviet Union in the 1950s are sketched out in Michael Kaser, *Comecon: Integration Problems of the Planned Economies* (London: Oxford University Press, 1965); and Robin A. Remington, *The Warsaw Pact: Case Studies in Communist Conflict Resolution* (Cambridge, Mass.: MIT Press, 1971), pp. 54–63.

8. The reasoning behind this conclusion is argued in Jeanne Kirk Laux, "Socialism, Nationalism and Underdevelopment: Research on Romanian Foreign Policy Making," in Hannes Adomeit and Robert Boardman, eds., *Foreign Policy Making in Communist Countries* (Farnborough, Hants: Saxon House, 1979).

9. Because of its seriousness, the impact of the Sino-Soviet rift on Eastern Europe could be considered "largely consummated," as is argued by Richard Lowenthal, "China's Impact on the Evolution of the Alliances in Europe," in *Western and Eastern Europe: The Changing Relationship*, Adelphi Paper 33 (London: Institute for Strategic Studies, 1967).

10. For example, the visit by Zhou Enlai in 1966 and the visit by Chairman Hua in 1978. For a fuller discussion of the importance of China in Soviet–East European relations see Edwina Moreton, "The Triangle in Eastern Europe," in Gerald Segal, ed., *The China Factor* (London: Croom Helm, 1982), esp. pp. 139–44.

11. For example, in 1964 and again in 1970, when the Soviet Union appeared to be seeking improved relations with West Germany at East Germany's expense. See Moreton, *East Germany and the Warsaw Alliance*, pp. 128 and 159.

12. For a discussion of the impact of economic factors and energy issues on Soviet–East European relations see Philip Hanson, "Soviet Trade with Eastern Europe," and Alan H. Smith, "Economic Factors Affecting Soviet–East European Relations in the 1980s," in Karen Dawisha and Philip Hanson, eds., *Soviet–East European Dilemmas: Coercion, Competition, and Consent* (London: Holmes and Meier, 1981).

13. The latest figures on Warsaw Pact defense spending are in *The Military Balance 1983–84* (London: International Institute of Strategic Studies, 1983).

14. For a fuller discussion of this propostion and the problems it raises see Chapter 3.

15. Smith, "Economic Factors Affecting Soviet–East European Relations in the 1980s," p. 122.

16. Hans-Adolf Jacobsen et al., eds., *Drei Jahrzehnte Aussenpolitik der DDR* (Munich: Oldenbourg Verlag, 1979), pt. 5, chaps. 3 and 4. East Germany's early contracts with national liberation movements are documented in Bernard von Plate, "Aspekte der SED-Parteibeziehungen in Afrika und der arabischen Region," *Deutschland Archiv*, no. 2 (1979). Two agreements were signed with the PLO, in 1973 and 1978, on the basis of which the GDR has provided "noncivilian equipment" and financial assistance to the organization. And Yasser Arafat has been a familiar visitor to East Berlin. See Michael Sodaro, "The GDR and the Third World: Supplicant and Surrogate," in Michael Radu, ed., *Eastern Europe and the Third World* (New York: Praeger, 1981), p. 130.

17. The costs and benefits of East German involvement are discussed in Edwina Moreton, "The East Europeans and the Cubans in the Middle East: Surrogates or Allies?" in Adeed Dawisha and Karen Dawisha, eds., *The Soviet Union in the Middle East* (London: Heinemann, for the Royal Institute of International Affairs, 1982), p. 15.

7. *Security through Detente and Arms Control*

1. Ronald H. Linden, *The Security Bind in Eastern Europe* (Pittsburgh: University Center for International Security Studies, 1980).

2. Peter Bender, *East Europe in Search of Security* (Baltimore: Johns Hopkins University Press, 1972).

3. A. Koveev, "Izuchenie problem evropeiskoi bezopasnosti," in *Obshchestvennye nauki*, no. 4 (1979), describes a "working collective" of institutes of international rela-

tions established in 1962 to coordinate Soviet and East European research on European security and arms control issues. I am indebted to Christopher Jones for an English translation of this article.

4. Panorama (East Germany), *Political Declaration of the States Parties to the Warsaw Treaty* (Prague, 5 January 1983), p. 24: "The [mutual renunciation of force] treaty would . . . free the members of both of these alliances of fear that the commitments of alliances existing within each of these alliances could be used for aggressive purposes against the member states of the other alliance and that these commitments could thus threaten their security."

5. For a concise history of the CSCE see Stephen J. Flanagan, "The CSCE and the Development of Detente," in Derek Leebaert, ed., *European Security: Prospects for the 1980s* (Lexington, Mass.: Lexington Books/D. C. Heath, 1979). For an East European view, see Adam D. Rotfeld et al., *Conference on Security and Cooperation in Europe: A Polish View* (Warsaw: Polish Institute of International Affairs, 1976).

6. Hans Peter Graf, "Does the German Democratic Republic Need NATO?" *Annals of International Studies*, vol. 10 (Geneva: Institut Universitaire Haute Etudes Internationales, 1979); N. Edwina Moreton, *East Germany and the Warsaw Pact: The Politics of Detente* (Boulder, Colo.: Westview Press, 1979).

7. Hansjakob Stehle, "Against the Division of Europe: Constructive Coexistence," in *The Independent Satellite* (London: Pall Mall Press, 1965), chap. 5.

8. "Address by the Polish Foreign Minister (Rapacki) to the UN General Assembly, December 14, 1964," United States Arms Control and Disarmament Agency, *Documents on Disarmament, 1964* (Washington, D.C.: U.S. Government Printing Office, 1965), p. 527.

9. *Pravda*, 3 April 1966.

10. "Address by CPSU General Secretary Brezhnev at Karlovy Vary Conference of European Communist Parties April 24, 1967," in United States Arms Control and Disarmament Agency, "Selected Background Documents Relating to Mutual and Balanced Force Reductions, Part I," (Washington, D.C.: ACDA Disarmament Document Series, no. 611, 17 May 1973), pp. 30–40.

11. Robin Remington, *The Warsaw Pact: Case Studies in Communist Conflict Resolution* (Cambridge, Mass.: MIT Press, 1971), pp. 54–55.

12. Nikolai Patolichev, Soviet minister of foreign trade, has also consistently supported an expansion of East-West trade through the CSCE. See Lawrence T. Caldwell, "CSCE, MFR, and Eastern Europe," in Charles Gati, ed., *The International Politics of Eastern Europe* (New York: Praeger, 1976).

13. Interviews with delegates to MBFR negotiations, Vienna, September 1982.

14. The Helsinki Final Act is reprinted in *Survival*, 17 (November–December 1975).

15. For apprehension about the dangers of ideological contamination from East-West detente in general and the CSCE in particular, see M. A. Suslov, *Pravda*, 21 January 1972; Vadim Zagladin and Vladimir Shaposhnikov, "The European Public and Peace in Europe," in *Kommunist*, no. 16 (August 1972); and Marian Dobrosielski, *Trybuna Ludu* (Warsaw), 5 December 1974.

16. "Declaration of Warsaw Treaty Member Countries," issued by the Warsaw Pact Political Consultative Committee meeting in Bucharest, 24–26 November 1976, reprinted in Robert King and Robert Dean, eds., *Eastern Europe's Uncertain Future* (New York: Praeger, 1977), pp. 15–17.

17. Thomas Heneghan, "Civil Rights Dissent in Eastern Europe," in King and Dean, eds., *Eastern Europe's Uncertain Future*, pp. 218–32.

18. Principles I, II, IV, and CI of the Helsinki Final Act, see *Survival*, 17 (November–December 1975).

19. *Scinteia* (Bucharest), 6 June 1980.

20. *Agerpress* (Bucharest), 7 June 1980, cited in Radio Free Europe Background Report 149, 18 June 1980.

21. Bradley Graham, "Eastern Europe Wants Ties to West," *Washington Post*, 6 March 1980; John Darnton, "Eastern Europe Trying to Breathe Life Back into Detente," *New York Times*, 24 May 1980.

22. "Nuclear Weapons in Europe: A Soviet View, President Brezhnev's Interview with *Der Spiegel* (Excerpts)," *Survival*, 24 (January–February 1982), 32–37.

23. For a summary of NATO and WTO negotiating positions at MBFR, see Jane Sharp, "Troop Reductions in Europe: A Status Report," *Armament and Disarmament Unit (ADIU) Report*, 5 (September–October 1983).

24. United States Control and Disarmament Agency, "Address by CPSU General Secretary Brezhnev at Tbilisi, May 14, 1971," *Documents on Disarmament, 1971* (Washington, D.C.: U.S. Government Printing Office, 1972), p. 293.

25. "Speech by CPSU General Secretary Brezhnev to World Conference of Peace Forces," Moscow Broadcast transcript, 6 October 1973, in United States Arms Control and Disarmament Agency, "Selected Background Documents Relating to Mutual and Balanced Force Reductions, Part II" (Washington, D.C.: ACDA Disarmament Document Series no. 619, 23 November 1973), pp. 47–48.

26. Bender, *East Europe in Search of Security*, passim.

27. Christoph Bertram, *Mutual Force Reductions in Europe: The Political Aspects*, Adelphi Paper 84 (London: International Institute for Strategic Studies, 1972).

28. These alliance problems help to explain the otherwise tortuous language of the invitation to the five Warsaw Pact states that NATO wanted as direct participants: "Governments of allied countries which issued the Declaration of Reykjavik agreed to propose that exploratory (MBFR) talks should be held beginning on 31 January 1973 in a place still to be agreed through diplomatic channels. The governments of Belgium, Canada, the Federal Republic of Germany, Luxembourg, the Netherlands, the United Kingdom, and the United States are communicating this proposal to the governments of Czechoslovakia, Poland, Hungary and the USSR. The Government of the Federal Republic of Germany is communicating this proposal to the Government of the German Democratic Republic also. The Governments of Denmark, Greece, Italy, Norway and Turkey will confirm their intention to be represented at the exploratory talks" (from "Statement by the North Atlantic Treaty Organization at Brussels, 16 November 1972," in United States Arms Control and Disarmament Agency, "Selected Background Documents, Part I," p. 185.

29. Interviews with NATO delegates to the MBFR talks in Vienna, London, and The Hague, Washington, D.C., 1982–1983.

30. For example, the upward adjustment of Polish manpower figures in *Military Balance, 1977–1978* from the previous year; and the campaign to temper the IISS judgment in its *Military Balance, 1979–1980* that "something very close to parity exists between the Theatre Nuclear Forces of NATO and the Warsaw Pact" (p. 117).

31. A. Ross Johnson, Robert W. Dean, Alexander Alexiev, *East European Military Establishments: The Warsaw Pact Northern Tier* (Santa Monica: Rand, 1980), p. 81.

32. Ibid., p. 115.

33. Helmut Schmidt endorsed the 50 percent solution in a speech to the Bundestag in March 1979 and at a meeting of the Social Democratic party on 13 November 1979.

34. John Erickson, "The Warsaw Pact—The Shape of Things to Come?" in Karen Dawisha and Philip Hanson, eds., *Soviet–East European Dilemmas: Coercion, Competition, and Consent* (London: Holmes and Meier, 1981), chap. 10, p. 169.

35. Jane M. O. Sharp, "Nuclear Weapons and Alliance Cohesion," *Bulletin of the Atomic Scientists,* 38 (June 1982), 33–36.

36. Johnson, Dean, and Alexiev, *East European Military Establishments,* p. 27.

37. Stehle, *Independent Satellite.*

38. Christopher D. Jones, *Soviet Influence in Eastern Europe: Political Autonomy and the Warsaw Pact* (New York:Praeger, 1981).

39. Condoleezza Rice, "Nuclear Weapons in Europe: Political Considerations in the Warsaw Pact," in *The Technology and Politics of Nuclear Weapons in Europe* (Cambridge, Mass.: Harvard University, Center for Science and International Affairs, forthcoming).

40. Reprinted in a research paper by Josef Hodic, "Military Political Views Prevalent in the Czechoslovak Army, 1948–1968" (Vienna, 1979).

41. United States Congress, 93d Cong., 2d sess., *Nuclear Weapons and Foreign Policy: Hearings before the Senate Foreign Relations Committee, March and April 1974* (Washington, D.C.: U.S. Government Printing Office, 1974).

42. As General James Polk put it: "We need to get over the 'firebreak' mentality and initiate a vigorous program to modernize our European stockpile" and "Just as the SALT talks demand that we push ahead with MIRV and Trident, so the MBFR talks require that we modernize our hardware, our thinking, and our tactical options available and required at the lower end of the nuclear spectrum" ("The Realities of Tactical Nuclear Warfare," *Orbis,* 17 [Summer 1973], 439–47).

43. Wojciech Multan, ed., *Rokwania Wiedenskie* (Warsaw: Polish Institute for International Affairs, 1980), pp. 274–78.

44. In August 1981, President Reagan announced that the United States would produce neutron warheads for the Lance missile and the 203mm artillery piece, though deployment to Western Europe would await a multilateral NATO decision (International Institute for Strategic Studies, *Strategic Survey, 1981–1982* [London: International Institute for Strategic Studies, 1982], p. 127). In 1983 the U.S. Congress denied the Reagan administration's request to produce 155mm neutron shells.

45. Soviet Committee for European Security and Cooperation, *How to Avert the Threat to Europe* (Moscow: Progress Publishers, 1983), p. 28.

46. Walter Andrews, "Defense Chief Said to Plan '80 Development of Medium Range Missile for Use in Europe," *Washington Post,* 25 February 1978.

47. Raymond Garthoff, "The SS-20 Decision," *Survival,* 25 (May–June 1983).

48. Leonid Brezhnev's 6 October speech in East Berlin, in *Pravda,* 6 October 1979; excerpts in *New York Times,* 7 October 1979, p. 12.

49. Soviet arguments against the new NATO missiles can be found in a number of Soviet publications. See, for example, Soviet Committee for European Security and Cooperation, *How to Avert the Threat to Europe.*

50. Defense Department spokesmen estimate an effective air defense system against cruise might cost the Pact up to $50 billion. See David Fairhall, "Strategies of the Strong Arm Men," *Manchester Guardian Weekly,* 8 May 1983.

51. *AVN News Service,* Berlin, 3 December 1981, cited by Rice, "Nuclear Weapons in Europe"; *Rude Pravo,* 15 January 1982, in ibid.

52. Whether Soviet nuclear warheads are stored in Eastern Europe was a matter of some dispute among intelligence analysts in the late 1970s and early 1980s. In February 1976 a Pact proposal at MBFR included a vague provision to withdraw an unspecified number of nuclear warheads. Some analysts took this to mean there must be warheads

deployed in the MBFR guidelines zone, most likely in East Germany. In his FY 1979 Posture Statement to the Congress, however, Defense Secretary Harold Brown stated that it was Soviet practice to store all warheads—including those designated for nuclear-capable delivery vehicles in Eastern Europe—on Soviet territory and to rely on warning to permit deployment to the theater of operations if and when necessary. The annual *Military Balance*, published by the International Institute for Strategic Studies (London), for 1979–1980, 1980–1981, 1981–1982, and 1982–1983, in 1979, 1980, 1981, and 1982 respectively, stated that there was no evidence that Soviet nuclear warheads were deployed in Eastern Europe. This language was omitted in the *Military Balance, 1983–1984*, published in 1983.

53. On the January 1983 meeting in Prague, see Panorama (East Berlin), *Political Declaration of the States Parties to the Warsaw Treaty*; on the June 1983 WTO summit meeting, see "That Mild Moscow Summit," *Christian Science Monitor*, 30 June 1983; see also the communiqué issued from the meeting of WTO defense ministers in East Berlin 21 October 1983, cited in "Eastern Bloc Defense Chiefs Warn against NATO Plan," *New York Times*, 22 October 1983.

54. As part of the Soviet campaign against the proposed deployment of Pershing and Cruise in the early 1980s, it was suggested that one countermeasure would be to introduce nuclear weapons into Eastern Europe (Serge Schmemann, "Soviet Warns NATO over Missile Plans," *New York Times*, 28 May 1983). About the same time Soviet spokesmen confirmed the general impression in the West that hitherto Soviet nuclear warheads had not been deployed outside Soviet territory (Associated Press report of interview with General Lebvedev, 15 April 1983).

55. See, for example, the address by Vasile Sandru, Romanian delegate to the CSCE Madrid review conference on 8 February 1983: "Romanian Delegate's Address," *Agerpress* (radio transcript from Bucharest) in Foreign Broadcast Information Service, 10 February 1983, p. BBI.

56. David S. Mason, "Romanian Autonomy and Arms Control Policies," *Arms Control*, 3 (May 1982), 13–36.

57. "Greece Asks Balkan Arms Parley," *New York Times*, 18 May 1983; "Greece and Romania Urge Talks to Rid Balkans of Nuclear Arms," ibid., 6 November 1982; "Yugoslavia and a Nuclear Free Zone in the Balkans," *RFE Background Report #113 (Yugoslavia)*, 14 May 1982.

58. *Baltimore Sun*, 27 June 1981.

59. Associated Press, "Sweden Is Urging Atom-Free Region," *New York Times*, 9 December 1982; also "Another Nuclear Non-Starter," *Economist*, 19 February 1983.

60. "GDR Delegate at CSCE Talks Cites Proposals," East Berlin ADN International Service, 15 February 1983; Foreign Broadcast Information Service, 15 February 1983.

61. Bender, *East Europe in Search of Security*, p. 141.

62. See the correspondence between Vaclav Racek and Edward P. Thompson in Edward P. Thompson, *Beyond the Cold War* (New York: Pantheon, 1982), pp. 81–107.

63. John Burns, "11 Russians Open Antinuclear Drive," *The New York Times*, 5 June 1982.

64. "Thoughts from Charter 77" excerpts statements from two documents which the group addressed to the Federal Assembly and the government of Czechoslovakia, *END Journal of European Nuclear Disarmament* (London), no. 1 (December 1982–January 1983), pp. 25–26.

65. Dezzo Miklos and Ferenc Ruzsa, "Towards a Nuclear-Free Hungary," *END Journal of European Nuclear Disarmament* (London), no. 2 (February–March 1983), pp. 24–25.

66. Soviet Committee for European Security and Cooperation, *How to Avert the Threat to Europe*, pp. 90–91.

8. *The Future of Political Relations within the Warsaw Pact*

1. The succession question has already spawned a small library. Still among the best studies is Myron Rush, *Political Succession in the USSR* (New York: Columbia University Press, 1965). Two more recent studies are Seweryn Bialer, *Stalin's Successors: Leadership, Stability and Change in the Soviet Union* (Cambridge: Cambridge University Press, 1980), and Jerry F. Hough, *Soviet Leadership in Transition* (Washington, D.C.: Brookings Institution, 1980). Hough is considerably more optimistic about the prospects of a smooth, well-ordered transition than most of his colleagues.

2. For more on this subject see J. F. Brown, *Relations between the Soviet Union and Its Eastern European Allies: A Survey* (Santa Monica: Rand, 1975). See also Robert L. Hutchings, "The Soviet Bloc in Transition, 1968–1975" (Ph.D. dissertation, University of Virginia, 1979). An expanded edition of this work, going up to 1980, is shortly to be published by the University of Wisconsin Press.

3. The slowness of the Soviet awareness of the seriousness of the situation in Czechoslovakia in 1967–1968 is a case in point here.

4. Politically the best example of the Soviet jealousy goes back to 1947–1948, when the Soviets opposed Dimitrov's concept of a Balkan association involving Bulgaria, Yugoslavia, and Romania. In CMEA also the Soviets have tended to dominate all economic groupings.

5. This generalization could be dangerous, but most observers would agree that irredentist feelings are strongest in the age group over fifty.

6. These developments of the first half of the 1970s are reviewed in Brown, *Relations between the Soviet Union and Its Eastern European Allies.*

7. The best study of the Hungarian New Economic Mechanism is by William F. Robinson, *The Pattern of Reform in Hungary* (New York: Praeger, 1973).

8. For an excellent account and analysis of these riots see Thomas E. Heneghan, "The Summer Storm in Poland," Radio Free Europe Research Background Report, 16 August 1976.

9. For a moving description of the fate and aims of the Charter movement some three years after its foundation, see former Foreign Minister Jiri Hajek in *Die Presse* (Vienna) 28 January 1980. For recent Chapter 77 activity, see "Czechoslovak Activists Call for Continued Arms Talks," *New York Times,* 16 November 1983, and the bimonthly *END Journal of European Nuclear Disarmament* (London) through 1983.

10. For a succinct study on this and related topics, see A. Ross Johnson, Robert W. Dean, and Alexander Alexiev: *East European Military Establishments: The Warsaw Pact Northern Tier* (New York: Crane Russak, 1982), pp. 143–49.

11. These price increases had been expected only for the beginning of 1976, when the new five-year planning cycle in CMEA began. The Soviet determination to apply them one year earlier undoubtedly shocked its East European allies.

12. See *Financial Times* (London), 5 March 1982, for a good analysis of the East European debt.

13. For an excellent analysis of this point, see Philip Windsor, *Change in Eastern Europe* (London: Royal Institute of International Affairs, 1980).

14. Little is known about these Soviet subsidies, but they are believed to have gone mainly to Czechoslovakia after 1968 and to Poland after the upheavals of 1970.

15. According to the West German financial paper *Handelsblatt* of 28 July 1982, the International Monetary Fund had calculated Hungary's net foreign debt at about $8 million.

16. Several books are being written about the rise of Solidarity. A good—and short— one that has already appeared is Denis MacShane, *Solidarity: Poland's Independent Trade Union* (Nottingham: Spokesman, 1981).

17. One of the most convincing assessments so far is by Frane Barbieri, "Andropov: The Nebulous Frontier," in *La Stampa* (Turin), 19 August 1983.

18. Aspirations toward this effort must have been given a boost by the key role played by the Polish security apparatus on, and since, the coup of 13 December 1981.

19. Whether the Soviets have already indulged in this policy is a matter for conjecture. Many Romanians are privately convinced that the Soviets have quietly encouraged Hungarian irredentism with regard to Transylvania. Irredentism is an issue, however, on which the Soviet Union could be very vulnerable.

20. For a discussion of the cohesion-viability concept see Brown, *Relations between the Soviet Union and Its Eastern European Allies.*

21. As recently as 8 August 1982 major price rises were announced in Hungary on a series of basic foodstuffs. They were the third series of price rises in 1982.

22. For a review of the Bulgarian economy see Mark Allan, "The Bulgarian Economy in the 1970's," *East European Economies Post-Helsinki: A Compendium of Papers Submitted to the Joint Economic Committee of the Congress of the United States* (Washington, D.C.: U.S. Government Printing Office, 1977). The most balanced recent review of the East German economy is by Helmut Loethoeffel in *Süddeutsche Zeitung* (Munich), 3 August 1982.

23. John B. Oakes, "A Chip off Soviet Bloc," *New York Times,* 1 September 1982, p. A23, refers to the Soviets supplying Bulgaria with cut-rate coal and oil.

24. For an excellent account of Czechoslovak economic difficulties see Vladimir V. Kusin, "Husak's Czechoslovakia and Economic Stagnation," *Problems of Communism,* 31 (May–June 1982), 24–37.

25. *Financial Times,* 5 March 1982, put the amount of West German subsidies to the GDR at DM 1.5 billion. To these direct subsidies should be added the benefits to the GDR from the "swing" credit agreements, an interest-free foreign credit; from trade benefits accruing from the GDR's de facto membership via the FRG in the Common Market; and from the so-called *Menschenhandel,* the process by which Bonn buys people out of the GDR. These additional benefits are difficult to estimate, but they are appreciable.

26. See Cam Hudson, "Reorganizing a Decrepit Economy: Poland Ambivalent to Economic Reform," *Radio Free Europe Research, Background Report,* 25 August 1982.

27. See Cam Hudson, "Bulgarian Economic Reforms: Between the Devil and the Deep Black Sea," *Radio Free Europe Research, Background Report,* 2 July 1982.

28. *Financial Times,* 4 May 1982, put the figure at $2.3 billion.

29. See Kusin, "Husak's Czechoslovakia."

30. Y. G. Liberman, "The Plan, Profits and Premiums," *Pravda,* 9 September 1962.

31. See J. B. de Weydenthal, "Anatomy of the Martial Law Regime in Poland: The Institutions," *Radio Free Europe Research, Background Report,* 2 February 1982.

32. Rudolf Barak was stripped of all his posts and arrested in February 1962.

33. George Tsankov was stripped of all his posts at the eighth Bulgarian party congress in November 1962.

34. Alexandru Draghici was criticized in April 1968 and subsequently lost all power and influence.

35. Mieczyslaw Moczar was removed from his Politburo position in June 1971. He was reelected to the Politburo after the fall of Gierek in September 1980 but was removed at the Eighth Party Congress in July 1981.

36. Alexander Ranković was stripped of all posts in June 1966.

37. It looks even taller after the riots of 31 August 1982, which shook the country. But in a longer perspective it still remains a possibility.

38. See, for example, Viktor Meier in *Frankfurter Allgemeine Zeitung*, 18 December 1981.

39. For a good discussion of this see "oo" in *Neue Zuercher Zeitung*, 19 February 1982.

40. See Z. Brzezinski and W. E. Griffith, "Peaceful Engagement in Eastern Europe," *Foreign Affairs*, 39 (July 1961), 642–54.

9. *Intrabloc Economic Relations and Prospects*

1. The calculations can be found in Paul Marer, "Soviet Economic Policy in Eastern Europe," in U.S. Congress, Joint Economic Committee, *Reorientation and Commercial Relations of the Economies of Eastern Europe* (Washington, D.C.: U.S. Government Printing Office, 1974).

2. Klara Beke and Laszlo Hynyadi, "A magyar export importanyag tartalma," *Kulgazdasag* (Budapest), no. 7, (1977).

3. Michael Marrese and Jan Vanous, *Soviet Subsidization of Trade with Eastern Europe: A Soviet Perspective* (Berkeley: Institute of International Studies of the University of California, 1983).

4. This view is stated by Philip Hanson in "Soviet Trade with Eastern Europe," in Karen Dawisha and Philip Hanson, eds., *Soviet-East European Dilemmas: Coercion, Competition, and Consent* (London: Holmes and Meier, 1981).

5. Ibid.

6. The statements in this and in the next paragraph were made in general terms by Albert O. Hirschmann, "Beyond Asymmetry: Critical Notes on Myself as a Young Man and on Some Other Old Friends," *International Organization*, 32 (Winter 1978), 45–50.

7. J. F. Brown, *Relations between the Soviet Union and Its Eastern European Allies: A Survey* (Santa Monica: Rand, 1975).

8. Wlodzimierz Brus, "Economic Reform and COMECON Interaction in the Decade 1966–1975," in *Wirtschaft und Gesellschaft* (Berlin: Duncker and Humblot, 1979).

10. *The Warsaw Pact in the International System*

1. Andropov's speech to the Central Committee, 15 June 1983, in *Pravda*, 16 June 1983, excerpted in *Current Digest of the Soviet Press*, 35 (20 July 1983), 7.

2. *Soviet and East European Aid to Third World Countries* (Washington, D.C.: Department of State, 1983), p. 16.

3. Tikhonov's speech to the CMEA, Budapest, 8 June 1982, in *Foreign Broadcast Information Service Daily Report Soviet Union* (FBIS-SOV), 9 June 1982, p. AA8.

Index of Names

General Index